INIGO

OF

RANCHO POSOLMI

Frontispiece: Mission and Chapel of Santa Clara in 1856 (Bancroft Library)

Ballena Press Anthropological Papers No. 47
Thomas C. Blackburn, Series Editor

INIGO

OF

RANCHO POSOLMI

THE LIFE AND TIMES OF A MISSION INDIAN

by
Laurence H. Shoup and Randall T. Milliken
A BALLENA PRESS PUBLICATION

Ballena Press

General Editors: Sylvia Brakke Vane
                 Lowell John Bean

Volume Director: Leslie P. Webster

Ballena Press Anthropological Papers Editors:
    Thomas C. Blackburn
    Sylvia Brakke Vane
    Lowell John Bean

```
E
99
.C8744
I557
1999
```

Library of Congress Cataloging-in-Publication Data

Shoup, Laurence H.
    Inigo of Rancho Posolmi : the life and times of a mission Indian / by Laurence H. Shoup and Randall T. Milliken.
        p. cm. -- (Ballena Press anthropological papers ; no. 47)
    Includes bibliographical references and index.
    ISBN 0-87919-143-0 (hc; alk. paper): $29.95
    ISBN 0-87919-142-2 (pa.; alk. paper): $19.95
    1. Inigo, Lope, 1781-1864. 2. Costanoan Indians--Biography.
    3. Santa Clara Mission. 4. Indians of North America--California--Santa Clara Valley (San Benito County and Santa Clara County, Calif.)--History. 5. Indians of North America--California--Biography. I. Milliken, Randall, 1946-   . II. Title.
    III. Series.
    E99.C87441557 1999
    979.4'73004974--dc21   99-39758
                                                                  CIP

Copyright @ 1999 by   Laurence H. Shoup
                         609 Aileen Street
                         Oakland, CA 94609

        Orders: Ballena Press Publishers' Services
                         P.O. Box 2510
                         Novato, CA 94948

All rights reserved. No part of the book may be reproduced in any form or by any means without prior written permission of the copyright holder, except brief quotes used in connection with reviews written specifically for inclusion in a magazine, newspaper, or scholarly work.

Printed in the United States of America
First Printing

TABLE OF CONTENTS

Table of Contents	v
List of Figures	vi
List of Tables	vii
Foreword	xi
Prologue: The Land of Lope Inigo	1
Chapter 1. Before Inigo, 1750-1781	3
Chapter 2. Indian Childhood and Mission Youth: From San Bernardino to Santa Clara, 1781-1797	25
Chapter 3. Maturity: A Mission Indian, 1798-1828	49
Chapter 4. Middle Age: War, Mission Secularization, and Return to San Bernardino, 1828-1847	87
Chapter 5. Old Age: Squatters, Land Transfers, and Final Years, 1847-1864	127
Chapter 6. After Inigo: Rancho Posolmi from Walkinshaw to Moffett Field, 1860s-Present	141
Epilogue. The Legacy of the Past	155
References	157
Index	175

List of Figures

Cover: Lope Inigo in 1856
(Santa Clara University Archives)

Frontispiece: Mission and College of Santa Clara in 1856
(Bancroft Library)

Fig. 1. Genealogical Reconstruction of the Family of Lope Inigo viii-ix
(Randall Milliken, based on Mission registers)

Fig. 2. The Geography of San Bernardino, Inigo's World
(Alan K. Brown) xiv

Fig. 3. Rancho Posolmi, About 1850
(Alan K. Brown) 115

Fig. 4. Plat of the Rancho Posolmi, September 1859
(United States Surveyor General 1859) 132

Fig. 5. Lope Inigo in 1856
(Santa Clara University Archives) 140

Fig. 6. The "Ynigo Reservation" in 1876
(Thompson and West 1876) 144

Fig. 7. Posolmi, 1895-1899
(United States Geological Service, 1899) 147

Fig. 8. Posolmi, 1897-1900
(United States Coastal and Geologic Survey 1900) 150

Fig. 9. Posolmi and Moffett Field, 1953
(USGS Mountain View, Calif., 7.5 min., 1953) 152

Fig. 10. Posolmi and Moffett Field, 1981
(USGS Mountain View, Calif. 7.5', 1961, revised 1981) 153

List of Tables

Table 1. Baptisms and Deaths of Children from Santa Clara Valley Villages, Mission Santa Clara, 1777   23

Table 2. Mission Santa Clara Animals, 1798-1828   52

Table 3. Births, Deaths, and Convert Recruitment of Indians at Mission Santa Clara, 1798-1828   63-64

Table 4. Language Groups Represented at Mission Santa Clara at the End of 1817 and 1827   82

Table 5. Central Attributes of the Colonial Mission System vs. Slave, Feudal, and Capitalist Systems   84

Table 6. Mission Santa Clara Indian Rebels Killed in the Estanislao-Cipriano Rebellion, May-June 1829   93

Table 7. Indian Births, Deaths, and Convert Recruitment at Mission Santa Clara, 1829-1847   96

Table 8. Livestock on Hand, Mission Santa Clara, 1834-1840   98

Table 9. Californio Births (Baptized at Mission Santa Clara), Pueblo Population, and Santa Clara County Private Land Grants, 1810-1845   105-106

Table 10. Key Grants from Mission Santa Clara Lands, 1829-1845   113

Table 11. Agricultural Returns and Values for Three Farms on Rancho Posolmi, 1860   138

Table 12. Agricultural Returns and Values for Five Farms on Rancho Posolmi, 1870   143

viii   *Inigo of Rancho Posolmi*

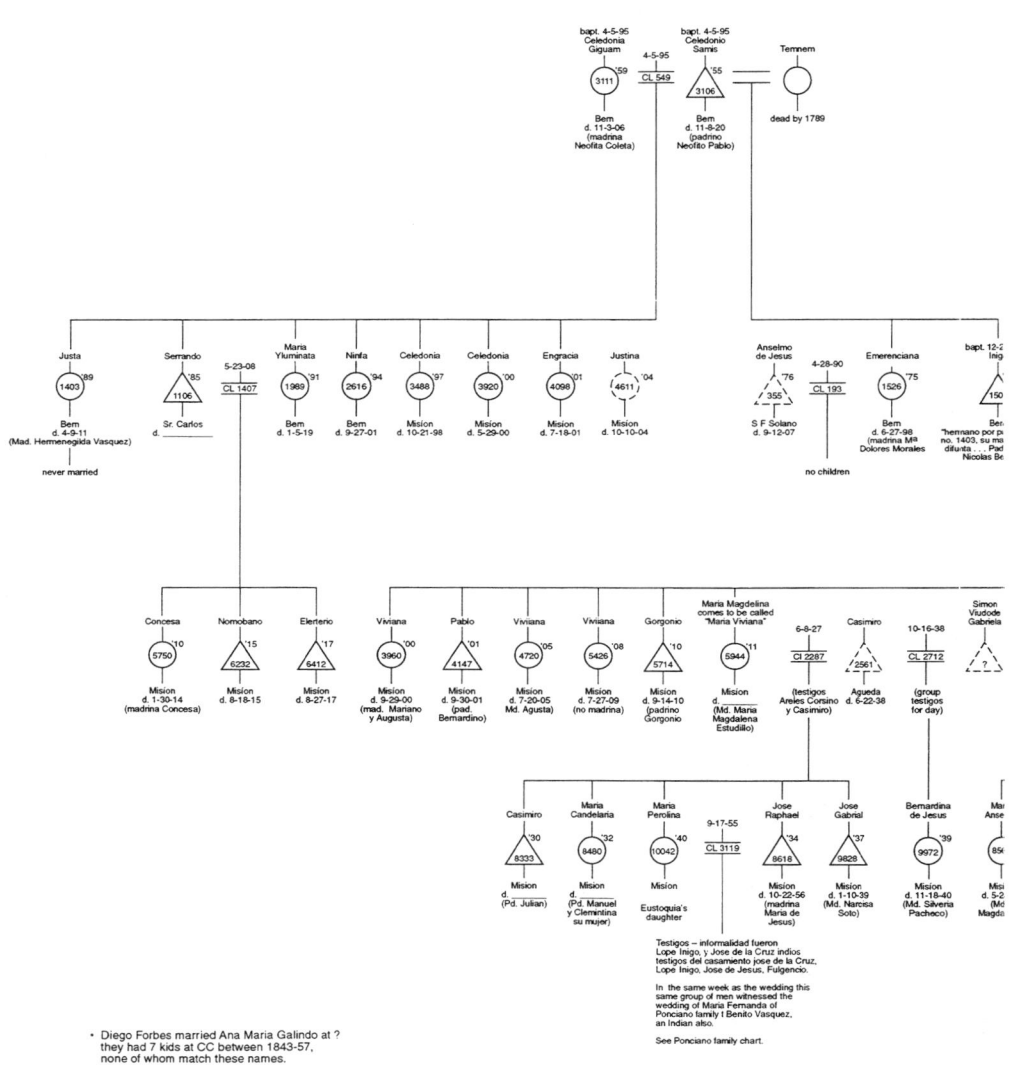

Fig. 1. Genealogical Reconstruction of the Family of Lope Inigo

Inigo of Rancho Posolmi

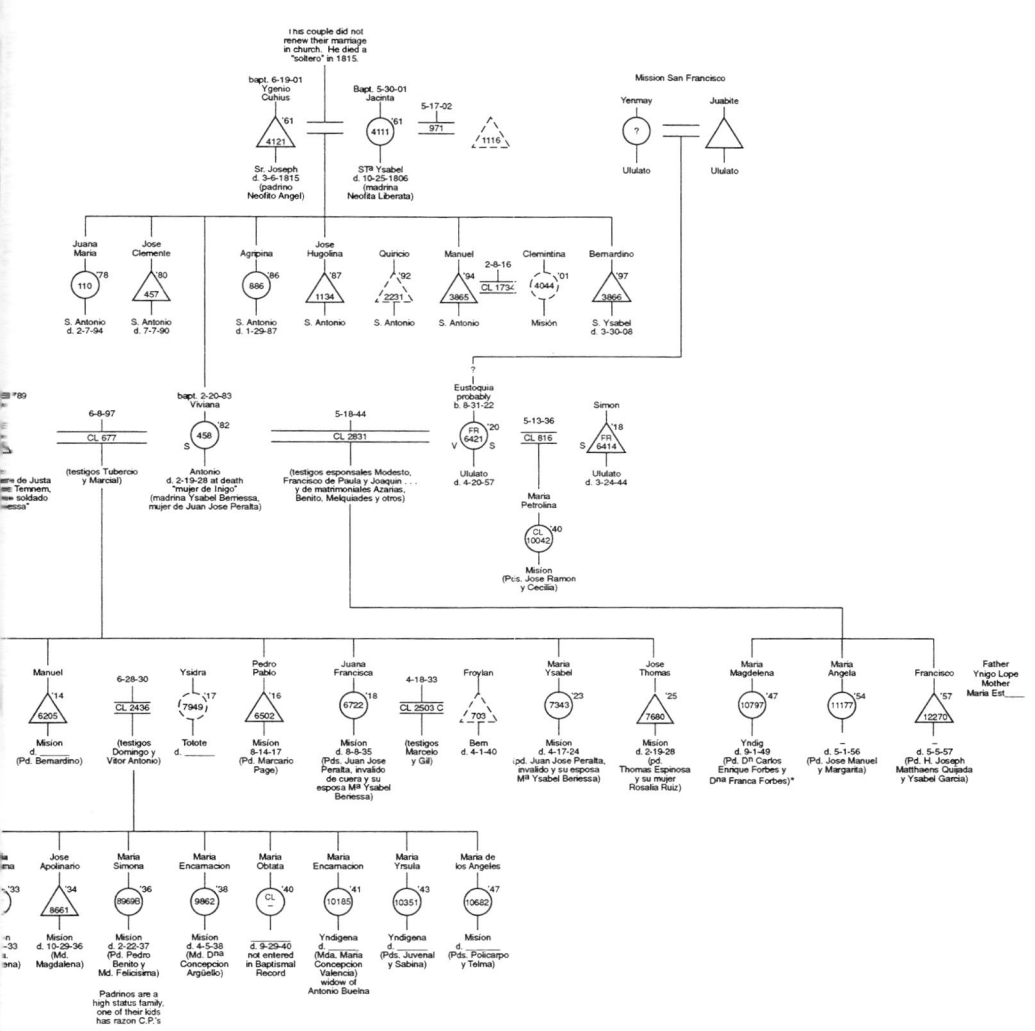

FOREWORD

This book began as a cultural resource management project, one of several mitigation-level studies completed as part of the Tasman Corridor Light Rail Section 106 Compliance Project, conducted for the Santa Clara Transportation Agency. It documents the history of Rancho Posolmi, located about two miles northeast of Mountain View, and especially this rancho's first owner, an Ohlone (Costanoan) Indian whose Christian name was Lope Inigo (1781-1864). For a number of reasons, biographies of Native Americans are rare in American historiography. It was possible to successfully complete this one because Lope Inigo was an important Native American and he lived a long life.

Henceforth we will use the terms Ohlone and Costanoan together in the text to reflect both historical and contemporary usage. When the Spanish arrived in this section of California, they called the Indians who lived in the area "Costanoans" or "Coast People." This term was later adopted by linguists to describe the language spoken by this group of Indians. The term "Costanoan" is not pleasing to many Indian people today, however; they prefer Ohlone, after one of their former villages. Thus the term Ohlone/Costanoan is used in the text of this book.

During the course of this study, we have had to deal with the central problem of a lack of adequate primary source materials. This is a common difficulty when telling the story of an individual who was a member of a group at the bottom of the social and economic hierarchy. Lope Inigo was a leader at Mission Santa Clara and among the most acculturated of Indians, a man who identified with the foreign way of life of the Christian missionaries and Spanish Empire. As we shall see, however, he nevertheless usually operated from a position of socially structured powerlessness. During his long life, he was often forced to choose from an array of undesirable choices. He and his people are mostly invisible and voiceless in the historical record. We thus know almost nothing of what he actually thought and felt. In this and other respects he is quite representative of the hundreds of thousands of Native Americans at that time and place, who lived, loved, worked, and died, both inside and outside the missions. Reconstructing his life, his times, and his relationship to Rancho Posolmi has been a challenge. It has involved a dual focus, both on the specifics of what is known about the man's life and on the historical context of that life. This history thus presents both our limited information about and our analysis of Inigo's birth, marriage, family life, work, land ownership, and death, within the context of the often dramatic historical events and great changes to which he had to adapt in order to survive.

Prior to conducting this research, the authors prepared a research design which would consciously and efficiently guide the investigation and analysis. The key questions posed by this research design focused on three areas: (1) Native American life in the Santa Clara Valley; (2) the life of Inigo and his immediate family; and (3) world system-related transformations in the Santa Clara Valley, including the socioeconomic and political power structures constraining the lives of Indians in this section of California during the 1770s-1860s. During this period, social and economic changes were very rapid. The 10,000-year historical development from a pre-agricultural to an industrial economy and society was compressed into only a relatively few decades in California.

This report is based on both traditional and innovative approaches to the archival record. The more traditional approach consisted of archival research at the following locations, all in California:

>Bancroft and Map libraries, University of California, Berkeley
>Orradre Library, University of Santa Clara
>San Jose Historical Museum
>Library of the Academy of American Franciscan History, Pacific School of Religion, Berkeley
>Mountain View Public Library, Mountain View
>Mountain View Pioneer and Historical Association, Mountain View
>Santa Clara County Free Library, Santa Clara
>Sutro Library, San Francisco
>California State Archives, Sacramento
>Bureau of Land Management, Sacramento

One innovative approach consisted of genealogical reconstruction based on a detailed computerized analysis of Mission Santa Clara baptismal, marriage, and death registers.

The sources for these historical events are virtually all non-Indian. The scarcity of hard data from the Native American viewpoint has, at times, forced us to stop short of drawing conclusions which are probable but not certain and to leave it to the reader to make his or her own judgments about what probably took place. We hope this will stimulate the reader's own historical imagination.

It should be noted that Lope Inigo's name was spelled in various ways. Since the "I" of old Spanish looks like a "Y", his name was frequently recorded as "Ynigo" or "Ynego." Other, less common, spelling variants included "Inygo" and "Indigo."

This book is a result of the joint research of historian Laurence H. Shoup and anthropologist Randall T. Milliken. Dr. Shoup was in overall charge of the project, conducted general research, organized the structure of the report, and wrote chapters 2-6 as well as parts of the Prologue and the Epilogue. Dr. Milliken conducted the mission register research, provided data and an analysis on Mission Santa Clara and its Native American inhabitants, developed the genealogical reconstruction of Inigo's family, and wrote Chapter 1. Dr. Alan K. Brown helped with the Prologue and Epilogue and provided several of the maps used in the report. We would like to thank Suzanne Baker of Archaeological/Historical Consultants and Sally Salzman Morgan of Woodward-Clyde Consultants, who provided insightful comments, helpful suggestions, and unfailing support during the editing of the entire manuscript. The original cultural resource management project was supervised by Sally Salzman Morgan of Woodward-Clyde Consultants.

We wish to express our appreciation to the institutions listed above who permitted the use of their archival resources. We also wish to thank each of the following individuals and institutions for granting permission to quote excerpts from their publications: Academy of American Franciscan History; Alan K. Brown; California Historical Society; Garland Publishing, Inc.; Randall Milliken; Santa Barbara Mission Archive-Library; Santa Clara University; University of California Press; University of Nevada Press; and University of New Mexico Press.

We also wish to express appreciation to the University of California Press for permission to quote from *Font's Complete Diary: A Chronicle of the Founding of San Franciso* by Herbert Bolton, copyright (c) 1931 by the Regents of the University of California; and from *Up and Down California in 1860-1864* by William H. Brewer, edited and translated by Francis Farquar, copyright (c) 1949, also by the Regents of the University of California.

We thank Garland Publishing, Inc., for permission to quote from *Native American Perspectives on the Hispanic Colonization of Alta California*, edited by Edward Castillo, copyright (c) 1991; and Anne McMahon, University Archivist, Santa Clara University, for permission to quote from the papers of Arthur Dunning Spearman.

We are likewise grateful for permission from the San Mateo Historical Association to quote from *Who Discovered the Golden Gate* by Frank M. Stanger and Alan K. Brown, copyright (c) 1969.

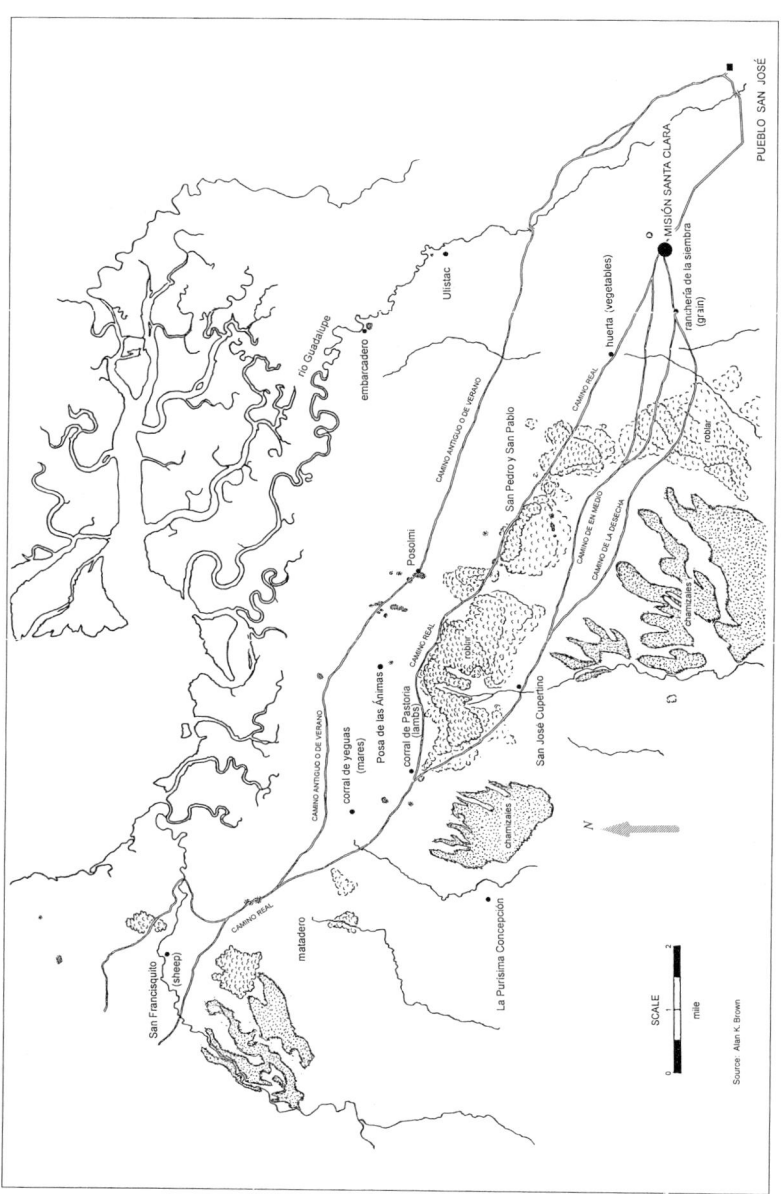

Fig. 2. The Geography of San Bernardino, Inigo's World

PROLOGUE

THE LAND OF LOPE INIGO

Before modern changes to the landscape, the view across the northern Santa Clara Valley from the top of the western mountain ridge was one of large zones of pastel colors, changing with the seasons but luminescent more often than matte. An observer looking out over the predominantly pale green late winter and spring landscape would have seen contrasts milder than those during the early summer, which then would develop slowly, through the long, sober late summer and autumn, into the early winter's near-colorlessness, before the annual spring rejuvenation. Nearest at hand, the viewer's eye would skim the dark, brush-covered mountain wall steeply down onto the park-like foothills. Beyond on the valley floor were gray-green expanses of brush and live oak groves merging into dark masses of deciduous valley (white) oaks, whose clumps, necks, and forests ran forward to end abruptly at a wide sweep of bayside grassland colored pale tan, pale yellow, or pale green depending on the time of year, with heavier broad green patches indicating willow jungles. In an irregular narrow strip just beyond the edge of the hard ground, natural salt-pans lay glaring white in late summer and autumn, followed by the wide zone of bay marsh that, always in contrast to the rest of the landscape, stood out with russet color in winter, green in summer, within its lacework of uncounted tidewater creeks along the nearer side of the southernmost basin of the bay. Then beyond the saltwater bowl's usual blue and the shifting gray of its tidal flats, details of the farther side became diminished by distance until swallowed into the background sweep of grassland with darker seams of wooded gulches rising up over the far ranges. Looking from the eastern ranges, from Mission Peak, another view of the valley was described by W. H. Whitney of the state geological survey in 1861: "The valley looked like a map, and the head of the bay, with its swamps intersected and cut up with winding streams and bayous crossing and winding in every direction, made by far the prettiest arabesque picture of the kind I have ever seen. It was wonderful" (Brewer 1966:174-175).

Ninety-two years earlier, the first Spanish expedition to explore this great sea-arm had advanced southeastward from the Peninsula hills, viewing the "large plain . . . all grown over with white-oaks large and small and some live-oaks . . . . We saw three or four smokes within these woods from heathen (Indian) villages, of which the scouts say there are many . . . the soldiers report that down next to the large estuary there are many lakes and little inlets with countless fowl, ducks, geese, cranes and others." The expedition's chronicler added his own observation of the sweep of bay lands: "To the south, the sea-arm or estuary turns into great numbers of other inlets, and I suppose lakes as well. I had a clear view of it from the height, and it looks like a maze" (Crespí in Stanger and Brown 1969:103-105). This watery world was, like the land, also filled with life—seals, mussels, oysters, salmon, steelhead, shrimp, sturgeon, stingray, and many other kinds of species.

A person traveling overland across the Santa Clara Valley prior to 1769 would have had to detour around marshes, bogs, and ponds, and also cross many watercourses, as standing and flowing water was quite abundant in the valley. Much of the valley was covered with groves of large oaks and other trees. Due to patterns of Indian burning, soil, water, and other factors, some parts of this forest were park-like—open and without significant undergrowth—and other sections dense. Overgrown brushlands of chaparral and poison oak existed, as did meadows, especially in a belt near the Bay. The land was inhabited by numerous animals—deer and foxes, bear and mountain lion, rabbits, squirrels, and smaller mammals.

This, then, was the land to which Lope Inigo was born in 1781. His land was rich and productive, so foreigners forcibly occupied it and established a mission there. Lope Inigo joined this mission (Santa Clara) late in 1789 and lived most of his life in its confines. Late in his life, following the demise of the mission system, he applied for and was granted his own land—Posolmi—which was probably his birthplace. He then lived at this location until his death in 1864. His land of Posolmi and the surrounding countryside was thus the setting for the great historical events of his life, the lives of his people, and of the other human beings who came from great distances to live on this piece of the earth.

CHAPTER 1

BEFORE INIGO, 1750-1781

Introduction

Inigo's parents were born in the lower Santa Clara Valley during the 1750s. Samis (Mission Santa Clara Baptism Number 3106 [SCL-B 3106]), Inigo's father, and Temnem (SCL-B 3111), his mother, were born into a tribal culture unaffected by the western civilization that was spreading around the world at the time. They grew up within a multifamily community, a group composed of 200 or 300 people that held a fixed area some eight miles across, including bayshore marshlands, open grasslands, and oak woodlands. Within their tribal lands, families moved from one spot to another through the seasons to harvest a variety of wild plant and animal foods. The families engaged in feuds with neighboring groups from time to time, but also gathered with their neighbors for regional trade feasts and ceremonies. Before Samis and Temnem reached their thirties, that way of life had begun to change inexorably.

Native Subsistence and Material Culture

Prior to the arrival of the Spanish, Inigo's parents and other eighteenth-century Santa Clara Valley people relied upon a great variety of wild seeds, greens, animals, birds, and fish for their sustenance (Fages 1937 [1775]:71-80). They neither domesticated animals nor tilled the soil. The available ethnographic data indicate that the division of labor was generally based on sex, with men predominantly responsible for gathering animal resources and women predominantly responsible for gathering plant resources.

Women gathered seasonal acorns, hazelnuts, strawberries, blackberries, soap plant root, and dozens of other crops (Palou 1913 [1786]:209). They spent a good deal of time processing acorns from their storage granaries to remove poisonous tannic acid and produce a fine edible flour. Less difficult to prepare, but perhaps just as important in the diet, were the tiny seeds of buttercups, clarkia, and red maids, flowering plants of the open fields. When not gathering in the fields, cooking food, or dealing with their children, women worked on their baskets, woven from sedge roots and other prepared plant fibers. Each household needed many different kinds of large and small baskets, for gathering, storing, and preparing foodstuffs.

Men hunted and fished as their contribution to the food supply. Larger animals were hunted with obsidian- and chert-tipped arrows and sinew-backed bows; small animals were caught in traps. Communal drives for antelope, deer, elk, quail, rabbits, and even grasshoppers accounted for a large proportion of the protein supply in most areas. Steelhead and smaller fish were captured in the creeks with nets and basket traps. Nets were also used to capture ducks and geese in the marshes. Twine and rope were made by men. Twine was necessary for producing such items as hunting and fishing nets, dance regalia, capes, and twisted rabbit-skin blankets. Hemp, milkweed, and nettle are all mentioned in the California ethnographic literature as sources of fiber for cordage.

This division of labor was not, however, necessarily rigid, and varied with age. Even though it appears that men were largely responsible for hunting, women participated in communal hunting drives, often surrounding an area and running and making loud noises to frighten game into the open or into the path of large nets. Likewise, shellfish may have been collected by both sexes. Both men and women appear to have been involved in processing animal resources (butchering, cooking, and hide processing).

Similarly, during intense harvest periods men likely participated in acorn and seed collection, and also shared with female relatives information gathered during hunting trips about plant maturation and abundance. Both men and women harvested and processed vegetable fibers for basket and twine production. In sum, while a functional division of labor existed, the exact extent and rigidity of this division is not explicit in the ethnographic record and it appears that many tasks were shared by both men and women.

Cutting tools used by both sexes were made from chert and obsidian. Chert sources are common in and around the Santa Clara

Valley, while obsidian was traded into the area from the Napa Valley north of San Francisco Bay.

The dress and style of ornamentation of the Santa Clara Valley people have not been described in detail. However, throughout Central California, men wore no clothing at all on most occasions, while women wore skirts of shredded plant fiber or deer skin (Palou 1926 [1786]:3:258). Men pierced their ears and nasal septums and wore a variety of ornaments; women commonly tattooed their faces and upper chests.

Houses were made from conveniently available local materials. In most places they were smallish hemispheric huts thatched with bundles of bulrush or grass (Fages 1972 [1772]:346; Vancouver 1798 [1792]:13). In 1769 Juan Crespí did see a large ceremonial house in a village of 200 people in the Point Año Nuevo vicinity, 30 miles west of the Santa Clara Valley:

> At this village there was a very large grass-roofed house, round like a half-orange, which, by what we saw of it inside, could hold everyone in the whole village [Crespí 1969 (1769):88].

Large earth-covered ceremonial houses, ubiquitous in Central California to the north of the San Francisco Bay, were not documented for the contact period in the southern San Francisco Bay Area.

Population Density and Land Use

The precontact population of the Santa Clara Valley when Inigo's parents were young was at least three, and at most six, persons per square mile, a figure that is quite sparse by today's standards. The available data do not allow us to be any more precise given the weakness of the only two available sources of information, explorers' comments and mission record baptismal counts.

An unknown number of villages dotted the valley at contact. In the spring of 1776, the Anza expedition noted four villages, each with about a hundred people, in the general vicinity of the northern Santa Clara Valley. On March 30, Anza moved south and east from the Palo Alto area toward the Guadalupe River. At Stevens Creek he passed through the first of the four villages, "a settlement of about a hundred heathen" (Anza 1930 [1776]:133). The expedition camped somewhere north of present downtown Santa Clara on the Guadalupe River:

> In the place where we are camped there are three good-sized villages, each about as large as the last one mentioned, composed of people like the foregoing, and by whom, according to the paths and trails, the region upstream appears to be populated [Anza 1930 (1776):134].

This quote tells us that a town of 100 people was considered "good-sized" to the well-traveled Spanish explorers, but is of little help in trying to understand the density and size of villages in the Santa Clara Valley at large. It provides no sense of scale, no information about the distance between the three villages near Anza's Guadalupe River camp, and doesn't give the number of other villages further upstream.

We can reconstruct a general picture of the contact period population density of the Santa Clara Valley by combining Anza's observations with information on Indian conversions recorded in the Mission Santa Clara baptismal register through the late 1700s. Seven local villages supplied converts to Mission Santa Clara from the 1770s through the 1790s. Four of the seven villages near Mission Santa Clara supplied enough converts to suggest that they originally contained more than 100 inhabitants; these were (1) *San Bernardino*, located in the general area where Inigo's parents lived (see Fig. 1)—this location was perhaps the same as the "Yñigo Mounds," but just as likely was on lower Stevens Creek, in what is now Mountain View—which supplied 44 adult married converts between 1784 and 1793; (2) *San Francisco Solano*, probably located on the lower Guadalupe River at or near present Alviso, which supplied 44 adult married converts between 1778 and 1800; (3) *Santa Ysabel*, probably located on the lower Coyote River or Penitencia Creek, in what is now north San Jose, which supplied 40 adult married converts between 1794 and 1802; and (4) *San Jose Cupertino*, probably located on Calabazas Creek or upper Stevens Creek, in what is now Cupertino, which supplied 50 adult married converts between 1780 and 1797.

The other three were smaller villages, as follows: (1) *Our Mother Santa Clara*, which was probably located west of the Guadalupe River within a few yards of one of the Mission Santa Clara sites, and supplied six adult married converts between 1780 and 1781; (2) *Our Patron San Francisco*, probably located on the Guadalupe River near *Our Mother Santa Clara* and *Santa Ysabel*, east of present downtown Santa Clara, which supplied 12 adult married converts between 1778 and 1791; and (3) *San Juan Bautista*, probably located on the Guadalupe River in the Willow Glen area south of present downtown San Jose, which supplied 12 adult married converts between 1780 and 1802.

The four valley villages of 100 inhabitants each which Anza saw while camped on the Guadalupe in March of 1772 may be the same villages as the four larger ones listed above that were noted in the Mission Santa Clara registers. But other evidence suggests that specific villages were merely temporary living sites for local populations that moved from place to place over the years, even over the seasons, in ways that we do not as yet understand.

Village populations seem to have dispersed and come back together in different places at various times of the year. Spanish explorers often found abandoned villages or newly settled ones. For instance, Father Palou visited the San Andreas Valley of the San Francisco Peninsula in November of 1774:

> The first expedition that passed here did not give it a name on account of not finding any villages, while now, in the short stretch that we have traveled, we have found five large ones. From this it is inferred that the country is well populated and that the inhabitants move their villages readily from place to place [Palou 1926 (1773-1783):272].

Mission San Francisco baptismal information also mentions family movement within local landscape areas on the San Francisco Peninsula:

> Like all the aforesaid [*Ssalson* people], they prefer to live at times along the tributaries of the San Mateo River, at other times at the aforesaid village, as well at Sycca. And they come up as far as Guriguri and San Bruno [SFR-B 178].

In some Bay Area districts semipermanent main village sites were maintained year-round while in other districts village populations continually moved among seasonally appropriate sites. Permanent villages seem to have been maintained in areas with a variety of habitats and many types of resources in close proximity (T. King 1974:45).

Although we cannot reconstruct the seasonal movement of populations from one spot to another along the southern San Francisco Bay shoreline and interior, we can propose a population density of four or five people per square mile, living in villages of 20 to 250 people three to five miles apart (Cook 1957; Brown 1973:7; Milliken 1983: 120).

Santa Clara Valley Tribelets

Firsthand ethnographic information about the territories of political groups before the Spanish arrived in the Santa Clara Valley is almost entirely lacking. The priests at Mission Santa Clara stated in 1777 that the "place of the Mission is called Thamien in the language of the natives" and that "there exist four Rancherias in the vicinity of [5 or 2] leagues" (Murguía and Peña 1777). The Spanish used the term *rancheria* indiscriminately to refer to villages and to the multivillage communities that anthropologists call tribelets. A. L. Kroeber (1932:133) coined the latter term to refer to the most common form of political organization throughout aboriginal west central California.

Tribelets were clusters of unrelated family groups that formed cooperative communities for ceremonial festivals, for group harvesting efforts, and—most importantly—for interfamily conflict resolution. In some parts of Central California, such multifamily communities lived for much of the year in a single large village centrally located on their lands. This was true among Pomo groups on Clear Lake, and among Patwin speakers along the Sacramento River. In other parts of Central California, the communities lived in two, three, or as many as five semipermanent villages. Such independent territorial groups can be shown to have existed around Mission San Juan Bautista just to the south of the Santa Clara Valley (the *Uñijaima*, the *Ausaima*, and the *Motsun* were multivillage tribelets) and in the areas around Mission San Francisco to the north of the Santa Clara Valley (the *Huimen* of the Marin Peninsula, the *Huchiuns* of the East Bay, and the *Ssalsons* of the San Francisco Peninsula were also multivillage tribelets).

The word "Thamien" that Murguía and Peña attributed to the region of Mission Santa Clara has a suffix that one would expect to indicate a tribelet. Chester King (1978) offered the first reconstruction of contact period tribelet geography for the Santa Clara Valley. King's map was based upon intermarriage patterns between the various rancherias mentioned in the Mission Santa Clara registers. Unfortunately, the rancherias mentioned in the Santa Clara baptismal register were sometimes villages, sometimes tribelets, and (in four cases) started out referring to specific villages but came to represent huge territorial expanses corresponding to "north" (Santa Agueda), "south" (San Carlos), "east" (San Antonio), and "west" (San Bernardino). Thus the directional assignments made by the priests at Mission Santa Clara are useless for the specific documentation of tribelet locations in the Santa Clara Valley.

Data and analysis suggest the following possible relationships between Mission Santa Clara rancherias and possible tribelet configurations in the lower Santa Clara Valley. First, the rancheria of San Francisco Solano, a specific village at Alviso, may have been part of a tribelet centered near the mouth of Coyote River, or it may have been part of a bayshore tribelet that included the first San Bernardino village in the lower Stevens Creek area. Second, the rancheria of San Bernardino, the term applied to a village on Stevens Creek, may have been part of a tribelet that included the *Puichon* group on lower San Francisquito Creek (baptized at Mission San Francisco de Asis) or it may have been the center for a small Stevens Creek tribelet. Third, the rancherias of San Jose Cupertino, Our Mother Santa Clara, and Our Patron San Francisco, all specific villages, probably comprised a single tribelet (the *Tamien*) that controlled most of the Guadalupe river system, and therefore the core of the Santa Clara Valley. Fourth, the rancheria of San Juan Bautista, a specific village just to the south or east of the original town of San Jose, was the farthest downstream town of a group of villages that were otherwise converted under the regional term "San Carlos"; it probably belonged to a tribelet that included the upper drainage of the Guadalupe River, and the present south San Jose, Campbell, and Los Gatos areas. Finally, the rancheria of Santa Ysabel seems to have been a specific village along the Coyote River to the east or northeast of the town of San Jose. It may have belonged to the *Tamien* tribelet of the Central Santa Clara Valley, or have been the center of an east valley tribelet that also included some family groups from the hills that came to Mission Santa Clara under the regional term "San Antonio."

It cannot be stressed strongly enough that any single configuration of territorial boundaries would be a very shaky approximation. The tribelets, however they were arranged, probably included fixed territories similar in size to those in the central Bay Area, in that each controlled a territory of some eight to ten miles in diameter, including a stretch of some major creek drainage or a group of springs and intermittent rivulets.

The Ohlone/Costanoan Language

Inigo's family and the people of the Santa Clara Valley at the time of the Spanish invasion spoke a language of the Ohlone/Costanoan language family that has been referred to as "Tamyen" by Richard Levy (1978:485). The Ohlone/Costanoan language family is a group of languages once spoken on the Pacific Coast and in the Coast Range valleys from Big Sur northward to the Golden Gate. "Tamyen" was one of eight hypothetical languages of that family. We say that "Tamyen" is a hypothetical language because very few vocabularies exist which would make it possible to reconstruct regional differences between Ohlone/Costanoan dialects.

Levy (1978:485) wrote that the eight Ohlone/Costanoan languages were "separate languages (not dialects) as different from one another as Spanish is from French." Spanish missionary and linguist Felipe Arroyo de la Cuesta (1976 [1821-1837]), on the other hand, warned that the differences between the Ohlone/Costanoan languages spoken at contiguous missions were the result of gradual changes from one group to the next:

> When one rancheria neighbors another, most of their sounds are the same in the one as the other. Although the differences increase with distance between rancherias being compared, the mechanism, or syntax, seems to remain the same.

Arroyo de la Cuesta learned the Ohlone/Costanoan language of Mission San Juan Bautista quite well and he interacted with Indian speakers of the other Ohlone/Costanoan dialects. He stressed the mutual intelligibility of Ohlone/Costanoan languages over a great distance:

> Though they appear to speak distinct languages this is only accidentally true; that is, some of the words are different only because of the manner of pronunciation, in some cases rough, in others agreeable, sweet and strong. Hence it is that the Indians living in a circumference of thirty or forty leagues [eighty to one hundred miles] understand one another [Arroyo de la Cuesta 1976 (1814):20-21].

The differences between neighboring dialects may have been no more distinct than those between, for example, Castilian and Andalusian Spanish. Only by comparing dialects separated by many intervening groups might one find differences as profound as those between Spanish and French.

Political Authority

Spanish commentators provided conflicting information about the nature of political authority among Central California tribelets. Explorers often mentioned interactions with *capitanes*, male village leaders. Anthropologist J. P. Harrington was told by descendants of the aboriginal people of Monterey County that their "captains" or chiefs were responsible for feeding visitors, providing for the impoverished, and directing expeditions for hunting, fishing, gathering, and warfare. The chief acted as the leader of a council of elders (Levy 1978:487). The Monterey area description of political organization is reminiscent of those for most other parts of central California, and probably applies equally well to the Santa Clara Valley.

Tribelet chiefs came from only one of many intermarried lineages within a tribelet. Primary allegiance for individuals was to the authority of the eldest members of one's own descent group. But we do not even know how descent groups were organized among tribelets in the Bay Area. Residence was ambilocal (i.e., married couples could live with either the husband's family or the wife's family) on the San Francisco Peninsula; residence with the husband's group was selected in 60 percent of the cases studied, and with the wife's group in 40 percent (Milliken 1983:58). Such ambilocal residence does not preclude strict unilineal inheritance patterns for certain positions or obligations, but we have no real information regarding such questions.

The processes that kept multiple lineages together under a single chief had everything to do with the native philosophy of how the world works. Father Narciso Duran of Mission San Jose, when asked by the Spanish government in 1812 to characterize native political organization, described an egalitarian people guided by their religious leaders:

> They recognize neither distinction nor superiority at all. Only in war do they obey the most valiant or the luckiest, and in acts of superstition they obey the sorcerers and witch-doctors. Outside of these they do not recognize any subordination, either civil or political . . . [Duran in McCarthy 1958:274].

Duran's statement reflects his lack of interest in the subtleties of native decision-making processes, but it does point out the importance of beliefs regarding supernatural powers as a key element in political power in aboriginal California.

Early writers, all male, failed to mention any leadership roles for women in the native society. Monterey area consultants told J. P. Harrington that the position of chief was handed down through the male line and that when there were no male heirs the office went to a man's sister or daughter (Levy 1978:487). Such a practice is not documented for any other area of west central California. However, there can be no doubt that elder women held power and respect through their understanding of proper rules for dealing with unseen forces. When the first Spanish explorers came into the Bay Area, it was sometimes the women who made speeches to them. Fages encountered a woman leader on the Fremont Plain during an exploration from Monterey in November of 1770:

> On the way close to a little creek about twenty heathens met us and some of the women commenced a dance for our entertainment, with many gestures of joy; one of the women harangued us at no little length [Fages 1969 (1769):120].

Throughout aboriginal North America, political action was intermixed with religious ritual action, although not always in a public way.

A status system probably existed within and among the tribelets of the Santa Clara Valley that was partially expressed through access to prestige roles in ceremonial dances. In all areas of California where ethnographers have explored the matter, rules of proper behavior surrounded every area of human activity. In ambiguous situations, young people had to rely upon more knowledgeable elders, thus granting political power to those elders. Chiefs, male and female, probably controlled recruitment into prestige roles at ceremonial dances. People who failed to meet their expectations in broader aspects of tribal life could be punished by being excluded from positions of honor at these ceremonies.

World View and Ritual Practice

The only written historical information about ritual and world view among eighteenth-century people in the Santa Clara Valley appears in cursory overviews recorded by hostile western writers (Arroyo de la Cuesta 1976 [1814]; Fages 1937 [1775]), and in fragmentary material from early twentieth-century interviews (Harrington 1921-1938). According to native Central California oral traditions, the world of ordinary human beings was preceded by a time of creation, when a supernatural race of beings appeared in time and space to create the world. Gifford (1927) has called these beings "bird people" because they were subsequently represented by feathered entities. After they created humans with their many languages, the bird people went away. In some stories creation time and the present are intimately bound. Settings and characters that in one story seem to have been set in the murky past seem in other stories to be present in parallel worlds at the edges of the known physical world, or in psychic worlds lying behind the visual (Gayton 1935). Doors between the visual world and the supernatural world allowed some powerful personified beings to travel between worlds. Among those doors were specific ones at the four cardinal points, and others in the top of the sky, various deep springs, pools, and other bodies of water.

Origin stories and stories about the first bird people stress the application of specific proper ritual songs and actions, and specific materials, in the creation of a properly ordered world. When the agents of creation did not follow the rules, tragic events occurred. The same was true for humans. They were supposed to follow a set of customary rules in every aspect of life. Proper behavior did not just include a proper way to do jobs, but also proper songs and ritual acts to accompany practical action. People who were particularly good at anything—weaving, hunting, sports, gambling, singing, fighting, or healing—were assumed to be receiving aid from supernatural allies, aid which came to people in dreams.

Throughout Central California, dancing and its associated ceremonial activities were the main forms of expression and were equivalent to what Europeans call religious ritual. Each local group had a fairly fixed schedule of seasonal ceremonies to which they invited their neighbors. The Franciscan priests of Mission Santa Clara recognized that dance ceremonies were given as a form of worship: "They worship the devils offering them seeds and they fast and dance in their honor to placate them" (Catalá and Viader 1976 [1814]:50). Dances were considered as more than mere acts of veneration; they were activities which maintained an undistorted world order. Each region had its own series of ceremonies, with specific dances (choreographed movements, costumes, and accompanying songs) performed in a specific order. Dancers were invested with supernatural powers, and only properly prepared individuals could touch them or their costumes after they were sanctified. Dance regalia was also specially endowed. Upon being ritually blessed, regalia seems to have been considered a part of the parallel supernatural world, as were the dancers when wearing blessed regalia.

People expressed distress at the death of a family member through culturally prescribed actions, such as those described in 1814 by Father Arroyo de la Cuesta at Mission San Juan Bautista:

> In their pagan days the deceased were buried by their relatives in a deep hole after their spine was broken and their bodies doubled up like a ball. As soon as a

pagan died, the wailing began with a most dismal chant. This was continued for the succeeding two nights. All the mourners were bedaubed. The nearest relatives would cut their hair with a sharp stone or a burning stick. They divested themselves of every kind of adornment about the neck, ears and nose and burned all the wearing apparel of the deceased and scattered the ashes at some distance from the village. At times, the survivors would invite their friends and present with shells these who had wailed for the deceased who then agreed to wail for the person a third time [Arroyo de la Cuesta 1976 (1814):99].

Early Spanish explorers thought they recognized cemeteries in three different areas near the Santa Clara Valley. At Pescadero Creek on the Pacific Coast, Father Francisco Palou described a cemetery near an abandoned village:

> Near the two large arroyos we found vestiges of villages, with a cemetery, in which were planted two slender poles, straight and very high. From the point of each one hung a small cape made of grass of the sort used by the heathen, which doubtless belonged to those who were buried there, as is their custom [Palou 1926 (1774):293].

The following day Palou reported another cemetery near Point Año Nuevo:

> We found vestiges of a deserted village, with its cemetery, in which was planted a high pole, this being the monument used by the heathen for the sepulchres of the chief men of the village [Palou 1926 (1774):295].

Eighteen months later, in March of 1776, Pedro Font described a cemetery in the present San Martin area of southern Santa Clara County:

> On passing near the village which I mentioned on the road we saw on the edge of it something like a cemetery. It was made of several small poles, although it was not like the cemeteries which we saw on the [Santa Barbara] Channel. On the poles were hung some

things like snails and some tule skirts which the women wear. Some arrows were stuck in the ground, and there were some feathers which perhaps were treasures of the persons buried there [Font 1930 (1776):322].

More recent ethnographic accounts for the Konkow Maidu people farther north in California describe the practice of yearly burning ceremonies for five years after a person's death. Poles were hung with clothing and baskets, then burned to honor the dead (Riddell 1978:382-383). The presence of poles at abandoned villages suggests that the contact-period people of the Santa Clara and San Mateo county areas left materials to honor the dead intact.

Mortuary practices were variable within tribelets. The Franciscans at Mission San Jose described the non-Christian funerary practices in an 1812 report:

> In their mourning for and burial of their dead they do not have much ceremony beyond a great deal of weeping and groaning and wailing, and wrapping the dead man in all of his clothes, jewels, etc., which they assume will be of service to him, for they are not without some idea (albeit a rather ridiculous one) of the immortality of some part of the man. Immediately after death, or at times even before death (of which there have been a few instances), they either bury or cremate the body [Duran and Fortuny 1958 (1814):274].

The death register of Mission Santa Clara contains many entries documenting burials in villages (Santa Clara Death Register, entries 336, 544, 574, 578, and others). Fewer entries mention cremation (Santa Clara Death Register, entries 134, 429, 1641, 3221). A group entry in mid-January of 1802 states that ten people "have died in their non-Christian villages and their non-Christian relatives or their own parents have buried or cremated them" (Santa Clara Death Register, entries 2707-2716).

Regional Interactions

Speaking of the entire area of west central California, Pedro Fages wrote in 1775:

> The land also provides them with an abundance of seeds and fruits . . . although the harvesting of them and their enjoyment is disputed with bow and arrow among these natives and their neighbors, who live almost constantly at war with each other [Fages 1937 (1775):70].

Langsdorff also conveyed an impression that a low level of warfare was prevalent: "The great endeavor of the contending parties in all their conflicts is to steal away the young girls and the wives of the enemy" (Langsdorff 1814 [1806]:107). Similar comments were repeatedly made by visitors during the period of Spanish and Mexican colonization. Beechey, for example, noted in 1827:

> The tribelets are constantly at war with one another, often in consequence of trespasses upon their territory and property; and weak tribelets are sometimes wholly annihilated or obliged to associate themselves with those of their conquerors [Beechey 1968 (1831):77].

These observations by outsiders do not tell us all that we would like to know about the dynamics of aboriginal warfare in the Bay Area. Around the world groups in small-scale societies lacking regional judicial institutions settle conflicts through reprisal. When injury and reprisal occur between groups of blood relatives, the struggle is called a feud. When unrelated groups band together to fight others, the fighting may be termed warfare (Otterbein 1977:924). The observations of outsiders, who probably did not know the details of any given conflict, do not help us generalize regarding the extent to which hostilities in the region took place as interfamily feuds, or as true political warfare between multifamily tribelets. Nor do we have any ethnographic information regarding processes of feud settlement or other types of conflict resolution.

Despite territoriality and intergroup hostility, people of the region were bound in a regional genetic fabric. At least 25 percent of the married adults in the tribelets of the San Francisco Peninsula were born to families from neighboring groups and moved to the group of their spouse at marriage. Most intertribelet marriages occurred between adjacent groups, no farther than ten or twelve miles apart. Only occasionally did people move to villages as far as 25 miles from their home (Milliken 1983:125). If Inigo's mother and father were not from the same tribe, they may have met during some regional ceremonial or trade gathering.

The Spanish Colonial System

In 1769, the foundations of the traditional world of Inigo's parents and the other native people of the Santa Clara Valley were shaken. The entry of Spanish missionaries into the Bay Area in that year marked a new era. Within the Ohlone/Costanoan world there was now an alien force, active, aggressive, and relatively dynamic—the Spanish colonial system.

While for over 200 years the various institutions of this colonial system had had a mild interest in Alta California (the lands north of Baja California), the expansion of the rival imperial systems of Russia and England along the West Coast were a spur that moved Spanish power into action. The moment of crisis came in the 1760s, when the severe defeat of France and Spain at the hands of England and her allies in the Seven Years War motivated fears of further British and Russian expansion at the expense of the far-flung Spanish empire. Taking advantage of this atmosphere and relying on the availability of the military reinforcements which the government of King Carlos III had sent to the New World, the king's powerful inspector-general in Mexico, José de Galvez, developed a colonization plan for Alta California (Brown in Companys 1983:24). The plan, which was also signed by the viceroy and the archbishop, had as its ultimate goal to occupy for Spain ". . . territories so extensive, abundant and rich by nature, that they may in a few years constitute a new Empire equal to, or better than this one of Mexico" (Cook 1973:43).

Galvez and his fellow imperial planners had a grand vision of a rich and thriving economy on the North American continent northwest of Sonoran Mexico. However, they found no enthusiasm among the general population of their empire, and very little in the central government in Madrid, for a move into distant lands possibly besieged by hostile Indians and lacking any modern infrastructure. Among the few enthusiastic supporters of the plan were the Franciscan missionaries. By a historic coincidence, just at this time these missionaries were in the process of replacing the Jesuit order of priests in the management of Catholic missions to the natives of northwestern Mexico. These Spanish-born Franciscans, supervised and ultimately under the authority of a military commander and governor directly appointed by the Viceroy in Mexico, would be point-men in the vanguard of colonialism.

In practice, the way the system evolved resulted in the first colonists being the small number of soldiers who occupied the country in company with the missionaries. As soon as possible, the soldiery would assume a police function, as the mission stations, drawing on native converts as a labor source, became agricultural plantations supported by Indian laborers. Soldiers and their families who were especially favored by the missionaries would often serve as instructors for the 'missionized' natives, so that the agriculture and primitive industry of the missions could become the economic backbone of the colony. There would be few settlers other than the military. As it transpired, in the small towns where civil colonists began the development of individualistic, small-scale farming, the population was mainly composed of retired soldiers' families. This Spanish-speaking population, from padres and mission military guards to retired farmers and ranchers, would gradually control more and more of the land. In time, this would force an end to native hegemony, resulting in a radical transformation of the economy and society of California, first in localities around the missions and subsequently in wider and wider areas. Eventually, Indian people as far east as the Sierra Nevada were impacted by the power emanating from the missions and pueblos. It is worth noting that the dual structure of Spanish colonialism—the missionaries with their relatively "soft line" toward the native people and the military with its often violent "hard line"—was generally very effective in preventing successful Indian uprisings.

Period of Spanish-Indian Contact, 1769-1776

Inigo's parents were in their early twenties when the Spanish colonists first entered the lower Santa Clara Valley in the fall of 1769. On November 10 of that year, at the end of a long exploration up through the California coast ranges and along the San Mateo coast from San Diego, the Portolá expedition camped on San Francisquito Creek, about seven miles north of the "Yñigo Mounds." According to the diarist Father Juan Crespí:

> At once upon our reaching here, several very well-behaved heathens, most of them well-bearded, came to the camp, giving us to understand that they were from three different villages, and I do not doubt there must be many of these, from the many smokes seen in different directions [Crespí in Stanger and Brown 1969:105].

In 1770, the Spaniards established a town and mission on Monterey Bay, some eighty miles south of the Golden Gate. From Monterey they sent new exploratory parties north to San Francisco Bay, through an inland route up the Santa Clara Valley. Pedro Fages led the first inland exploration into the Santa Clara Valley, through the lands of the local Indian groups known as the *Matalans* and *Tamiens*, thence northward into the East Bay area, in November of 1770. Fages did not record his interactions with Santa Clara Valley people on that trip.

On March 24, 1772, Pedro Fages again came up along the east side of the Santa Clara Valley to camp at Scott Creek, where people came to visit him from two nearby villages, one of seven huts, the other of nine huts. After an exploration of the Carquinez Strait and Diablo Valley areas, the party moved back south along the east side of the Santa Clara Valley on April 4:

> We encountered heathen who as soon as they saw us got scared and ran inside their two little houses. (I wanted to give them) some little strings of beads, but there was no way we could make them receive the gift [Fages 1972 (1772):354].

Bay Area tribelets were left undisturbed from April 1772 until the fall of 1774. During that two-and-a-half year period, Spanish troops and Christian missionaries worked on the new presidio at Monterey Bay and Mission San Carlos Borromeo on the nearby Carmel River. The Monterey Peninsula is some forty miles south of the Santa Clara Valley, just beyond the direct spheres of social interaction of the southernmost Bay region tribelets. However, indirect news about the Spanish settlements must have arrived in the Bay region, passed northward from village to village.

In the late fall of 1774, a group of *Matalan* hunters in the upper Santa Clara Valley encountered a group of mounted Spaniards under the command of Captain Fernando Rivera y Moncada:

> We passed a patch of willows and cottonwoods, and now found running water in the creek. Here, all at once, there were heathens standing with their weapons in hand, [though] they made no show of them. In people such as these, who have no knowledge of others and live like wild beasts at bay, it is second nature to snatch them up [Moncada 1969 (1774):133].

Moncada's expedition was looking for possible locations for a mission and military base on the San Francisco Peninsula. The party was not warmly received by hunters further along in the western Santa Clara Valley:

> In a little grove of those trees, about one in the afternoon, we came to three heathen with bows and arrows. Apparently they had been hunting, for we did not see in all that vicinity either village or smokes, although on the plain we came across many well-beaten paths . . . . We passed not far from them and I called to them, but they did not wish to come near, even though I showed them some beads, but they made signs that I should throw them, which I did, but not even then did they approach. Seeing this, the commander alighted and took the beads, and gave them to them; we then went on our way, leaving them at their work [Palou 1926 (1773-1783):III:262].

The *Puichons* on San Francisquito Creek, on the other hand, received the Rivera party warmly. On November 29, the Spanish party left them and continued north through *Lamchin* and *Ssalson* lands.

Inigo's parents were definitely together and starting a family by 1775. In that year, Inigo's older sister, Ronsom, was born. We do not know if she was their first child, but she was the oldest of his siblings ever to be baptized (SCL-B 1526).

In the spring of 1776, Juan Bautista de Anza led a group north from Monterey into the San Francisco Bay Area in search of a site for a military base and a mission. His group included Franciscan priest Pedro Font, eleven soldiers, and seven servants and muleteers. The diaries of the expedition indicate that by 1776 the local people were becoming increasingly familiar with the Spaniards and, in at least two places, increasingly antagonistic.

Matalan people of the southern Santa Clara Valley met the Anza party on March 25, 1776, and reacted with annoyance when the Spaniards did not stop with them:

> On seeing us they shouted amongst the oaks and then came out naked like fauns, running and shouting and making many gestures, as if they wished to stop us, and signaling to us that we must not go forward. Although they came armed with bows and arrows, they committed no hostility toward us . . . . Their method was to run, one behind the other in single file, until they got ahead of us, and then, halting, they began to shout and even to shriek, making many gestures and signs as if they were angry and did not wish us to go forward. Then, seeing that we continued on our way, without

paying any attention to them, they again started to run to get ahead of us. Then they went through the same performance . . . although we understood nothing of what they said. And so they continued for about a league, when all but a few of them went away, then, finally, little by little even these left us and we saw them no more [Font 1930 (1776):323-324].

The Anza party was the fifth Spanish group to pass through *Matalan* lands since 1770. The *Matalans* may have been tired of the foreigners wandering through their lands without even stopping to acknowledge them, let alone exchange gifts and receive formal permission to cross through.

Father Pedro Font reported two villages of "20 tule huts" in the southern Santa Clara Valley area (south of Coyote) in 1776 (Font 1930 [1776]:320). He saw a total of 100 people while passing up the west side of the Santa Clara Valley (Font 1930 [1776]:324).

The Anza party continued northward to the tip of the San Francisco Peninsula, where they explored the eventual presidio and mission sites of San Francisco. Next, they retraced their steps down the Peninsula, then turned eastward across a part of the Santa Clara Valley that had not been traversed by the earlier Spanish expeditions.

At a village of about a hundred people on or near Stevens Creek, they gave out beads to allay people's fears. One old woman, perhaps a shaman, reacted to the invaders as if they were spirit beings:

> One of the women, from the time when she first saw us until we departed, stood at the door of her hut making gestures like crosses and drawing lines on the ground at the same time talking to herself as though praying, and during her prayer she was immobile, paying no attention to the glass beads which the commander offered her [Font 1930 (1776):354].

The actions of the Stevens Creek woman suggest that some people viewed the invaders as supernatural beings or sorcerers. It is quite possible that this was the village of Samis, Temnem, and Inigo. Anza's party subsequently camped on the lower Guadalupe River:

> In the place where we camped there are three good-sized villages, each about as large as the last one mentioned, composed of people like the foregoing, and

by whom, according to the paths and trails, the region upstream appears to be populated [Anza 1930 (1776): 134].

Indigenous people of the San Francisco Bay region reacted in a variety of ways during their first encounters with the Spaniards. Curiosity and helpfulness were the most common initial reactions; in some areas, however, people showed great fear. By 1776, some tribelets were reacting with increasing warmth, while others were exhibiting scorn.

The Beginning of Santa Clara Missionization, 1777

The Spanish founded Mission Santa Clara on January 6, 1777, a few months after their movement through the valley to found Mission San Francisco some forty miles to the north (Palou 1913 [1786]:213). In the fall of that year a small number of settlers from Mexico founded the nearby town of San Jose Guadalupe. The local native people, including Inigo's parents, were given an abrupt introduction to the full range of European-style village culture, from language to livestock, house design, and daily life. They also learned the consequences of breaking Spanish law. In 1777, Spanish troops killed three local people who had butchered cattle and resisted arrest (Palou 1926 [1773-1783]:161).

No Indian people were baptized as Catholics during the first five months of Mission Santa Clara's existence. Palou (1913 [1786]:213) wrote, however, that the local Indian people visited the missionaries and presented them with gifts. In May of 1777 an epidemic struck the children of the local villages around the mission. "The Fathers were able to perform a great many baptisms by simply going through the villages" (Palou 1913 [1786]:213). The Franciscan priests baptized 54 sick and dying children between June 6 and June 22, 1777. The baptized children ranged in age from a few days old to seven years old (Santa Clara Baptisms nos. 1-54). Table 1 indicates the villages in which the children were baptized, as well as the number of those children who actually died during that spring and summer.

The true severity of this epidemic of 1777 is unknown. The figures for deaths represent only baptized children. There is no way of knowing how many children in these villages did not get sick, nor of knowing how many parents chose not to bring their sick children to the foreign priests. The recovery rates of the baptized children suggest, however, that the people from some of these villages, San Jose Cupertino and San Bernardino in particular, may have had a more positive attitude toward the newcomers by the end of the summer than did the people of the other villages.

Table 1
Baptisms and Deaths of Children from Santa Clara Valley Villages, Mission Santa Clara, 1777

Village	Children Baptized	Children Died
Santa Clara (downtown Santa Clara)	2	1
San Francisco (downtown San Jose?)	7	3
San Francisco Solano (Agnews/Alviso area)	5	3
San Juan Bautista (toward Campbell)	15	10
San Jose Cupertino (Cupertino)	13	3
Santa Ysabel (Milpitas/N. San Jose)	4	2
San Bernardino (Mountain View/Palo Alto area)	3	0
San Antonio (E. San Jose/Hall's Valley area)	2	1
Totals	51	23 (45.1 percent)

The first mission site was probably within the territory of San Francisco Solano, a large village of over two hundred near the mouth of the Guadalupe River. The first adult convert at Mission Santa Clara was an old man from this village, converted on June 26, 1777. By the end of that first year seven more children and five teenagers had been converted (Santa Clara Baptisms). Over the next three years, scores of children from the surrounding villages were baptized. The baptized children normally would continue to live in their native villages with their parents and only at their majority (usually at nine or ten years of age) become a part of the residential mission community. Only 53 adults, however, joined the mission, and only 22 of them were married. Not until 1789, twelve years after its founding, would the missionaries convince significant numbers of married adults to leave their villages and move to Mission Santa Clara. The long-term Spanish goal was to baptize all the natives and bring them under the control of the priests and into the developing self-sufficient mission communities, the main production unit of the colonial system. This goal was never significantly altered during the two-thirds of a century period of the mission's existence.

CHAPTER 2

INDIAN CHILDHOOD AND MISSION YOUTH: FROM SAN BERNARDINO TO SANTA CLARA, 1781-1797

Native Childhood

Inigo was born in 1781, on the cusp between the native world which had existed for centuries and the new reality being created by Spanish colonization. At Inigo's birth, his people's world, including the Native American philosophy and lifeways which had existed for centuries in this part of California, was still largely intact. The dominant political economy was still the native one and the vast majority of the people of the Santa Clara Valley still lived as they always had, by hunting and gathering. By 1781, however, there was also another reality. At Mission Santa Clara and the nearby secular town of San José Guadalupe, Spanish colonialism was entering Inigo's world. The conquest and domination of Native American lives, labor, and land was underway.

Both persuasion and force, of many varieties, went into this religious and economic conquest of native society. Under the rules of Spanish colonialism, persuasion, including gift-giving and the attraction of the unfamiliar and abundant foods produced by newly introduced agriculture and stock-raising, was emphasized, to induce people to voluntarily join the Spanish missions. Indian people were never supposed to be physically forced into conversion. In addition, unlike the Anglo-American concept of ownership in which land could easily be sold, land utilized by the Spanish missions was held to belong legally to the Indians. However, in the view of the Spanish missionaries and colonists, the local people were like children, ignorant of "rational" (civilized) behavior; the land was therefore to be held in trust for them by the mission and colonial authorities. Spanish military officers were willing to use all the force at their disposal in order to maintain their settlements, including the missions. In practice, Spanish authorities favored the "civilized" order enjoined by Spanish laws, and the natives were not viewed or treated as having equal status with the Spanish colonists.

The overall practical effect of Spanish hegemony, economically speaking, was to produce and maintain a large colonial labor force drawn from the native population, one which was to be constantly renewed by new Indian converts. This labor force consisted of local people recently separated from their own institutions who worked at relatively undifferentiated tasks for minimal material rewards. Among the missionized natives, only a handful of individuals stood out as personalities by their actions, accomplishments, or—ultimately, after the effects of epidemic disease and other aspects of colonialism—actual survival. The life of Lope Inigo, whose native name is unknown to us, spanned all but the earliest of the events that have just been described. His life—although not necessarily fully representative or typical of the whole Native American experience in coastal California—is certainly illustrative of the times and experiences of many of these colonized people during the founding period of California history.

Inigo was born four years after the founding of the mission station of Santa Clara. His family was part of a tribelet that lived a few miles to the northwest of the new mission's location, in an area to which the Spanish-speaking padres had assigned the name of "San Bernardino." The tribe's exact territory is not definitely known, but it probably included the place later known as "Ynigo Mounds," at or near archaeological site CA-SCL-12, near the southeastern edge of today's Moffett Field. Mission Santa Clara later stood in its various locations near the Guadalupe River about six miles to the east. The Moffett Field area was included in the Mexican-era land grant (given the native name of Posolmi) when Inigo received it, much later in his life. The Posolmi grant was also sometimes called "San Bernardino" in the 1850s land-grant case papers, verifying the connection between the two (United States 410 ND).

As a family group living in an intact village west of the new mission, Inigo and his family would have had numerous occasions to encounter the Spanish and their ways. As we have seen, the Spanish padres and military were very active in the area, beginning several years before his birth. Then, when Inigo was still a baby, dramatic events began to take place at the new mission site. In 1781, the year Inigo was born, Father Junipero Serra, assisted by Fathers Crespí, Peña, and Murguía, laid the cornerstone of a massive new church at Santa Clara. The construction of this new church over the following three years must have been an amazing thing for the local native peoples, for its size was impressive for its time and place. An early description of the church can be found in the old Baptismal Register:

The church walls are one vara and a half [4.2 feet] thick, of adobe, on stone foundations, supported by buttresses one vara [2.8 feet] thick. Its dimensions inside are eight varas [22.4 feet] high, forty and one-half [113.4 feet] long, and nine varas [25.2 feet] wide. The sacristy, which is in the rear of the chancel, has the same height and thickness of the walls as the church; its length is equal to the width of the church, and its width is six varas [16.8 feet]. A portico measuring five varas [14 feet] extends, as regards the roof, along the entire length of the building. In the church and the sacristy there is a flat ceiling of wooden beams on brackets with a planking of wood of *alerche*, commonly called redwood. Above this flat ceiling there is a pavement of adobe flags, and above all there is a slanting roof well adapted for drainage. The brackets extend beyond the walls, as also the thatch of the roof, to protect the walls from rains, which are very abundant. The main door and the cloister door, or side door, each have two leaves, are made of cedar and redwood respectively and each is provided with a lock. The two doors of the sacristy are of the same material (redwood), each having one leaf, and provided with locks. The church is whitewashed inside and outside. The walls inside are painted with a border above and below. The entire chancel and a great part of the ceiling are also painted. The whole floor is a pavement of adobe flags[1][Webb 1952:125].

On May 15 and 16, 1784, when Inigo was about three years old, an elderly Father Serra returned to Santa Clara for the blessing of the completed church, assisted by Fathers Palou and Peña (Webb 1952:124). One report states that this public event was well attended, with "all of the neophytes, many of the unchristianized Indians, the troops and many of the people from the Pueblo of San Jose . . . " in attendance (Hall 1871:420). None of Inigo's family had as yet been baptized into the mission, but they may have been there that day to visit and partake in the activities.

People from the area known as San Bernardino were baptized from 1777 on. The usual pattern was for the Indians to come to the mission for baptism, although sometimes the padres would go to villages to undertake this task. Most of those baptized were children under the age of seven. It was apparently very common in the 1780s for non-Christian Indian women to bring their children into the mission to be baptized, then raise those children in their native villages, with the children only moving to the mission later (Milliken 1991:139-140). In general, the convert population in this era was young. The San Bernardino area, for example, contributed mostly children. One study found that of the 161 baptisms of gentile (non-Christian) Indians from San Bernardino during the 1777-1788 years, only 35 were over ten years old. Fully 78.3 percent (126 individuals) were aged ten or younger (Jackson 1984:233). Some of these Indian children were apparently baptized because of their parents' fear of the Spanish, whose horses and armored riders with guns and lances were technologically far superior militarily to anything the native people could put forward in battle. In January 1783, for example, José Moraga led an expedition against some of the local rancherias, the causes and results being reported by Father Francisco Palou:

> He came back again to chastise some heathen in the neighborhood of Santa Clara who had killed some mares belonging to the settlers of the pueblo of San José. The heathen took up arms, and our soldiers killed two of them without having one of ours even wounded, and being frightened by this they voluntarily gave up some of their children for baptism [quoted in Winter 1978:440].

This incident indicates that the native people were carrying out a survival strategy that involved suing for renewed peaceful relations when they were defeated by superior military power. Indeed, mission baptism records show that a large increase in baptisms (31 total, all children under seven years of age) took place during the following month, February 1783 (Santa Clara Baptism Records). This was by far the largest monthly total of baptisms since the founding of the mission. This was a pattern which would later be repeated.

Moraga's punitive expedition also indicates that from an early date, the Spanish considered it criminal for the local natives to hunt the non-native animals brought in by the Spanish, or to trespass and damage settlers' fields (Milliken 1991:135). The mission padres sometimes protested that the settlers' livestock (which already numbered 600 head by 1780) were destroying the Indian food supply, and that the Indians therefore were justified in slaughtering such livestock. This protest was unheeded. Besides the two natives killed in the above-mentioned incident, two men who had killed horses were taken to the San Francisco Presidio where they were reportedly given lashes every three days for 15-20 days (Milliken 1991:135).

Despite isolated events which led to a temporary surge in children brought for baptism, the overall pace of mission conversions was slow during Inigo's childhood, a fact which, together with other problems, disturbed Fathers Peña and Noboa. On the one hand, by the end of 1786 the mission had been in operation for almost a decade and real economic and demographic progress had been made. The total Mission Santa Clara neophyte population was 557 people, including " . . . 61 families of married neophytes who live in a village of straw houses and they go to church mornings and afternoons . . . " (Noboa and Peña 1786:39). The Indian village, made up of people from various tribelets, was therefore in place next to the mission church by this time. Besides straw huts, there existed six rammed-earth palisade wall houses, at least one of which was used for the *monjeria*, or unmarried women's house, which was closely guarded and locked at night (Milliken 1991:153). The mission was also making economic progress. It had a variety of animals (horses, sheep, goats, pigs, cattle, mules), some in fairly large numbers, and was producing such crops as wheat, barley, garbanzos, lentils, peas, corn, beans, pears, apples, peaches, quince, and pomegranates (Noboa and Peña 1786:38; 1787:45).

On the other hand, the mission priests found the Indian adults reluctant to join the mission system. The priests complained as follows in their report dated December 31, 1786:

> There are innumerable heathen in the Rancherias that surround the mission and only a few of them know [Christianity] from those who have become baptized. We are denied the assistance of the guard in order to go out to allure them, flatter them, and charm them without which we are unable to assure the fruit, that we are after, as we have experimented, visiting from time to time the rancherias, to request them humbly [to submit] to the superiority . . . [quoted in Winter 1978:441].

It appears that the priests desired the guard for both security purposes and to impress the natives with the raw power of Spanish colonialism, thus helping assure a favorable result in their conversion efforts. Another hindrance to conversion, in the eyes of the missions, was that insufficient gifts were available to lure the natives. A June 30, 1784, report by the padres stated that they needed the following:

> . . . clothes to dress the neophytes who have none other than the ones given by the ministers. We cannot cover their nudity by other means, because even

if this Mission could sell enough seeds, and with the profits bring clothes to dress the converted ones, and therefore bring to our faith many gentiles, who are commonly attracted by clothing and food, we do not have these means since not even the soldiers and the presidios can obtain clothes [Noboa and Peña 1784:34].

Furthermore, the padres also saw native relations with the settlers of San Jose as a problem, arguing that unconverted Indians were being employed in the town and were not being properly disciplined there, resulting in "much sin," and damage to the mission. They added that the townspeople:

> . . . let them live in their old freedom and gentile customs and participate in them themselves, and teach them unworthy vices, because there is work and food, they refuse to submit to the bond of the gospel and the laws of Christianity . . . [Noboa and Peña 1788:47].

Thus it appears that the secular powers were more willing for the natives to remain on their land and continue traditional ways as long as they did not kill or harm the settlers' roving stock. The Church and its leaders were much more anxious to actually stamp out a native lifestyle which they saw as sinful.

During the mid-1780s there were also occasional food shortages at Mission Santa Clara, forcing the Indians to return to gathering native foods. Part of the reason was apparently because the mission had to feed the military. At the end of 1786, Noboa and Peña reported:

> This year nothing was built because of scarcity of food, and because with the food we helped the troops, that is why all the summer most of the neophytes were kept in the fields, and in the Mission only a few for the most necessary work [Noboa and Peña 1786:38].

In spite of shortcomings, Spanish material culture and practices must have been powerfully attractive for the native people. The variety of goods, the giant church building, the music and ritual of the church services, the different animals (all new to the natives), the tools and processes of agricultural production, and the great power of the Spanish military on horseback were impressive. The missionaries must have been viewed as having a close relationship with the supernatural powers. Their power and subsequent attraction for the Indians may have been most keenly felt by the more malleable youth, who were not as set in the ways of their forefathers as the adults. To them, the glitter of the mission and the new ways and adventure it represented may have made them at least interested in entering into a relationship with the institution and its leaders. Still, the decision to be baptized was a decision made mostly by adults for their children, since the vast majority of those baptized during the 1770s and 1780s were under ten years of age.

Though the adults also felt the attraction of the mission and feared the military, they were pulled by their own traditions and lifeways and by their strong ties to and intimate knowledge of their very specific territory and its natural features. The adults were thus terribly torn between two worlds and psychologically confused about what to do. It seems probable that bringing their children for baptism represented a kind of temporizing and compromise between the old and the new. In that way, they had a foot in both camps and a kind of insurance policy. They maintained their own villages and traditional lifeways, and at the same time, developed a relationship with a new and very powerful institution and the people who ran it. Different family groups must have responded differently to the dilemma posed by the arrival of the Spanish and their mission, with some entering the mission more rapidly or with more commitment than others.

In the case of Inigo, it appears that the influence of his stepmother may have been decisive. Inigo's mother Temnem died during his early childhood, sometime before 1789. His widowed father's new wife was named Giguam (later baptized with the name Celedonia) and in June of 1789 she gave birth to a daughter in Inigo's home village in the region of San Bernardino, west of the mission. At one month old, this daughter was taken to the mission for baptism. She was baptized with the name Justa (#1403) on July 13, 1789. Inigo may have made the trip to the mission with his stepmother, stepsister, and perhaps his father as well. With one member of the family baptized, and perhaps under the influence of his wife, Inigo's father Samis (Celedonio) agreed to allow both eight-year old Inigo and his 15-year old sister "Emerenciana" (her Spanish name) to be baptized at the mission. Inigo was baptized first, on December 26, 1789 (#1501), together with five other children from the San Bernardino area. Three of them (two boys and one girl) were seven or eight years old, and the others were much younger. So perhaps Inigo was baptized with two of his playmates.

Inigo had an Indian name which we do not know. His Christian name, "Inigo," was taken from Saint Ignatius, Bishop of Antioch, Syria, martyred on December 20, 107 A.D. Saint Ignatius was captured by the Romans during the period when Christianity was a proscribed religion and world view. After being interviewed by the Emperor Trajan, he was ordered to be taken to Rome to be publicly killed and eaten by lions for the "entertainment" of the people. Inigo was probably made aware of this history, as well as the fact that Saint Ignatius believed in humility and meekness, and was a strong promoter of unity, preaching that people must refrain from the "pernicious weeds" of heresy and schism (Butler 1961[1745]:I:145). Inigo may have been given his name by the Mission Santa Clara priests due to the proximity of the date of his baptism (December 26) to the date of the martyrdom of Saint Ignatius (December 20).

Less than a month and a half after Inigo's baptism, Inigo's sister Emerenciana was also baptized. However, it was five more years before their father and stepmother were baptized. These five years between 1789 and 1794 can be seen as the period of a decisive shift between the dominance of the native political economy—hunting and gathering—and that of the Spanish mission and colony in the Santa Clara Valley.

By the time Inigo was baptized, most of the children of the valley had been baptized and were in the process of developing a close relationship with the mission. Young people were typically considered adults at nine or ten years of age. At that age baptized Indians could come to live in the mission and fully participate in its activities. But by the end of 1789 most of the adults of the area had not yet been baptized. Only 84 neophyte families lived in the straw-hut town and worked on mission projects, collectively raising crops for themselves (Noboa and Peña 1790:54). In their report for 1789, written in January of 1790, Fathers Noboa and Peña of Mission Santa Clara made it clear that while the mission population was increasing, there were still masses of Indians who were resisting joining them. As their report expressed it:

> Everywhere there is much heathendom, not even in the closest ranches is a lack of heathens, even though many have been baptized and live in the Mission. In the area 15 to 20 leagues (45 to 60 miles) around, the same language is spoken, it has only a very small variety of terms and accents. Among the people there is no diversity of nations. Because of lack of communication they have no news (know nothing) about far away tribes. They distinguish their neighbors by families and last names [Noboa and Peña 1790:54].

The two padres also reported that of the 787 individuals who had by then been baptized and still lived at the mission, only 168 were married adults (21.3 percent), while another 180 were single persons nine years of age or older (22.9 percent). Fully 439 people (55.8

percent) were boys and girls under the age of nine (Noboa and Peña 1790:54). With so many unconverted adult Indians (heathens or "gentiles" as the padres called them) living outside the mission, there was for a few years a situation of more or less dual power (in economy, society, and political strength) in the valley between the mission and the still independent Indians. This situation, of course, did not last.

Mission Youth

The mission of Inigo's childhood and youth was developing rapidly in the early 1790s. It had a growing population, a complement of substantial buildings, a political economy, a religious world view, and a set daily routine. It was also an extremely paternalistic system in which the Indians were treated as eternal children. All of these aspects of the mission would have affected a young and impressionable person like Inigo, and molded his ideas and personality into those of a "mission Indian," a type of colonized persona, who willingly served the padres, the mission, and the Spanish Colonial system. Over time this service resulted in more important roles and increased responsibility for Inigo.

During Inigo's first year or two as a convert to the mission, he probably still lived with his family at his village site, only gradually becoming a full-time member of the mission community. By 1791, when he was ten, he was probably a full member. This was the common procedure for the missions during this early period. The mission population was growing rapidly during the early 1790s, from 787 in 1789 to 910 in 1790, 957 in 1791, 1,001 in 1792, and 1,062 in 1793. It continued to be a youthful mission, however, as the bulk of the adults in the Santa Clara Valley continued (until 1794-1795) to maintain their independent ways. During the early 1790s the youth continued to supply the great majority of the converts, but adults individually or in small groups were increasingly entering the mission during these years. During the first years of the 1790s, 70 percent of the neophyte Indians living at Mission Santa Clara were under 15 years of age (Milliken 1991:172). Inigo was part of this group.

As the population grew, so did the need for buildings for economic purposes, for housing, and for carrying out the mission's activities. Besides the large church and adjacent straw-hut village mentioned above (and discussed further below), by the early 1790s the mission had the following structures (Jackson 1994:186):

-- A residence for the missionaries
-- Several grain warehouses for holding the gathered crops

-- Offices
-- A kitchen
-- A residence for the *mayordomo* (overseer)

The main part of the mission formed an incomplete square, with some outbuildings nearby. The British sea captain George Vancouver visited Santa Clara in 1792 and later described the place as follows:

> We arrived at the mission of Santa Clara, which according to my estimation is about forty geographical miles from San Francisco. Our journey, excepting that part of it through the morass, had been very pleasant and entertaining; and our reception at Santa Clara by the hospitable fathers of the mission, was such as excited in every breast the most lively sensations of gratitude and regard. Father Tomás de la Peña appeared to be the principal of the missionaries. The anxious solicitude of this gentleman, and that of his colleague Father José Sanchez, to anticipate all our wishes, unequivocally manifested the principles by which their conduct was regulated. Our evening passed very pleasantly, and after a most excellent breakfast next morning, the 21st, on tea and chocolate, we took a view of the establishment and the adjacent country.
>
> The buildings and offices of this mission, like those of San Francisco, form a square, but not an entire enclosure. It is situated in an extensive fertile plain, the soil of which, as also that of the surrounding country, is black productive mould, superior to any I had before seen in America. The particular spot which had been selected by the reverend fathers for their establishment, did not appear so suitable for their purpose as many other parts of the plain within a little distance of their present buildings, which are erected in a low marshy situation for the sake of being near a run of fine water; notwithstanding that within a few hundred yards they might have built their houses on dry and comfortable eminences.
>
> The stream of water passes close by the walls of the fathers' apartments, which are upon the same plan with those at San Francisco; built near, and communicating with the church, but appearing to be more extensive, and to possess in some degree more comforts, or rather

less inconveniences, than those already described. The church was long and lofty, and as well built as the rude materials of which it is composed would allow, and when compared with the unimproved state of the country, infinitely more decorated than might have been reasonably expected.

Apartments within the square in which the priests resided, were appropriated to a number of young female Indians; and the like reasons were given as at San Francisco for their being so selected and educated. Their occupations were the same, though some of their woolen manufactures surpassed those we had before seen, and wanted only the operation of fulling, with which the fathers were unacquainted, to make them very decent blankets. The upper story of their interior oblong square, which might be about one hundred and seventy feet long, and one hundred feet broad, were made use of as granaries, as were some of the lower rooms; all of which were well stored with corn and pulse of different sorts; and besides these, in case of fire, there were two spacious warehouses for the reception of grain detached from each other, and the rest of the buildings, erected at a convenient distance from the mission. These had been recently finished, contained some stores, and were to be kept constantly full, as a reserve in the event of such a misfortune [Vancouver 1801 (1792):30-32].

Vancouver also visited the straw-hut village, which had six rammed-earth palisade walled houses, and observed the ongoing construction of new houses for some of the Indians:

Our attention was next called to the village of the Indians near the mission. The habitations were not so regularly disposed, nor did it contain so many, as the village at San Francisco; yet the same horrid state of uncleanliness and laziness seemed to pervade the whole
. . . .
A certain number of the most intelligent, tractable, and industrious persons, were selected from the group, and were employed in a pleasant and well-adapted spot of land facing the mission, under the direction and instruction of the fathers, in building for themselves a range of small, but comparatively speaking

> comfortable and convenient habitations. The walls, though not so thick, are constructed in the same manner with those described in the square at San Francisco, and the houses are formed after the European fashion, each consisting of two commodious rooms below, with garrets over them. At the back of each house a space of ground is enclosed, sufficient for cultivating a large quantity of vegetables, for rearing poultry and for other useful and domestic purposes. The buildings were in a state of forwardness, and when finished, each house was designed to accommodate one distinct family only . . . [Vancouver 1801 (1792):34-37].

During the years 1792, 1793, and 1794 Indian housing was the central focus of construction activity of the mission (Jackson 1994:186). In 1793, for example, 14 adobes, each with a thatched roof, were constructed for Indian housing (Noboa and Peña 1793:63). It is likely that Inigo eventually lived with his family in one of these early adobes.

Early Economy

At the same time that the mission was rapidly expanding numerically and physically, the institution's ability to produce the necessities of life was also growing apace. The main areas of work included, first and foremost, agricultural labor, including plowing the soil using oxen, planting, and harvesting, as well as tending to the various animals. Vancouver is again our best source for a description of the mission's field agricultural activities during this period:

> They cultivate wheat, maize, peas and beans; the latter are produced in great variety, and the whole in greater abundance than their necessities require. Of these several sorts they had many thousand bushels in store, of very excellent quality, which had been obtained with little labour, and without manure. By the help of a very mean, and ill contrived plough drawn by oxen, the earth is once slightly turned over, and smoothed down by a harrow; in the month of November or December, the wheat is sown in drills, or broadcast on the even surface, and scratched in with the harrow; this is the whole of their system of husbandry, which uniformly produces them in July or August an abundant harvest. The maize,

peas, and beans, are produced with as little labour; these are sown in the spring months, and succeed extremely well, as do hemp and flax, or linseed. The wheat affords in general from twenty-five to thirty for one according to the seasons, twenty-five for one being the least return they have ever yet deposited in their granaries from the field; notwithstanding the enormous waste occasioned by their rude method of threshing, which is always performed in the open air by the treading of cattle. The product of the other grains and pulse bears a similar proportion to that of the wheat. I was much surprised to find that neither barley nor oats were cultivated; on enquiry I was given to understand, that as the superior kinds of grain could be plentifully obtained with the same labour that the inferior ones would require, they had some time ago declined the cultivation of them. The labours of the field are performed under the immediate inspection of the fathers, by the natives who are instructed in the Roman Catholic faith, and taught the art of husbandry. The annual produce is taken under the care of these worthy pastors, who distribute it in such quantities to the several persons as completely answers all the useful and necessary purposes.

Besides a few acres of arable land, which we saw under cultivation near the mission, was a small spot of garden ground, producing several sorts of vegetables in great perfection and abundance. The extent of it, however, like the garden at San Francisco, appeared unequal to the consumption of the European residents; the priests, and their guard consisting of a corporal and six soldiers. Here were planted peaches, apricots, apples, pears, figs, and vines, all of which excepting the latter promised to succeed very well [Vancouver 1801 (1792): 32-34].

Apparently in this time period, little was done to take care of what had become a large number of animals—Jackson and Castillo (1995:127), for example, report that 4,200 cattle, 800 sheep, and 610 horses were present in 1792. As Vancouver noted:

In complement to our visit, the fathers ordered a feast for the Indians of the village. The principal part of the entertainment was beef, furnished from a certain number of black cattle, which were presented on the occasion to the villagers. These animals propagate very fast, and being suffered to live in large herds on the fertile plains of Santa Clara, in a sort of wild state, some skill and adroitness is required to take them [Vancouver 1801 (1792):38].

Cattle, as well as horses, sheep, pigs, goats, and mules, were growing in number and all apparently allowed to roam at will, and the Indians were not allowed to harm them. This meant that part of the valley's ability to sustain the native population with naturally growing foods was rapidly being impacted. Probably most affected were the various small herbal and seed plants gathered during certain seasons, along with animals such as deer which depended upon the same plants. Acorns, and shellfish and other sealife were probably less impacted. The overall decrease of natural food sources was undoubtedly a key factor in the sudden mass migration of valley adults into the mission in 1794-1795, a topic we will return to below.

Handicraft production was also increasingly important. As Vancouver mentions above, Indian women were already engaged in "wooien manufacturers" in 1792. In 1793, Indian labor on the two looms known to be present produced 400 blankets and some sackcloth (Noboa and Peña 1793:63). Also in 1793, six shoemakers and carpenters, Indian craftsmen from San Francisco, were assigned as instructors at Santa Clara (Archibald 1978a:149). The Indian women were also responsible for grinding the grain in primitive stone mortars, a carryover from their work regime during precontact days (Hall 1871:114). It appears that men's occupations changed much more than women's in the transition from native to Spanish colonial lifeways.

World View and Daily Routine

The Indians who came to the mission were taught in catechism class the Spanish language and the Catholic religious doctrine of the time. The latter typically included the Acts of Faith, Hope, Charity, and Contrition, which were necessary for salvation, as well as . . . "the Pater Noster, Ave Maria, the Credo, the Salve, the Ten Commandments of God, the Precepts of the Church, the Sacraments, and the General Confession, or Confiteor" (Webb 1952:47). A biography of Father Magín Catalá, who arrived at Mission Santa Clara in 1794, states that this padre:

> ... was detailed to guide the Christian Indians in their religious instruction of the new-coming Gentiles from the Rancherias. After a usual three months of instruction, he would then baptize those nine and over who were ready, and the infant children. The teachings of the Faith were deepened daily through the gathering of the adult neophytes and the children for morning and evening prayers in the church. The program, described in the Annual and semi-annual reports or *Informes*, was *La Instruccion Doctrinal y Racional*, which included not only religious training, but also the secular or *Racional* which included the Spanish language, and later, for the more promising boys, the reading of musical notation for use in instrumental and vocal work. Self-development and facility in spoken Spanish were also obtained through dramatics in the form of *Pastorelas* or Shepherd Plays of Christmas, *La Passion*, the full outdoor dramatization of the Passion of Christ, and other group activities such as the solemn celebrations of Corpus Christi, processions on Rogation Days to bless the field crops and other festive occasions [Spearman n.d.:59].

A lack of common language skills and very different cultural traditions probably made the content of the doctrine obscure to the native people. In addition, it must have been very difficult for the Indians baptized during this period and later to comprehend that by this act they were henceforth to be required to live and work at the mission forever except when the padres gave them passes to leave. If they left without permission, they were considered runaways and were subject to being returned by force by the Spanish military (Milliken 1991:161-163).

Religious pageantry was also an important aspect of Indian education. One source of such pageantry was the Christmas Eve nativity play or *Pastorela*:

> At Mission Santa Clara, according to legend, there were two rooms which adjoined the church on the cemetery side. The first was the baptistry and is shown in a daguerreotype of the early 1850s. The second was known as the "Bethlehem" from the fact that the manger, or crib, was represented in it each year at Christmas. One may picture the "Pastorela" being enacted just without this room, a velvet curtain concealing the Nativity scene until the conclusion of the play. Then, the

screen being dramatically drawn aside, the manger, the figures of the Child, Mary and Joseph, with perhaps an animal or two, are displayed within the room. Christmas hymns are sung by the Indian choir accompanied by violins, bass-viols, flutes, trumpets, bandolas and the joyful sound of the mission bells fills the church. This was an event that the Indians long and eagerly awaited. And how coveted and striven for were the actor's parts in that appealing drama![2][Webb 1952:263].

Religious activities and work tasks made up the bulk of the overall daily routine of Inigo and the other Indians at Mission Santa Clara in the early 1790s and later as well. A key to this routine was the use of the clock and mission bells to signal the appropriate activity. Where the natural rhythms of daylight and darkness, hunger and thirst, and the seasons had largely governed Indian life prior to the arrival of the Spanish, now the clock had a key role. The mission bells were used to tell the Indians what the clock and the schedule set by the padres dictated. A clock was brought to Mission Santa Clara at the founding of the mission in 1777, and the yearly report for that year recorded as part of the goods present: "A wooden clock with little bells, or chimes for striking the hours and quarter hours" (Webb 1952:36). The mission also had a sundial, to back up the clock and perhaps to teach the Indians the connections between the position of the sun, time, the ringing of the bell, and their activities (Webb 1952:37-38). Edith Webb reports on the use of the mission bells at each and every California mission:

> That the task of the bell-ringer was an important one is readily seen, for records state that the mission Indians were governed for worship, for labor, for meals, and for sleep by the sound of a bell. The Indians' day began at sunrise when the Angelus bell called them to prayers in the mission church. About an hour later another bell announced breakfast, whereupon each family sent to the community kitchen for its share of the food that had been prepared. After breakfast another ring of the bell sent all who were old enough and able to work to their appointed tasks. There were no laggards in this community. From the small boy who scared birds away from the orchard or straying animals from drying adobes to the little girl who helped prepare the wool for spinning, and the old woman who gathered wood for the kitchen fires, all who were able to work had some spec-

ial task to perform. In the forenoon and again in mid-afternoon, one of the Padres gathered together all the children over five years of age and instructed them in the Doctrina. Following the morning period with the children the Padre visited the fields and shops to see that no one was absent from work. Shortly after eleven o'clock, the Padres had their noonday meal. From twelve until two o'clock the Indians ate their meal and enjoyed the inevitable siesta. Then back to work they went until about five o'clock, when it was time for prayers and devotions. At six o'clock came the ringing of the Angelus. Supper was then served. For the remainder of the evening until Poor Souls' Bell was rung at eight o'clock, the Indians were free to do as they wished within certain limitations, of course. Thus it was that day after day, week after week, and year after year, the life of the mission community was regulated by the ringing of a bell[3][Webb 1952:35].

Food at Santa Clara was typical for the missions: *atole* mush (cooked flour) for breakfast, *pozole* (a gruel of cooked grain, corn, and peas, with some meat) for lunch, and *atole* again for dinner (Webb 1952:40; Gieger 1976:88).

A final aspect of life at Mission Santa Clara and the surrounding countryside during the initial years of Inigo's association with this institution was the role of violence as a form of social control. Floggings were the most common form of violence directed at the natives. Such beatings showed other Indians what could happen if they failed to follow the directions and orders of the Spanish padres and soldiers (Milliken 1991:152). Putting people in stocks and shackling them were also punishments used to discipline the Indians. This police/military type authority and violence had, at least by the late 1780s/early 1790s, and probably well before, been extended beyond the mission Indians to the non-Christian Indians. One purpose was to try to enforce peaceful relations between the different and still independent Indian groups. As Lieutenant José Arguello wrote in a letter to Governor Fages in April 1788:

> He verified that a pagan named El Caporal, who works at the Pueblo, was found to be putting a group together to go make war on some other pagans over a woman. He was seized and given a few lashes. After

three days under detention he was put at liberty [Arguello (1788) as quoted in Milliken 1991:167].

In its new role as a regional police force, the Spanish military also suppressed any local leaders still resisting Spanish control. Seen as lawbreakers, such individuals and groups were subject to violent suppression (Milliken 1991:166-168, 185-191).

The young Inigo, along with his family, tribal group, and Santa Clara Valley Indians in general, must have been well aware of all these developments, both in the mission and the larger valley. The bulk of the adult Indians of the valley had been temporizing and postponing a decision about either rebelling against the growing colonial power or joining the mission, and they were confused and unsure about what to do. Any course had both positives and negatives, but events were forcing a decision. In late 1794 and early 1795, all aspects of the problem suddenly came to a head and the cultural landscape of the valley underwent one of its most profound changes ever.

The Transformation of 1794-1795

During the six-month period between the end of September 1794 and the first days of April 1795, an economic, social, and political transformation took place in the Santa Clara Valley. During this short period of time no less than 586 people were baptized at the mission, many in groups as large as 46 people in one day. Almost 80 percent (437) of these 586 people were adults. This was a striking reversal from the 17 years of previous experience at the mission where the overwhelming majority of those baptized had been children (Milliken 1991:202-203). Inigo's father and stepmother were among these new converts. This meant that the entire family was now part of the mission for the duration. The mass conversion depopulated all the Indian villages for miles around the mission, as well as much of the Santa Clara Valley.

The total mission population was only 1,062 at the end of 1793, but it had jumped to 1,541 at the end of 1795, most of the increase due to the mass conversions from September 1794 to April 1795. More important than the raw numbers of people was the fact that an analysis of baptism records shows that the elders of all tribelets and most of the prime-of-life adults remaining in the Santa Clara Valley were converted during this short period. What made it a transformation which approached a revolution was that it signaled the death of native lifeways in the Santa Clara Valley and the absolute victory of the new colonial system. Henceforth, for many decades, the political economy of the place would be dominated by the mission agricultural plantation and craft economy and society, politically commanded by the padres and the colonial political/military authorities. The Indians would, for the following half-century, effectively be the serfs/slaves of this system and those who ran it, existing at the bottom of a rigid racial caste system.

The key question is this: Why did the independent Indians of 1794-95 (including Inigo's parents) decide to give up their independent lifeways and subordinate themselves to the mission? They were clearly reluctant to do so, and had resisted this decision for over a decade and a half. As is usually the case with any important historical event, an adequate explanation is complex, involving environmental and economic, political and military, cultural, and psychological aspects. Beginning with what are perhaps more objective factors, we can say that while adequate data are lacking, some evidence does exist that the traditional Indian economy of the valley was breaking down. The numbers of imported animals alone must have had a serious impact on the adequacy of native seeds, plants, acorns, animal, and other food supplies, even given the loss of large numbers of people to the mission and to additional deaths caused by the new diseases brought by the Spanish. In order to protect their animals, the Spanish had also stopped the practice of native fire management, resulting in a further decline in native food sources (Milliken 1991:325). In addition, a drought reportedly had ruined the remaining wild seed crops during 1794 (Milliken 1991:198, 208). Little information is available about the severity of this drought, but studies have shown that availability of food at other missions during this same time period was an attraction for native peoples, causing an increase in mission conversions (Milliken 1991:208). In addition, the arrival of the Spanish resulted in the serious disruption of the native trade system, making it more difficult to get needed items in short supply locally. Another factor is that the number of younger generation conversions and removals to the mission must have seriously undermined the strength and stability of native society. Indian leaders could see the difficulty of continuing the old ways in these new circumstances.

Perhaps knowing or sensing the Indians' new vulnerability, it was precisely at this point in time that both aggressive preaching and violence were used to encourage conversion. For example, Father Manuel Fernandez, a new padre at the mission, was guilty of both threats and violence against the non-Christian Indians. As an October 1794 letter from Commissioner Gabriel Moraga reported:

> I give you notice that, as a result of various trips made by the Reverend Father Manuel Fernandez, minister of Mission Santa Clara, to the villages neigh-

> boring this town, the pagans have abandoned them and have retired into the mountains. It is common knowledge among the Indians, confirmed by remarks made by the soldiers that have escorted said religious, that Indians who refused to become Christians were severely threatened. In some cases he went beyond threat to actual punishment. Confirming this was he who the Father came upon at the cornfield of soldier Ygnacio Soto, and in whose presence the Father called to one of several pagans who were gleaning corn. Because the man did not come over immediately, he [Father Fernandez] asked a soldier who accompanied him for a lance, then proceeded to horsewhip the Indian with it to the utmost. Following this and other incidents, the pagans really credited the threat of the Father to the effect that if those who told him (out of fear) that they would go to be baptized failed to fulfill this promise, he would have to burn their villages down.
>
> One pagan inhabitant of this pueblo, called El Mocho, came to me to complain that said Father had gone to his village and, because he would not go to the mission and because he was accused of dissuading his relatives, had ordered him tied up and given many lashes, first with a halter rope and then with a leather riata. The Indian was left in such bad condition that he came in supporting himself by a cane, unable to stand upright, with waist and buttocks covered with swollen wounds [Moraga 1794, quoted in Milliken 1991:530].

Along with the threats and violence came a visit from Lieutenant Hermenegildo Sal, a leader of the San Francisco Presidio. Sal, Moraga, and others were concerned that Father Fernandez's violence against the non-mission Indians could spark a violent rebellion. There was a faction which apparently wanted to follow this course and one relatively minor incident did take place near the Pueblo of San Jose (Milliken 1991:199). The main effect of Sal's visit was, however, to calm the situation by meeting with and offering Indian leaders gifts and assurances of protection, including protection against priestly abuses (Milliken 1991:201). This added up to a kind of "good cop/bad cop" approach that was apparently very effective.

The overall effect of the ecological, economic, political, and military impacts on the traditional people of the valley was to severely weaken their culture and potential for unity against Spanish colonialism.

The lack of overall unity among large groups that was already a feature of aboriginal society was reinforced by the Spanish, which meant that any uprising was doomed to failure against superior Spanish military tactics and technology. The Indians were also probably increasingly unable psychologically to gather the will to resist what was a powerful alien force. It was easier for them to attempt to find a niche in the new mission-based economy and society. The transformation of 1794-95 which brought the rest of Inigo's family into the mission and ended the system of dual power in the valley was the product of all these factors.

Young Adulthood in a Missionized Valley

In 1795 Inigo was 14 years old, a full-time mission resident and probably already an able worker. With a large number of new adult converts, the two padres who controlled the mission (Father Fernandez had been removed and Magín Catalá added in 1794-95, so Catalá and Francisco Miguel Sanchez were the two priests in charge in 1795) were faced with both an opportunity and a potentially serious problem. With more workers, the priests could produce more food and other products for the use of the missions, as well as the presidios and pueblos, but the danger was that, if the Indians could not be fed adequately, the threat of rebellion, higher death rates, or escape would grow. So it was decided to increase agricultural production by building irrigation works to bring water from the Guadalupe River to the mission and its fields. This was reportedly one of the first great public works projects at any mission and must have required an immense amount of Indian labor. As Edith Webb reported:

> The first improvement of any great magnitude was made at Santa Clara where, in 1795, a zanja, or trench, half a league long, nine feet wide, and five feet deep was dug by the neophytes to carry water from the Guadalupe River to the mission. The water-course followed the line of the famous "Alameda," the shaded carreta road and walk that connected the pueblo of San Jose with Mission Santa Clara at its second site. According to an early map, this zanja passed between the pear orchard and the rear wing of the quadrangle of the second site. Apparently it intersected the stream seen by Vancouver and the two were combined to furnish an ample supply of water for all the mission's needs. Surplus water from all sources (there were many springs

in the vicinity) joined an ancient water-course that led to a marsh, or cienega, not far to the north. The marsh was marked by a large grove of sycamore trees[4][Webb 1952:67].

Since Indian labor was now abundant (and, of course, unpaid), Padre Catalá soon thought of another public works project—the *Alameda* linking the Mission and the Pueblo of San Jose. Arthur Dunning Spearman writes about this famous road:

> It was along the westerly side of this already completed zanja that Padre Magín Catalá conceived the project of an arboreal way, or *Alameda* that would encourage the pueblo dwellers to come more faithfully to church on Sundays. It could also protect the women and children from the rather wild long-horn cattle grazing in open meadowlands along the way.
> The beginning of the planting of the long lines of black willows, laurels, swamp elms and occasional sycamore was made soon after 1795. An early American visitor was informed that four rows were first planted. One row later was removed to insure a wide lane for *carretas*. The narrow lane remained on the east side and become the route of the first American horse-cars.
> Senorita Encarnacion Pinedo took part as a little girl in the Corpus Christi processions that stopped for the blessings at *altares de enramada* along the *Alameda*. She described them as located at determined distances where the trees at the sides had been planted so as to form recesses for the erection of the processional altars within them. Those *altares* when built in the open plaza were framed over with boughs and were lined with exquisite shawls of imported Chinese embroidery, or with delicate lace mantillas of white and other appropriate colors. The antique mantillas, large and square, bore long decorative fringes, as did the handsome long *rebosos*, the face and neck scarves. Their long fringes were utilized to give finish to the altar decorations. The altar table was covered with fine linen clothes and edged with Spanish drawn-work patterns. Frontals of embroidered silks stretched on frames were hung or set before the under portion of the altar tables. At these *altares de enramada* or Benediction Stations, the procession of the

Blessed Sacrament would stop while the priest rested the Sacred Host in its monstrance on the altar table during a hymn. The Blessing was then given and the people moved on [Spearman n.d.:117-118].

Construction of the *Alameda* was apparently ongoing until about 1800 (Spearman n.d.:125).

A final construction project of the mid-1790s was work on a warehouse, prison, and barracks for the soldiers stationed at the mission. The report for 1796 noted that "the guardhouse, the warehouse and the houses for the troops have been built, all of adobe and tile" (Sanchez and Viader 1796:70).

Inigo and his father probably worked on both the *Alameda* and the giant ditch, which was over a mile long and entailed the movement of large volumes of earth. They also perhaps worked on the soldiers' barracks. All this work was done at the direction of one of the padres and one or more Indian foremen. The Indians, of course, did all of the labor at the missions and even in the pueblos. As Webb reported:

> All these writers agree that it was the Indians, directed by one of the Padres, a mayordomo, or Indian foreman, who performed the labors not only at the missions but for the people of the pueblos as well. One Padre, we are told, attended to affairs spiritual while the other visited the various workshops and fields to see that work was progressing and that no laborer was absent. This Padre could not, of course, spend all his time with one group of workers; consequently, there was the foreman, often an Indian himself, to direct the work. Men of Spanish or Mexican decent, who were not serving as soldiers, were often hired by the Padres as overseers, gate-keepers, stewards, etc. They had, apparently, no objection to such employment, but as has been noted in substance by more than one writer of that period, they did no work themselves that could not be accomplished on horseback. The Indians, therefore, were the laborers in the shops and fields[5][Webb 1952:84].

By the summer of 1797, Inigo was 16 years old and ready to take a bride. He and a 15-year old girl named Maria Viviana, (or "Bibiana") of a tribelet in the San Antonio area, to the east of San José, were married on June 8, 1797. Maria Viviana, or simply "Viviana," (SCL-B 458) had been baptized at one year of age in early 1783. Her parents, Yginio and Jacinta (later renamed José and Isabel, SCL-B 4121 and 4111, respectively), were both born about 1761 and neither had yet submitted to baptism and joined the mission, although they had brought all eight of their children in for baptism. Nothing is known about Inigo's and Viviana's courtship, if there was one. Within a few years, however, they did begin to have children.

Endnotes:

1. Reprinted from INDIAN LIFE AT THE OLD MISSIONS by Edith Buckland Webb by permission of the University of Nebraska Press. Copyright 1952 by the heirs of Edith Buckland Webb.

2. ibid.

3. ibid.

4. ibid.

5. ibid.

CHAPTER 3

MATURITY: A MISSION INDIAN, 1798-1828

The 30 years from 1798, when he was 17, to 1828, when he was 47, represent the period of Inigo's maturity. During that time he and his wife Viviana had all of their 11 children. Both Inigo and Viviana labored at and served the mission. Inigo obtained a position of responsibility at Mission Santa Clara during this period. At the same time the mission itself also passed from a position of relative youth (21 years old in 1798), through and beyond maturity (51 years old in 1828). This era may be labeled the "Classic Mission Period." Mission Santa Clara was, in many ways, a typical representative of an Alta California mission of the time. The life experience of Inigo during these years was also, in many respects at least, representative of tens of thousands of other Native Americans of this era.

This chapter begins with a review of the material base and political power structure of Mission Santa Clara, develops in depth known details of the life of Inigo and Viviana during these years, and then generalizes about the nature of the mission.

The Material Base of Mission Santa Clara, 1798-1828

In its relations of power and authority, Mission Santa Clara was similar to all the missions of Alta California. The mission as an institution had a definite and unchanging hierarchy of power. Those at the top supervised and enforced their will on the people under them. Near the top of this hierarchy during this entire era were the two priests—Magín Catalá and José Viader—who were in turn subordinate to the more distantly located president of the Missions and the governor of California. Catalá was in charge of spiritual matters and Viader of temporal ones (such as economic affairs). Below them were the military commander of the mission and the soldiers under him. Then came several settlers, called *mayordomos*, who acted as organizers, administrators, and supervisors. All of the above were considered the "people of reason," as distinct from the Indian workers who labored at the mission and whose status was that of children without full rights. The Native American laborers thus amounted to a distinct and separate class of people, a caste apart from the Spanish rulers. The Indians had their own leaders called *alcaldes* (magistrates) and *regidores* (councilmen).

The practice of installing Indian leaders went back nearly to the beginning of all missions, when Governor Neve decreed that the neophytes of each mission should elect two *alcaldes* and two *regidores* from their ranks (Engelhardt 1912 II:336-346). While the ideal was to move the Indians toward self-government, this did not mean that native culture was to be encouraged; the priests " . . . saw to it that only the most acculturated and trusted of the neophytes become *alcaldes* (Phillips 1981:23). One ex-mission Indian later stated that the padres " . . . appointed *alcaldes* from the people . . . that knew how to speak Spanish more than the others and were better than the others in their customs" (Phillips 1974:295). "Better" in this case implied, of course, "more Spanish."

In 1797, the same year that Inigo and Viviana were married, a land conflict developed between the settlers of the Pueblo of San Jose—established as a civilian agricultural settlement in 1777—and the leaders of Mission Santa Clara. During that year, members of the pueblo tried to expand onto lands that the mission claimed to be holding in trust for the Indians. The two priests, Magín Catalá and José Viader, responded with the argument that the mission had about 1,400 Christians (much larger than the pueblo population of a few hundred) and that there were thousands more non-Christian Indians in more distant villages, as far away as the eastern Coast Ranges and the margins of the great Central Valley. The priests argued that these Indians, especially those to be converted later, would need this land in the future to maintain themselves by the product of their labor (Hall 1871:63). Catalá ended by warning that the gentile (i.e., non-Christian) Indians were especially upset, hinting that rebellion could be the result:

> . . . I myself, can swear that I have heard the Gentiles complain among themselves of the manifest injustice of the settlers in desiring to appropriate to themselves . . . [what] they have no right [to] whatever; that the Christian Indians note this, and speak of it publicly, is not strange; but a complaint of this character

from the mouth of a Gentile, argues much inquietude, and something more [Hall 1871:66].

The California governor at the time, Diego de Borica, wrote to his superior, the viceroy, that the Santa Clara priests had greatly overestimated the number of non-Christian Indians within Mission Santa Clara's sphere of influence, and that many of these Indians actually "belonged" to other nearby missions (Hall 1871:73-74). Nevertheless, due to the central importance of the missions in the Spanish colonial system, the governor recommended that the viceroy set the Guadalupe River as the boundary between the pueblo lands (on the east) and the mission lands (on the west), a decision favorable to Mission Santa Clara. In September 1800, the viceroy ratified the governor's recommendation with the proviso that the settlers would have the right to get timber and wood in the coastal mountains miles west of the mission (Hall 1871:78). The result was that during this entire period, Mission Santa Clara lands consisted of the area lying between the Guadalupe River on the east, San Francisquito Creek (near today's Palo Alto) and the Coast Range on the west, San Francisco Bay on the north, and the Coast Range Mountains on the south (Bowman n.d.:29). This area contains a large part of the Santa Clara Valley and encompasses the land occupied by today's communities of Santa Clara, Sunnyvale, Mountain View, Palo Alto, Los Altos, Los Altos Hills, Cupertino, Campbell, Saratoga, Los Gatos, and the western part of San Jose (see Fig. 1). It should be remembered, however, that the mission's Indian converts were increasingly drawn from distant areas, eventually even from the foothills of the Sierra Nevada, about 150 miles to the east of the mission.

Although occupying a large area, by the late 1820s the mission reportedly had barely enough land to graze the thousands of cattle, sheep, horses, and other animals that the mission had at that time (Bowman n.d.:3-6, 29; Kotzebue 1830:93). Table 2 (after Jackson and Castillo 1995:128) offers some statistics on the numbers of animals present at times. These statistics indicate that the mission herds were depleted by the frequent levies imposed by the government and army during the years of the War for Mexican Independence (1811-1821).

Table 2
Mission Santa Clara Animals, 1798-1828

Year	Number of Cattle	Number of Horses	Number of Sheep
1798	3000	500	3150
1801	4000	1000	5000
1805	6050	2312	7000
1808	6900	2095	9000
1811	6550	2800	10250
1815	5200	1260	10100
1818	3120	925	10200
1823	6050	795	13000
1828	14500	850	15500

Mission lands were also used to grow the main crops of wheat, corn, peas, beans, vegetables and fruits (Hall 1871:119; Bowman n.d.:29; Kotzebue 1830:93-94; Geiger 1976:88). A visitor at Mission Santa Clara during the mid-1820s described its agriculture as follows:

> Agriculture, as I have before observed, is the copious source of revenue to the monks, and they farm on an extensive scale. The yearly crop of wheat at Santa Clara alone produces three thousand fanegos, about six hundred and twenty English quarters, or three thousand four hundred Berlin bushels; and from the extraordinary fertility of the soil, the harvest, on an average, is forty-fold, notwithstanding the roughness of their mode of cultivation. The field is first broken up with a very clumsy plough, then sown, and a second ploughing completes the work. Under the hard clods of earth thus left undisturbed, a great part of the seed perishes of course. How unexampled would be the harvest, if assisted by the capital and industry of an European farmer! The monks themselves confess that they are not good agriculturists; but they are content with their harvests. Their carelessness is however unpardonable, in

having never yet erected a mill. There is not one in all California; and the poor Indians are obliged to grind their corn by manual labour between two large, flat stones [Kotzebue 1830:99-100].

While it is not true that no missions had mills, it is true that Santa Clara apparently did not have one, despite the fact that the technologies for both water and wind power were well-known in Spain. They were apparently little used in California because the price of human (Indian) labor was so low. Missions where mills were built, such as Santa Cruz (which built the first known mission mill in 1796), were also generally those with a relatively short supply of Indian laborers (Webb 1952:153).

A number of seasonal activities at Mission Santa Clara, such as branding and wheat threshing, are portrayed in the following passage of the remembrances of Nasario Galindo, born about 1810 and the son of Leandro Galindo, who was a *mayordomo* at the mission during this period:

> Every year, in the months of June and July, the calves that had been born that year were branded. There were times when 10,000 head were branded, other times about 8,000. During the winter, many calves, sheep and horses were found dead, killed by coyotes and wolves. Before the beginning of the winter, all the sheep were sheared and the wool was woven on the looms to clothe the Indians, and as soon as November arrived, all the big and little children were also clothed.
>
> There were at Santa Clara about 2,000 souls, and to sustain them it required sowing a great area with all varieties of seeds. Santa Clara, having an abundance of water for irrigation, did not fear the dry years so that all the crops flourished, filling the storehouses at harvest time with all that one could wish. Some of these storehouses were about 500 varas in length and about 50 varas wide and contained wheat, barley, corn, beans, lentils, garbanzos and horse beans. All of these were piled up in the granaries because there were no sacks in those times. When the time arrived for harvesting the grain, 100 Indians were employed to clean it before putting it in the storehouses. They had one measure which when used twice made a fanega, as it was called in Spanish. Each Indian would take about 50 pounds in

his blanket, so that it was filled, and conveying it in this manner they filled the storehouses with grain, cleaner than that which was threshed by machines, because the winnowing was done on the threshing floor. When the wheat was spread on the floors, mares were used to treat it, then about 40 Indians, called paleros, piled it with wooden shovels called palas and threw it in the air so chaff and straw would separate. Indian women with brooms swept the chaff away after the spears of grain had come out whole and these were flailed by Indians so as to produce the grain. To clean it further, it was shoveled into a savanda or crib, a square container fashioned of rawhide that had been hardened in the sun and then pierced with many little holes made with a hot iron instrument having many points, and through these holes the grain was sifted. This was the manner of cleaning all the harvested grain. Indians also were taught to take care of the orchard, supplying the priests with fruit when it was ripe.

In a large house there were six copper ollas that could hold two or three barrels of water and to this was added a fanega of mixed grain with horse beans. This was the noon-day meal and when the bell was rung, all the Indians came with their little baskets to receive their ration of food. Every evening, three or four fanegas of pinole were made, to which was added a gruel of barley, and again the bell was rung, summoning the Indians for their evening meal. The young girls, known as nuns, were fed separately, each receiving a ration of posol at noon and a meal of pinole in the evening. Every day of the year, this was the customary manner of feeding the Indians at all the missions in California [Galindo 1883].

Another key economic activity at Mission Santa Clara was the cattle industry. As the decades passed, it became more and more important and reached into every corner of mission life. The slaughtering season (*la matanza*) was "perhaps the busiest time of all at the old missions . . . " (Webb 1952:188). The food which resulted from the killing of a part of the cattle herd was an important source of protein at the mission, and the hides were bartered with trading ships from New England especially for many items that the padres wanted for the mission and the Indians. These hides were often carried on the heads of Indian laborers all the way from the mission storehouses to the embarcadero near the mouth of the Guadalupe River. There the foreign ships were met and trade conducted. One observer of this process later reported:

> But often in winter, there being no roads across the valley, each separate hide was doubled across the middle and placed on the head of an Indian. Long files of Indians, each carrying a hide in this manner, could be seen trotting over the unfenced level land through the wild mustard to the embarcadero, and in a few weeks the whole cargo would thus be delivered . . .[1][quoted in Webb 1952:188-189].

Another type of Mission Santa Clara production was wine making. Indian men crushed the juice out of the grapes by stamping on them in large tubs. A wine cellar also existed at Mission Santa Clara (Webb 1952:221).

Other economic activities at the mission during this period included production of fabrics, soap, blankets, saddles, tanned hides, shoes, and tallow (Stodder 1986:31). Some of these items were consumed by the Indians, soldiers, and priests at the mission itself; the remainder were used to support the presidios and pueblos and occasionally to trade with the Russian, English, American, and Spanish captains of the sailing vessels which arrived off the coast (Stodder 1986:31). This trade, together with giving products to the presidio, allowed the padres to obtain needed items, including tools and household goods, as well as the trinkets, such as beads, which were used to attract the unchristianized Indians. Shell beads had long been a wealth and currency item for the native population and so the new glass beads brought by the Spanish were undoubtedly highly prized.

Construction of buildings was less frequent during the 1798-1828 period than had been the case during the first 20 years (1777-1797) of the mission's existence. The major structures had already been completed, and the mission population reached its all-time peak (1,541 people) in 1795. Periodic construction did, however, take place during the 1798-1828 years, beginning with the building of housing for Indian families in 1798. These tile-roofed adobe houses were reportedly arranged in barrack-like rows with separate small apartments for each family. The tule-grass structures characteristic of the early-day Indian village at the mission had apparently been replaced by then (Webb 1951:15; Jackson 1994:186). In 1801, Father Fermin de Lasuen, the president of all the Alta California Missions, reported how many of these Indian-occupied houses were furnished:

> . . . the houses of the Indians of San Francisco and Santa Clara are now fitted out, many of them, with grinding stones, pans, pots, stew-pots, and even small ovens for baking bread, and the others will soon be supplied in that fashion [Lasuen 1801 in Kenneally 1965:206)]

In 1813 new barracks for the soldiers stationed at the mission were built. These apparently replaced the barracks built for the mission's soldiers in 1796 (Jackson 1994:186).

In 1812 an earthquake damaged the old 1784-era church, and another earthquake finally destroyed it in 1818. A temporary church was then quickly constructed while plans were laid for a more permanent new building. By 1822 plans were complete and in that year, "Indian crews were sent with their Indian . . . foremen, to the . . . foothills to cut the redwood for beams and scantling and roof rafters, or for gate and door and window lintels" (Spearman 1963:62).

Construction on the new church and the central quadrangle of which it was a part continued until 1825, when the new structures were completed and dedicated. Adobe bricks were reportedly used for the walls and kiln-fired tiles for the roof and floor (Spearman 1963:62). The new church was then painted with the "red earth" of cinnabar (mercury ore) from what was later to become the New Almaden Mine (Hall 1871:397). The Indians of the area had reportedly known about the cinnabar at the site for many years. As Frederick Hall reported in 1871:

> Nearly all of the Indians in their region, and those of Santa Cruz, were in the habit of visiting the hill in which the New Almaden Mine was first opened and worked, to obtain red paint to adorn their faces and bodies. The cinnabar is of a reddish hue, and when moistened and rubbed, easily produces a red pigment, highly esteemed [by the Indians] . . . [Hall 1871:44].

They reportedly believed that the place was sacred and apparently only told of it in 1824 when paint was needed for the new church. In 1857, 60-year-old Antonio Suñol related that he first heard about the New Almaden Mine location in 1824 and said that the "Indians went there to get paint; they had an idea that the place was sacred. They used to drop feathers there or other little offerings, and they used to say the devil was there" (Suñol 1857:83).

The new church seems to have been completed by the time the traveler Otto von Kotzebue visited Mission Santa Clara during the mid-1820s. Kotzebue reported on the complement of buildings and their uses:

> The mission, which was founded in the year 1777, is situated beside a stream of the most pure and delicious water, in a large and extremely fertile plain. The buildings of Santa Clara, overshadowed by thick groves of oaks, and surrounded by gardens which, though carelessly cultivated, produce an abundance of vegetables, the finest grapes, and fruits of all kinds, are in the same style as at all the other missions. They consist of a large stone church, a spacious dwelling-house for the monks, a large magazine for the preservation of corn, and the Rancherios, or barracks, for the Indians, of which mention has already been made. These are divided into long rows of houses, or rather stalls, where each family is allowed a space scarcely large enough to enable them to lie down to repose. We were struck by the appearance of a large quadrangular building, which having no windows on the outside, and only one carefully secured door, resembled a prison for state-criminals. It proved to be the residence appropriated by the monks, the severe guardians of chastity, to the young unmarried Indian women, whom they keep under their particular superintendence, making their time useful to the community by spinning, weaving, and similar occupations. These dungeons are opened two or three times a day, but only to allow the prisoners to pass to and from the church. I have occasionally seen the poor girls rushing out eagerly to breathe the fresh air, and driven immediately into the church like a flock of sheep, by an old ragged Spaniard armed with a stick. After mass, they are in the same manner hurried back to their prisons. Yet, notwithstanding all the care of the ghostly fathers, the feet of some of these uninviting fair ones were cumbered with bars of iron, the penal consequence, as I was informed, of detected transgression. Only on their marriage are these cloistered virgins allowed to issue from their confinement and associate with their own people in the barracks [Kotzebue 1830:94-95].

Another topic involves the question of Indian labor, and the ways in which the priests often served as labor brokers for the colonial system, arranging for mission Indians to be sent to the various pueblos and presidios to work, or denying such labor on occasion. As President of the Missions Fermin Lasuen wrote in 1801, "Every time the presidios and private individuals ask for Indians, as a rule they are given to them, and this does not happen just rarely, but very very often" (Lasuen 1801 in Kenneally 1965:211). Lasuen complained that the presidios especially overworked the Indians and said that it cost a great deal to influence the Indians to go there to work, because they did not want to go, but at the same time wanted to obey the priests (Lasuen 1801 in Kenneally 1965:208). Lasuen added that the Pueblo of San Jose had recently asked Mission Santa Clara to supply Indians to build a large aqueduct, which was a lot of work. The mission supplied the Indian labor, then the pueblo could not pay the agreed-upon cost and the mission had to absorb the loss (Lasuen 1801 in Kenneally 1965:213). During 1796 and again in 1802 large numbers of Indian laborers were also sent from Mission Santa Clara to Monterey to work on the presidio there (Pueblo of San Jose 1796, 1802).

The non-Christian Indian labor force in the Santa Clara Valley and the nearby mountains to the east continued to diminish during the 1800-1810 decade, as conversion to the mission was complete. As a result, increasing conflict over Indian labor arose between the Pueblo of San Jose and Mission Santa Clara. In 1807 the mission priests complained to the governor that the pueblo settlers were luring Christian Indians from the mission to work for them in San Jose. The governor agreed with the Franciscans, reaffirming the traditional government position that mission Indians belonged to the priests, and ordered punishment meted out to the Indians for the misdeeds of the townspeople:

> In light of the repeated complaints made by the reverend Father ministers of Mission Santa Clara regarding the townspeople of the pueblo secreting away Indians of the mission, I advise you to give all such Indians, men or women, twenty-five lashes and then send them back to their mission, if they are over age twelve [Arrillaga 1807a in Milliken 1991:297].

Since the padres were, in this case, not accommodating about releasing Indians to help the settlers, and due to the need of the pueblo population for cheap Indian labor, in 1807 the governor allowed the townspeople to recruit non-missionized Indian workers all the way from the San Joaquin Valley (see Milliken 1991:297-299).

A final issue during the "Classic Mission Period" was the conflict which developed due to the constant requests from the governor of California for more and more supplies from the missions. The background to this conflict was the Mexican War for Independence which resulted in the cutoff of most supplies to California after 1811. The shortfall had to be made up and the governors ordered the missions to assist in the support of the presidios, since they had the bulk of the land and labor force. One source estimated that unpaid contributions made by the missions to the California government during this period amounted to nearly $500,000, an immense sum for the time and place (Engelhardt 1912 III:313-314). Engelhardt stated that " . . . the missions . . . proved the salvation of the territory in that they furnished subsistence for the military from the governor down to the last soldier in the ranks, who but for the managing friars and their neophytes must have starved or abandoned the country" (1912:III:313).

At Mission Santa Clara, padres Catalá and Viader strongly protested the constant government levies, in at least one case refusing to supply the materials requested. In a letter to Governor Sola dated May 3, 1820, the two mission priests stated that in 1819 the mission was itself short of food and had to request charity from Mission San Juan Bautista and might have to do the same in 1820. They added that the oxen used to transport supplies to the Presidio of San Francisco were in short supply and were needed at the mission. Tools for farming, clothing, and other supplies for the neophytes were also lacking and the request from the government for more blankets could, therefore, not be fulfilled. In order to not "overwork the unfortunate neophytes whose lot is to go naked" and not make an "almost insurmountable burden for these unhappy Christians," Catalá and Viader wanted to exempt Mission Santa Clara from these "extra duties" because, although "great sacrifices" had been made, "How . . . can we do it all?" (Catalá and Viader 1820). These issues must have directly affected Inigo and his family, and must have been a key part of the larger context of their lives during this period.

In sum, the missions constituted such a powerful institution in Colonial California because they were the main landholders, producers of food and raw materials, and also controlled the bulk of the Indian labor force. The missions were also favored (vis-à-vis conflicts with the Pueblo of San Jose, for example) because they were the chosen political, economic, and social institution used to convert and pacify the Native Americans. The governor and leading colonial authorities assumed, apparently correctly, that the secular powers and persons of towns like San Jose would exploit Indian labor so ruthlessly that long-term problems (including rebellion) would be created. Looked at from one perspective then, the missions were protecting the natives from secular exploitation and were at least making some small attempts to integrate them into a new culture and society. From the perspective of most Indians, however, the entire colonial experience was a complete disaster because people were uprooted and forced to work on colonialist projects, and because so many died. As we shall see, the lives of Inigo and Viviana are instructive in this regard.

Inigo and Viviana: A Young Married Couple at Mission Santa Clara

While we have no direct and concrete evidence, it is likely that Inigo and his wife Viviana at some time occupied one of the family-style adobe houses constructed in 1798. It is also virtually certain that they participated in the round of work characteristic of the period—construction, agricultural field work, animal husbandry, cooking, craft production, weaving, and so on. Based on what is documented regarding his later life, we can sure that during his tenure at the mission Inigo learned these and other skills, including logging and sawmilling (United States 410 ND:35-36). In short, he acquired many of the skills for economic independence that the mission had sought to teach.

It was probably early in this era that Inigo became an *alcalde* (magistrate or Indian leader) at Mission Santa Clara. His appointment or election to this position meant that he joined the lower level of the power structure of the mission and was one of those responsible (with the priests, soldiers, and other male Indian leaders) for governing and controlling the Indians at the mission and ensuring that all necessary work was completed.

In 1814 a conflict developed between the Indian leaders Inigo and Marcelo on the one hand and Padre Viader on the other. Details about the dispute are unavailable, but Alvarado gives the following brief remarks in his *History of California 1769-1824*:

> In 1814, he [Viader] was suddenly attacked by the Indians Marcelo and Inigo. Father Viader captured them, strengthening with this deed the belief that the Great God protects those who serve him on this earth. The Christian generosity with which Father Viader treated the two neophytes made such a favorable impression on the culprits that from that day on they kept a watchful eye whenever danger menaced men of reason [Alvarado n.d.:37].

While Inigo was involved in what was defined as man's work, Viviana took care of what were considered women's tasks, among them spinning and weaving. As early as 1792 the Indian women of Mission Santa Clara were weaving good woolen blankets. One report stated that the Mission Santa Clara blankets were white with yellow stripes, the yellow being obtained from wildflowers (Webb 1952:209, 214). Viviana undoubtedly learned these crafts along with roasting and grinding grain, which the priests also considered to be appropriate labor for women. The latter work was long and tedious, due to the primitive technology employed, and may have been the main labor of women at the mission (Stodder 1986:27-28).

The fact that Indian women were assigned the tasks of processing vegetal foods and weaving, and that Indian men were taking care of animal husbandry, indicates that some of the gendered division of labor used in the mission system was carried over from precolonial times. However, other work assignments apparently crossed traditional native labor divisions; for instance, men, not women, appear to have been primarily involved in growing vegetable crops during the mission period, a pattern consistent with preferred European practices at the time.

Overall, one effect of the missionization of the Indians seems to have been an increasingly rigid structuring of gender roles, particularly in the exertion of corporate control over female sexuality through the seclusion of unmarried women and girls and the close supervision of married women. Restrictions on women's mobility and association with men limited their opportunity to carry out traditional "women's work," such as vegetal food gathering, and also prevented men and women from working together. Similarly, mission priests, in assigning labor tasks and overseeing the work of neophytes, may have formalized and enforced labor patterns that were originally more flexible social and cultural guidelines for behavior.

Women were also responsible for the care of children, so Viviana had this job as well. However, eight of Inigo's and Viviana's eleven children died before they reached their third birthday (see Fig. 8); these were:

Viviana	Born	08-01-1800	Died	09-29-1800
Pablo	Born	09-04-1801	Died	09-30-1801
Viviana	Born	04-10-1805	Died	07-20-1805
Viviana	Born	02-25-1808	Died	07-27-1808
Gorgonio	Born	07-06-1810	Died	09-14-1810
Pedro Pablo	Born	12-19-1816	Died	08-14-1817
Maria Ysabel	Born	02-03-1823	Died	04-17-1824
José Thomas	Born	06-06-1825	Died	02-19-1828

The three children of Inigo and Viviana who survived past childhood were:

Maria Magdalena	Born	10-13-1811	Died after 1855
Manuel	Born	06-24-1814	Died after 1847
Juana Francisca	Born	10-20-1818	Died 08-08-1835

High infant and child mortality was commonplace at Mission Santa Clara and the other Alta California missions. The death rate for Indian people of all ages was very high, a fact not lost on those responsible for maintaining an institution that played a key role in the Spanish/Mexican colonial system. The missions were responsible for attracting, training, and acculturating the labor force that produced most of the food and other items needed to keep the entire system going. The production of Mission Santa Clara and other missions had become even more crucial once supplies from Mexico were largely cut off by the War for Independence against Spain which began in 1810-11 (Bean 1973:57-58). The high death rate for the mission Indians was thus a key concern.

Because of the high numbers of deaths (and an accompanying low birth rate), Mission Santa Clara (and the other Alta California missions as well) did not have a self-sustaining population. This in turn meant that recruitment of new converts was a constant necessity. It was necessary both because the missionaries wanted to save souls and because an attractive, functioning institution (with places to live, food, and clothing) was central to attracting native people to Christianity and then keeping them Christian. The Spanish colonialists, including the priests, believed that the entire native way of life had to be eliminated and the native population transformed. This transformation had ideological, cultural, political, and economic aspects. There also had to be an adequate population to carry out the overall program. For all these reasons, bringing in new converts was always necessary.

Because all nearby Indians had already been converted, the priests, soldiers, and Indian leaders of the mission had to travel increasing distances to find new converts. Locating new converts and, especially, keeping them at the mission tended to become more difficult over time due to the long distances involved and the nature of mission economy and society. Table 3 offers a statistical picture of Indian births and deaths, the net loss of Indians each year (excess of deaths over births), the number of new converts, and the total Mission Santa Clara population on a yearly basis for the entire 1798-1828 period.

The yearly figures, while instructive, are less important than the totals for each category, which collectively illustrate key facts about the

Table 3
Births, Deaths, and Convert Recruitment of Indians at Mission Santa Clara 1798-1828

Date	No. of Indian Births	No. of Indian Deaths	Deficit	No. of New Indian Converts	Total Rec. Population
1798	47	170	123	146	1382
1799	43	194	151	113	1343
1800	41	161	120	92	1318
1801	45	137	92	89	1322
1802	39	248	209	185	1291
1803	34	144	110	92	1271
1804	34	126	92	67	1240
1805	47	109	62	289	1469
1806	47	231	184	181	1406
1807	43	142	99	94	1401
1808	45	132	87	93	1410
1809	32	102	70	57	1398
1810	22	147	125	63	1332
1811	51	150	99	142	1371
1812	44	115	71	57	1348
1813	46	89	43	39	1347
1814	34	87	53	13	1306
1815	33	115	82	81	1306
1816	34	109	75	102	1336
1817	31	108	77	76	1336
1818	33	104	71	52	1321
1819	33	114	81	72	1313

1820	43	91	48	87	1359
1821	33	89	56	87	1388
1822	39	141	102	115	1394
1823	37	125	88	81	1395
1824	34	97	63	115	1450
1825	37	148	111	63	1403
1826	46	114	68	99	1428
1827	31	115	84	118	1462
1828	32	189	157	92	1369
Totals	**1190**	**4143**	**2953**	**3052**	**42215**
Annual Average	**38.4**	**133.6**	**95.3**	**98.5**	**1361.8**

mission experience. First of all, the number of recorded Indian births at Mission Santa Clara during the 1798-1828 period was 1,190 (38.4 a year average) and includes the 11 children born to Inigo and Viviana. The number of recorded Indian deaths at this mission during the same period was 4,143, an average of 133.6 a year, a figure that included nine members of Inigo's family. So while a baby was being born at Mission Santa Clara about every 9.5 days on the average, an Indian died at this mission every 2.7 days on the average. This was much higher than the mortality of the settlers at the Pueblo of San Jose and that of the gentile or unconverted Indians. Both of the latter populations were steadily growing, not declining.

Many of the deaths were of babies, and an unknown additional number were of new recruits who lacked immunity to diseases common at the mission. But those who stayed alive did not successfully reproduce at a rate nearly adequate to offset the very high death rate. The already low numbers of births slowly declined on the average from a total of 41.25 a year during the 1798-1813 years to 35.3 a year during the 1814-1828 period. This decline took place even though the total population average was slightly lower during the 1798-1813 period (1,353.06 per year) than the 1814-1828 years (1,371.07). The slow decline in the birth rate was probably partly due to the gradual aging of the Mission Santa Clara population, but the point is the same—the mission's core population was not only unable to reproduce itself, it was in fact rapidly declining.

Maturity: 1798-1828

One study found mean life expectancy at birth at Mission Santa Clara to be only 3.2 years (Jackson 1994:104). Put another way, during this period about ten percent of the total population of Mission Santa Clara was dying each year; the average population was 1,361.8 and the average yearly death rate was 133.6, which is a horrific figure. By comparison, about 0.5 percent of California's population dies in a given year today (*San Francisco Chronicle* April 5, 1994:A17).

The excess of deaths over births at Mission Santa Clara, as shown in the Deficit column of Table 3, created a situation requiring a constant influx of new converts recruited from Native Americans still living in traditional ways. Without new converts, the mission would have completely disappeared in about a decade and a half, since the average deficit (excess of deaths over births) was 95.3 people a year (7 percent each year on average). New converts, therefore, had to be acquired for the mission to continue. During the 1798-1828 years, Mission Santa Clara recruited 98.5 converts per year on average, very close to and a little higher overall than the deficit it faced due to the high mission death rate. These facts raise two of the key issues that need to be addressed in order to fully understand both the nature of the mission system generally and Santa Clara specifically, as well as the experience of Inigo himself: (1) why was the death rate so high? and (2) what recruitment situations and techniques could ensure a steady supply of new converts given the high death rate at the mission?

Why a High Death Rate?

A number of factors—biological, socio-economic, and psychological—account for the high death rate at Mission Santa Clara, and by extension Alta California missions generally. The key overall context is the colonial system and its labor force needs. To maintain this system native people had to be concentrated into mission centers so that they could be converted to Christianity, acculturated to the Spanish language and lifeways, and work to produce under colonial tutelage the food, clothing, shelter, and other necessities of life. Indians thus had to rapidly give up their old lifeways and culture and adopt new ones. A new work regime was imposed and violence (in the form of whippings, stocks, and shackles) was used to punish rule infractions or running away.

Neophytes were forced to speak Spanish, as is indicated by the 1801 statement of Fermin Francisco de Lasuen, President of all the Alta California missions:

> Indians are obliged to use Spanish, exhorted to learn it, given prizes for speaking it, reprimanded for not using it, it is the custom to deny their request unless it is expressed in Spanish [Lasuen 1801 in Kenneally 1965:200-201].

The priests also engaged in a systematic campaign of denigration of native lifeways and beliefs. Views about the naturalness of nudity and sexual activity were sternly repressed. Dances and other native communal religious and other practices, while discouraged by the priests, were allowed to continue as a concession to the Indians. The 1814 report on Mission Santa Clara by fathers Catalá and Viader listed dancing and gambling as two of the "vices" the Indians still had. They also were said to be "very superstitious," "worship the devils," and "practice witchcraft" (Geiger 1976:50-51, 106). Neophytes naturally internalized such criticism, making them ashamed of themselves and therefore psychologically damaged. They came to believe " . . . that they deserved to be powerless, to be ordered about, to be punished" (Milliken 1991:330). The psychological cost of the move to the mission was very great, because in tribelet life people belonged to specific places and were accustomed to visiting them. Therefore, by going to the mission they left behind part of their identity (Milliken 1991:331). The result was often the psychocultural disintegration of the Indian person.

This sudden change in cultural patterns and lifestyles was brutal in its effects. A variety of enforced changes, particularly limited variety in diet, changed regime in dress and exercise, separation from extended family group, greater crowding, restrictions in movement, intensive labor (much more arduous than under native conditions), and introduced diseases all impacted the Indians' lives. This amounted to a kind of culture shock that created tremendous stress and often greatly lowered individual resistance to disease. The system's regimentation and extreme paternalism, together with the Indians' strong feelings of longing for their home territory, resulted in noticeable despondency. In 1792, Vancouver remarked that the Indians of Mission Santa Clara were acting in a very passive manner: "All the operations and functions both of body and mind, appeared to be carried on with a mechanical, lifeless, careless indifference . . . " (Vancouver 1792 quoted in Weber 1991:30).

A later visitor, Langsdorf, stated that the missionaries complained that

> . . . upon the least illness the Indians become wholly downcast and dejected, and giving themselves up to this depression of spirits, will not observe diet or

anything else recommended for their recovery [Langsdorf 1814 in Archibald 1978a:156].

Indian dissatisfaction was also reportedly manifested in both abortion and infanticide. As Padre President Lasuen stated in 1801:

> Knowing full well the inhuman crimes these Indian women so often commit . . . how they commit abortion and are guilty of suffocating their infants, we employ for their correction all care and vigilance, all the expedients, and all the diligence which a matter of such importance demands [Lasuen 1801 in Kenneally 1965: 210].

Their strong attachment to their homeland and the deep longing for it is indicated by a quote from Otto von Kotzebue's 1816 account of watching the Santa Clara neophytes return to their home villages:

> Twice in the year they receive permission to return to their native homes. This short time is the happiest period of their existence; and I myself have seen them going home in crowds, with loud rejoicings. The sick, who cannot undertake the journey, at least accompany their happy countrymen to the shore where they embark and sit there for days together mournfully gazing on the distant summits of the mountains which surround their homes; they often sit in this situation for several days, without taking any food, so much does the sight of their lost home affect these new Christians. Every time some of those who have the permission run away, and they would probably all do it, were they not deterred by their fears of the soldiers [Kotzebue 1816 in Castillo 1991:427].

In 1802, Padre President Lasuen wrote in a similar way about the Indians of Mission Santa Clara:

> For one who has not seen it, it is impossible to form an idea of the attachment of these poor creatures for the forest. There they are without a roof, without shade, without food, without medicine, and without any help. Here they have all of these things to their hearts' content . . . They see all of this, and yet they yearn for

the forest. Those who are attached to the mission are few . . . [Lasuen 1802 in Kenneally 1965:284].

Lasuen had stated earlier that the missionaries had the hard job of transforming a "savage race" to make them "human, Christian, civil and industrious," adding that the task could be accomplished only by "denaturalizing them," forcing them to "act against nature" (Lasuen 1801 in Kenneally 1965:202). Lasuen justified whipping and the other punishments inflicted upon the Indians by stating that punishments in a " . . . barbarous, fierce and ignorant country . . . are different from one that is cultured and enlightened," adding that the Indians are

> . . . people of vicious and ferocious habits who know no law but force, no superior but their free will, and no reason but their own caprice. They look on their own most barbarous and cruel actions with an indifference foreign to human nature . . . [Lasuen 1801 in Kenneally 1965:220].

The effect of the missionaries' negative attitude toward the Indians and the destruction of native lifeways and culture was to create a colonized people, most of whom had submitted to work in a slave plantation-like environment. The great majority of them were powerless in this situation. Closely supervised by those in charge, mission Indians had to choose among a range of bad options, from open rebellion (risking a violent response from the colonizer) to complete submission. Once enmeshed in the mission system, the Indians had no easy exit. Once baptized, they had to serve the mission and their colonial masters in perpetuity, for if an Indian ran away, the soldiers were sent to bring him or her back to the mission and probable punishment for escaping. The habit of a colonized mind-set was so ingrained that it continued long after the mission's demise. Thus, John Marsh, the early Contra Costa County settler, could in 1846 write a United States government official about the Bay Area California Indians:

> In many recent instances when a family of white people have taken a farm in the vicinity of an Indian village, in a short time they would have the whole tribe willing serfs. They submit to flagellation with more humility than the negroes. Nothing more is necessary for their complete subjugation, but kindness in the beginning, and a little well timed severity when manifestly deserved. It is common for the white man to ask the

Indian when the latter has committed any fault, how many lashes he thinks he deserves. The Indian with a simplicity and humility almost inconceivable, replies ten or twenty, according to his opinion of the magnitude of his offense. The white man then orders another Indian to inflict the punishment, which is received without the least sign of resentment or discontent. This I have myself witnessed or I could hardly have believed it. Throughout all California the Indians are the principal laborers, without them the business of the country could hardly be carried on [*Contra Costa Gazette* 12/21/1887].

On this continuum of rebellion/submission, Inigo was clearly on the submissive side. He wanted to and did assimilate into the Spanish colonial system, learning the Spanish language, customs, values, and technology. In borrowing from the Spanish he recreated himself, rejecting much of his "Indianness" in favor of being more like the Spanish. His identification with the Spanish and the colonial system was evidently complete enough that he did not feel the dejection and stress felt by many other Indians who joined the mission at an age older than he had. From the Spanish perspective, he was a success story; he eventually made it to the point of becoming a colonist himself. Inigo's assimilation was reinforced by his becoming an *alcalde*, a relatively favorable niche in the mission system. As part of the mission power structure, *alcaldes* reportedly got more and better clothing and other goods. Their jobs were like that of policeman, maintaining order among the Indians (Vallejo 1891:185). Although the Indian *alcaldes* reportedly punished other Indians at some missions, the 1814 report by the two Santa Clara priests stated that "here at the mission no Indian is allowed to punish another. All punishments are meted out under the supervision of the missionary fathers or the corporals of the guard" (Geiger 1976:115). The Indian *alcaldes* at Santa Clara may, however, have had a role in deciding on the form and severity of punishment (Archibald 1978b:175).

At Santa Clara the Indian *alcaldes* also had the responsibility for training the young people. Nasario Galindo related that during the 1820s fathers Catalá and Viader:

> . . . made it the custom to have all the boys and all the young girls, when they reached the age of ten years, separated from their Indian parents so that they could be put under the charge of one of the Indian alcaldes, who were elderly men, known to be of good

> repute. There were two houses where these children were assigned, one for the boys and one for the girls, and each alcalde had a list of their names. These names were written on a paper that was pasted upon a board and alongside each name was a correa or strip of leather that was worn around the neck.
>   It was custom for these children to say their prayers in the church both at night and in the morning, and they would attend when the bell rang at the accustomed hour. The alcalde, by looking over the list of names, could detect any that were missing because not only did they not answer their name when the roll was called but the correa would not be in place. When this occurred, the runaway was sought and when found was brought back to the Mission and punished. Besides the children that went daily to the church for Mass, all the Indians that lived outside the Mission also attended these services. There was one Indian who knew how to recite the prayers and he taught the rest in their own language and all followed him in praying in a loud voice. After the Mass was over, they all sang the "Santo Dios" and on Friday they sang the "Adorete Santa Cruz" [Galindo 1959 (1883):102].

While we can never know for sure, it is worth speculating that Inigo's assimilation perhaps allowed him to largely escape the great ambivalence and stress which most of the colonized Indians felt. He may have given up the memory of his own life, and that of his relatives, to avoid missing or mourning its loss, and thereby evaded the stress which decreased other Indians' resistance to disease. Thus, adaptation and assimilation were the road to personal survival in several respects.

Combined with the psychological deterioration which adversely affected most missionized Indians was the impact of contagious diseases and perhaps an inadequate diet. In regard to diseases, an 1814 report prepared by padres Catalá and Viader stated that "the dominant diseases of the Indians and the most devastating, are syphilis, which is chronic, and dysentery, which occurs during the autumn. They also suffer colds, fevers and typhus" (Geiger 1976:78-79).

In addition, there were at least three major epidemics: in 1802, when almost 20 percent of the entire Mission Santa Clara population died (a total of 248 people); in 1806, when the high total yearly death rate (231 or about 16 percent of the total population) was largely due to an epidemic; and finally, in 1827-28, when about 14 percent of the total

Maturity: 1798-1828

population (189 people) died. The 1802 epidemic was the result of a peste or plague of unclear nature. It has variously been suggested that it was pneumonia, diphtheria, scarlet fever, or tuberculosis (Milliken 1991:254). The 1806 epidemic was reportedly measles, which also affected Mission San Jose (Milliken 1991:288-289). The 1827-1828 epidemic, in which Inigo's wife Viviana and two-and-a-half-year old son José Tomás both died (on the same day, February 19, 1828), was also probably caused by an outbreak of measles (Jackson 1994:120). These and other epidemics can be traced to the overcrowding and lowered resistance caused by the colonial situation described above. Also important was the fact that the native people had no immunity to European diseases, making the death rate much higher than it would otherwise have been. Dysentery was perhaps due to the poor sanitation of the mission situation (Stodder 1986:43; Jackson 1994:127-132). The new clothing the Indians had to wear at the mission may also have been a factor. As Jackson points out:

> The missionaries also changed the style of dress of the converts living in the missions, substituting cotton, and particularly, woolen cloth for the traditional materials used by the Indians. The common practice was for the Franciscans to distribute a single set of clothing and blankets that the Indians wore until a new set was issued. Communal laundries were built at the missions, and Indian women made efforts to keep clothing and blankets clean. However, the new-style clothing easily harbored potentially dangerous parasites, and it could not be discarded with the same frequency as could traditional clothing. Finally, the missionaries attempted to establish new standards of dress, which required Indians to frequently wear the new garments. Although not necessarily an important factor in the elevation of death rates, change in clothing styles and materials exemplified the way in which the social engineering practiced by the missionaries damaged the health of Indian converts [Jackson 1994:135].

As padres Catalá and Viader stated in 1814, endemic syphilis was by this time a major health problem at the mission. The Spanish apparently brought this contagious disease from Baja California. It spread through the widespread rape of Indian women by soldiers and settlers, as well as through prostitution (Stodder 1986:41; Archibald 1978a:157; Rivera 1969 [1774]).

The question of the adequacy or inadequacy of the diet given people at the missions is less clear and subject to more controversy than that of disease. Sherburne Cook (1976:45) concluded that mission diets included at least one pound of meat per person per day. At least some early travelers also state that the food was abundant and nourishing (Langsdorff 1814:16). Ann Stodder, on the other hand, stresses that poor nutrition was a key factor in the high death rate at the missions (Stodder 1986). The evidence to prove her thesis does not appear to be adequate, however, so we must conclude that the role of nutrition, if any, in the high mission death rate remains unclear.

More important was the apparent higher death rate and lowered fertility for women living at the missions. Women died at such a high rate that the sexual ratio became very unbalanced at Mission Santa Clara and other Alta California missions (Jackson 1994:113-114). The reasons for the high female death rate are not fully clear, but death in childbirth and the special problems of being a woman in a culture which severely devalued them were undoubtedly factors. As Robert Jackson points out:

> Women and young children were the most vulnerable segment of the mission populations, and they suffered exceptionally high death rates out of proportion to their numbers in the total population. Women of childbearing age were perhaps most at risk. There appears to have been little or no prenatal care; and evidence suggests that the missionaries included women in the mission work force, which would have made pregnancies more dangerous. Moreover, the attempt by the missionaries to wipe out many of the native cultures may have denied young women access to traditional child-care knowledge. Children were born stillborn, or died shortly after birth due to the complications of birth or due to congenital illness such as syphilis. Dehydration also claimed many lives in the first year or two of life. Finally, qualitative evidence also suggests that abortion was commonly practiced in the mission communities; and the response by missionaries to apparent or real instances of provoked abortion contributed to the humiliation of Indian women, raised levels of stress, and only exacerbated the social conditions that had led women to abort in the first place [Jackson 1994:126].

It is unknown how many deaths are related to each of the various causes mentioned above. What is clear, however, is that Inigo's own

Maturity: 1798-1828

family and the Indian population at Mission Santa Clara generally suffered a horrible death rate. Very few Indians lived long enough to become an "old Christian" like Inigo. Given this fact, we need to explain how the religious and secular leaders were able to recruit, often from distant areas, the large numbers of Indians needed to maintain a viable population at Mission Santa Clara.

Recruitment Situations and Techniques

As was the case during the earlier period of Mission Santa Clara's history, recruitment of native peoples into the mission focused on luring the Indians with gifts and sending out Christian Indians and the mission fathers to preach the virtues of Christian and mission life. The idea was to treat the Indians with justice and try to win them over by stressing the benefits they could gain by cooperating with the Spanish. If such cooperation was not possible due to resistance on the part of the Native Americans, then Spanish military force was used to punish any native transgressions. Examples of each approach from the 1804-1807 period will be used to illustrate recruitment situations and techniques in some detail.

In 1807, the settlers of San Jose needed Indian laborers to help with the harvest. The governor gave them permission to recruit non-Christian Indians in the San Joaquin Valley. The Indians were to be paid with flannel, thread, needles, glass beads, and blankets. The governor issued very specific instructions to the townspeople about the need to treat the Indians well and not try to force them to become Christians, indicating that some settlers probably were tempted to use violence to hold the Indians as laborers:

> I wish them to be treated with all possible consideration so that, seeing the treatment that they receive, they will feel like coming in to reside in the future. The work assignments are to be moderate. Because they are not accustomed to it, it will be difficult to put much on them for the present . . . . Let them know that it is my desire that neither they nor their relatives should come to any harm. Rather, I want to maintain harmony. Let them know that they can come and go at will. I want no one to apply any violent pressure on them to become Christians. I desire that they enjoy their liberty, as they have done up until now. I

also want them to be paid a just wage for their work [Arrillaga 1807b in Milliken 1991:607].

Concerned about the possible negative effect on later relations, when a Mission Santa Clara Indian critically injured one of the children who had come along with the Indian work party, the governor was angry and ordered severe punishment meted out to the "thug" who did it:

> Regarding this incident I should tell you that although you have done very well to inform the pagans that they will receive just compensation for the transgression, it is important that you give them what you can. Given the situation, I order you to take the thug to the jail. If what you tell me is true, I will order you to punish him with twenty-five lashes for three or four mornings running, and if it be necessary, for still more days. If it seems they are not satisfied with that punishment, let the pagans know that I will banish him to a place where he will never do harm again. The strongest necessary punishment will be given him, short of execution [Arrillaga 1807c in Milliken 1991:298].

When native people rebelled and attacked Spanish military or civilian parties traveling into the interior, the response was very different. In Spanish eyes, Indian peoples did not have the right to prohibit the Spanish from exploring and recruiting in any part of California. If gentile (unconverted) natives forcibly resisted the passage or activities of exploration/recruitment parties through their territory, they were seen as lawbreakers or rebels and subject to full military retaliation and Indian defeat. Such retaliation was often followed by the mass conversions of the Indians who had been defeated, swelling the mission population.

A detailed review of the events of 1804-1806 shows how this policy worked in practice. Interestingly enough, Inigo himself was also involved in some of these events. He was in his early twenties at that time, and, as a loyal mission Indian, was a prime candidate for the role of an "Indian auxiliary." The auxiliaries were support troops who often accompanied the Spanish soldiers when they engaged non-Christian Indians in battle. Detailed evidence about this aspect of Inigo's career is, of course, unavailable, because military service records and most other records do not exist for Indians. But, when Inigo requested a land grant in late 1839, he listed among his services " . . . aid in the missions of Don Luis Peralta, Don José Sanchez, Don Mariano Vallejo, Don José

Tiburcia Castro, etc. etc." (United States Government 410 ND). Comparing these names to lists of military expeditions against various tribelets, in the eastern Coast Range and the San Joaquin Valley, we find that Peralta conducted four expeditions in 1804-1805; Sanchez led four in the 1811-1829 period; Vallejo led at least two expeditions in the 1829-1833 years; and Castro commanded one in 1839 (Milliken 1991: 270-271, 278-280; Cook 1976:245-250). We can conclude that Inigo went on a number of punitive campaigns against other Native Americans as an Indian auxiliary over a 35-year long period. The first was one of those led by Luis Peralta in 1804-1805.

The background context to these and several other expeditions during the same time frame was the declining mission population and relatively slow recruitment of the 1796-1804 years. Mission Santa Clara population hit its all-time peak at the end of 1795 at 1,541, largely due to the great influx (718 people) during 1794 and 1795. Recruitment fell off during the following years, averaging only 103.4 a year (931 total), during the 1796-1804 years (see Table 3). At the same time, deaths at the mission during this period totaled 1,602, or an average of 178 a year. The excess of deaths over recruitment, combined with an inadequate birth rate and some runaways meant that the total population of Mission Santa Clara was steadily dropping during the 1795-1804 period, reaching a low of 1,240 in 1804. This decline in population must have been of serious concern to the mission's leaders, since if it continued, the mission would disappear. The recruitment of "heathen" or gentile Indians, therefore, had to be increased and runaways recaptured.

In February 1804, a group of 20 Mission Santa Clara Christian Indians led by the *regidor* (councilman) Jorge (a 37-year old "Carlos" Indian who had been baptized in 1792) was sent out by Catalá and Viader deep into the mountains of the Coast Range east of the Santa Clara Valley. Their goal was reportedly to capture runaways, but they were probably also trying to convince gentile Indians to join them at the mission. The *Tayssen* tribelet, under Captain Joscori, attacked the group, killing Jorge and driving the rest out of their territory (Milliken 1991:268). A few months later, the Spanish governor wrote about the incident:

> The commander at San Francisco advises me that the priests of Mission Santa Clara sent out twenty Christians in solicitude of some runaways. The pagans killed the leader of the party. The rest fled to save themselves. I do not have enough troops to punish this insult [Arrillaga 1804 in Milliken 1991:268].

The resistance of the *Tayssen* group upset the priests at Santa Clara, since it set off a new round of fugitivism and therefore required military intervention. As the commander of the San Francisco Presidio later reported:

> The Fathers of the missions cry for assistance regarding runaway Indians who hole up as fugitives. They complain that because I do not go out looking for them it lowers the morale of the others, who then flee. Finally, Father José Viader of Mission Santa Clara is upset with me regarding the killing of the Christian George [Jorge] by the pagans of the mountains. I informed you about this last February 28. I found myself without forces when it happened, as I still do not have them, I have been unable to do anything [Arguello 1804a in Milliken 1991:270].

By the late summer of 1804, the Spanish military had enough troops (and probably Indian auxiliaries) to mount a punitive raid into the coastal mountains. The first expedition went out in September 1804. Its commander, Peralta, was not successful, so he went out again in October of 1804. While most details of these raids are lacking, this report on the October action did survive:

> The second expedition made by Sergeant Peralta in pursuit of the pagan Indians who killed the Christian Jorge did not succeed in capturing them. They did succeed in seizing eleven Christians of Mission San José and Mission San Francisco. After giving over the women and children to the Fathers, they arrived at the Presidio with thirty-two troublemakers [Arguello 1804b in Milliken 1991:271].

The male gentile Indians, accused of being "troublemakers" (i.e., those harboring runaways, harassing Christian evangelists, and those generally unwilling to submit to Spanish authority), were captured and forcibly taken to the Presidio. Their fate, perhaps a flogging, a work detail, or imprisonment for some time, is apparently unrecorded.

The year 1805 saw more Indian resistance in the East Bay mountains and Spanish retaliation. In January of 1805, a party from Mission San Jose, led by Father Pedro de la Cueva, traveled into the mountains south of today's Livermore Valley to hear confessions and baptize the sick. It probably was also a recruitment expedition or one in search of runaways, and Cueva ignored the advice of at least one soldier not to travel to the area. They ended up in the territory of a hostile group called the *Luecha* tribelet and were attacked by large numbers of Indians:

> The guide led them to a village of pagans, telling them they were Christians. Those from the village began to fire arrows with great enthusiasm—soon they got support from two other villages. They killed Ygnacio Higuera and two of our Indians. Father Cueva took an arrow in the eye and Joaquin Higuera another in the thigh. The pagans killed all the saddle horses . . . They kept firing arrows at the Father and the soldiers from midday until about dusk. The soldiers lost everything but their leather jackets, shields, and muskets. This took place yesterday, and some Indians brought back word on foot. This morning the Father and soldiers arrived on horses that had been sent out for them [Sanchez 1805 in Milliken 1991:278].

For the first time since the Spanish arrived in the Bay Area in force three and a half decades before, a Spanish person had been killed by a Native Californian. A priest had also been wounded. The Spanish leadership felt this required immediate retaliation, and on January 20, 1805, a punitive force (perhaps including Inigo) under the command of Luis Peralta was sent into *Luecha* territory. After two days travel, they

> . . . arrived at the point where the criminals had committed the crime. They did not find a single soul. They looked for the bodies, finding only that of the steward buried in a gully. Due to the rains that had recently fallen, it was impossible to find the trail by which the Indians had fled. The expedition went on into the mountains. They came upon and seized two pagan Indians. From them they verified the location of the village they sought.
> On the twenty-third in the afternoon they left for the place identified by the pagans. "We came upon it and came charging in with swords drawn. As we came upon them they were taking up arms. They began to fire. We struck them down, and five of the delinquents were killed at that place. The rest, with their women, fired at us from some ravines, one group from a nearby grove of trees. Presently everyone charged the grove,"

returning their fire because they had fired, thus killing five of the delinquents, including two captains and "and a little girl struck by accident." The grove was searched. "Twenty-five head, among them children and adults, all women, were brought out." Four adult males were also caught, two of them wounded. It is believed that some men suffering from gunshot wounds remained in the grove. After sunset the party retired to where they had left the horses, bringing the prisoners with them.

On the twenty-fourth they returned to the grove to see what they could find. Finding nothing, they returned. They recovered the body of the steward. They searched again [for the other bodies]. Not finding them, they retired.

On the twenty-seventh they freed one of the Indian men who had proved himself to be innocent [Peralta 1805 in Milliken 1991:279].

On this expedition, Spanish soldiers and mission auxiliaries killed 11 *Luecha* men, and four non-Christian men and 25 non-Christian women and children were captured and brought into Mission San Jose. Since another Peralta-led Spanish expedition entered their territory in mid-February 1805, the remaining *Luechas* could not resume normal tribelet life. In any case, most of the *Luechas*, with 11 of their people killed and others captured, were apparently ready to submit to the Spanish. Runaways gave themselves up and non-Christians asked to be baptized. After Sergeant Luis Peralta returned to the mountains, it was reported that "the expedition turned out well, in that before they even reached the mountains most of the runaways gave themselves up to their missions of San Jose and Santa Clara. Since then some pagans have asked to be baptized" (Arguello 1805 in Milliken 1991:279-280).

The newly baptized (at Mission San Jose) included both children and a few of the *Luecha* women captured during the previous raid. Later, more *Luecha* were baptized at Mission Santa Clara (Milliken 1991:280-281). With their rebellion defeated, they apparently felt that they had to enter the missions.

As another result of Peralta's mid-February 1805 expedition, other, more distant Indians gave assurances of past and future peaceful behavior: "One captain from the big village on the San Joaquin River called Pescadero came to give Sergeant Peralta assurances that neither he nor his people had taken part in the attack against Father Cueva and his escort" (Arguello 1805 in Milliken 1991:280).

The four arrested non-Christian *Luechas* were recommended for prison terms at Santa Barbara or San Diego, probably along with two Christians whom Peralta arrested in mid-February 1805 (Milliken 1991:280).

The dramatic events of 1805 continued in May when the threat of rebellion arose at Mission Santa Clara:

> In Mission Santa Clara a Christian Indian was captured on the roof of the Fathers' rooms. With him had come a pagan from the rancheria of the Seunens, to check out the entrance. They schemed to burn down Mission Santa Clara and kill the Fathers that very night. Their object had been to bring together the rancherias of the Bolbons and Seunens, a great number of pagans. All this was related by the Indian prisoner. Another five implicated Christians were also taken into custody [L. Arguello 1805 in Milliken 1991:281].

In response to this threat and the still unresolved *Tayssen* insurgency of early 1804, and also to quell any lingering *Luecha* rebellion, the Spanish government mounted the longest and most thorough campaign ever attempted up to that time. A group of 22 soldiers left Mission San Jose in mid-May 1805 under Luis Arguello. For a month the expedition's horses and armed men swept through 75 miles of the Coast Ranges from Mount Diablo south to Pacheco Pass. They apparently encountered little resistance. They struck at the *Luechas*, capturing four non-Christians, thirteen runaway Christians, and another nine non-Christians accused of various crimes against Spanish power. They attacked the *Tayssen* who had killed Jorge in early 1804, capturing six men who had been involved.

During and immediately after Arguello's expedition, *Luecha* and *Tayssen* families poured into Mission Santa Clara. While no members of these two groups are listed in Mission registers as being baptized prior to June 20, 1805, in the last ten days of June alone, 97 *Tayssen* and 13 *Luecha* were baptized at Mission Santa Clara. During the last six-and-a-half months of 1805, a total of 129 *Tayssen* and 63 *Luecha* were also baptized, these two groups making up a large percentage (63 percent) of the 289 new recruits of that year. The trend continued into 1806 when 94 additional *Tayssen* and ten more *Luecha* were baptized, 57.5 percent of the 181 total baptisms at Mission Santa Clara during that year. The large number who joined the Mission Santa Clara from these two groups indicates that, prior to 1805 at least, they were the most powerful still independent groups in the coastal mountains east of the Santa Clara Valley.

While the details of Spanish military tactics in Native American village areas during 1805 and 1806 are unknown, it is clear that they were engaging in a war with a foe that was very inferior technologically. Since the Spanish could act with impunity, almost all casualties were on the native side. The response on the part of the Indian people, especially the sudden switch of the *Luecha* and *Tayssen* groups from hostility to conversion to Christianity in a matter of a few months, indicates that they were terror-stricken and, in effect, begging for relief from attacks. They apparently decided that joining the mission would supply the relief and security they needed to survive.

The impact of the influx of large numbers of raw new recruits from a foreign group into Mission Santa Clara during the major recruitment years of 1805 and 1806 must have been dramatic. Approximately one-third of the total population of Mission Santa Clara entered the mission at that time and now had to be trained and led. The rapid change in ethnic makeup must have given Inigo and other experienced and loyal Christian Indians both a more central role and increased status. As the high death rate at the mission continued and more new recruits arrived, his role and related status probably increased. Those from early-recruited Ohlone/Costanoan groups must have also had higher status than recent arrivals.

Mission Expansion into the San Joaquin Valley

By 1806 the mission frontier had reached the western edge of the San Joaquin Valley. With the villages of the Coast Ranges almost exhausted as a source of converts, Spanish leaders began plans for new missions in the San Joaquin Valley. These plans came to nothing, however, since this source of Indians was needed to fill the ever-dying ranks of the existing missions. The explorations originally conducted to look for new mission locations, therefore, soon turned into simple expeditions to recapture runaways and recruit new converts. Initially, the Spanish were cautious about exercising their military muscle and the leaders of the initial ventures in 1806 were carefully instructed by the governor to act in a peaceful and judicious manner toward the natives:

> The object of the expedition that you will undertake is to reconnoiter to the north to gain knowledge of the rugged lands adjacent to our establishments, as well as to make peace with the pagans. The goal is to

relieve them of the horror with which they view our troops, for which they are not lacking in motives, since up to now we have never gone out except to punish them.

The present concept is different, in that I intend to create a situation in which the pagans will not oppose our coming to their villages or into their lands, that they will see that our sorties are not made with the object of punishment, but with the object of friendship. Likewise let them understand that they are not to admit runaways or criminals, and certainly not to shelter our enemies, just as we would not admit theirs, and that we are quick to receive them into our friendship and commerce. Leave them of a peaceful disposition in their villages, and offer them sincerely that we will listen to their complaints and castigate any Christians who maltreat them or do them any damage. All of this the sergeant is to make them understand as best as he is able [Arrillaga 1806 in Milliken 1991:296].

The idea behind this cautious approach was probably to determine the strength of the Indians, try to recruit them peacefully, and at the same time assert Spanish-defined rights. These included the rights to travel anywhere they wanted and to capture runaways wherever they might be. The 1806 expeditions were, however, only the beginning of Spanish penetration. Over the following 22 years there was on the average one expedition a year; some were exploratory (with no reported conflict) and others punitive, aimed at capturing runaways or punishing transgressions. While details are often lacking, there were reported incidents of heavy fighting with as many as 45 people killed and up to 100 captured in some instances. At times Indian habitations and food supplies were also burned.

Three of the most serious instances of fighting took place during the 1819, 1820, and 1826 expeditions led by José Sanchez. Inigo apparently participated as an Indian auxiliary on one or more of these sorties. All three were against the Sierra Miwok and all together resulted in at least 75 killed, 20 wounded, and 44 captured (Cook 1976:245-247).

The result of the extension of Spanish power to the San Joaquin Valley and beyond was that significant numbers of Yokuts and Ohlone/Costanoan/Yokuts borderlands people were entering the Santa Clara Mission by 1810 and 1811. As time went on and the Ohlone/Costanoan people at the mission died and were not replaced by new recruitment (since there were no longer any non-Christian Ohlone/Costanoans living outside the missions), the Yokuts and other San Joaquin Valley people became the dominant group at Santa Clara. Table 4 shows the evolution of this development over time.

Table 4
Language Groups Represented at Mission Santa Clara at the End of 1817 and 1827

Year	Ohlone/ Costanoan	Mixed Ohlone/ Costanoan /Yokuts	Yokuts	Mixed Yokuts/ Miwok	Miwok
1817	64 percent	5 percent	0 percent	31 percent	0 percent
1827	40 percent	3 percent	42 percent	11 percent	5 percent

It should be noted that by 1827, 58 percent of the population of Mission Santa Clara came from the San Joaquin Valley (the Yokuts and Miwok). This trend continued into the 1830s as the number of Ohlone/ Costanoan continued to decline.

The increasing dominance of San Joaquin Valley groups at Mission Santa Clara is also reflected in birth rates. Before 1819 the number of Ohlone/Costanoan births was always quite a bit higher than the number of births of San Joaquin Valley groups at the mission. During the 1819-1821 period the number of births was about the same, but from 1822 to 1828 the Valley groups always had a much larger number of births than the Ohlone/Costanoans. The increasing dominance of the San Joaquin Valley groups undoubtedly had some effect upon life at the Mission Santa Clara, but data are lacking to show what that impact was. Tension and low-level conflict probably arose between the different groups, conflict which undoubtedly had some role in the dramatic events of 1828-1829, which we will discuss in the following chapter.

Conclusion: What Kind of System?

This chapter has outlined basic aspects of the mission system in which Inigo and his family lived at Santa Clara during the 1797-1828 years. Still needed is a summary statement outlining the overall nature of this system in a comparative world-historical perspective. Table 5 compares central aspects of the mission system with slave, feudal, and capitalistic historical systems.

Maturity: 1798-1828

The colonial mission system, as practiced in Alta California, was similar to chattel slavery in eight of the twelve attributes listed in Table 5. They were as follows: an inability to leave; forced labor; physical abuse; declining population; deprivation of property rights; creation of a caste system; frequent resistance; and a general lack of technological development. The colonial mission system was unlike chattel slavery in four respects: mission Indians were not sold; the system did not mainly produce goods for sale on the market; children were not separated from their parents; and the Indians had some legal rights.

The colonial mission system, as practiced in Alta California, was also similar to feudalism in seven of the twelve attributes listed in Table 5. These were: an inability to leave; people were not sold; forced labor existed; there was little production for sale on the market; children were not separated from their parents before the age of ten; people were deprived of property rights; and there was a generalized lack of technological development. It was also unlike feudalism in five aspects: under feudalism physical abuse was uncommon; the population did not decline; a caste system rarely existed; resistance movements were infrequent; and the Indians had some legal rights.

Table 5
Central Attributes of the Colonial Mission System
vs. Slave, Feudal, and Capitalist Systems

Aspect	Colonial Mission System	Chattel Slavery	Feudalism	Capitalism
Right to leave	Absent	Absent	Absent	Usually present
Sale of people	Absent	Present	Absent	Absent
Forced labor	Present	Present	Present	Absent
Legal rights	Some present	Absent	Absent	Present
Physical abuse common	Present	Present	Absent	Absent
Declining population	Present	Present	Absent	Absent
Production for sale	Absent	Present	Absent	Present
Children often separated from parents	Absent	Present	Absent	Absent
Deprivation of property rights	Present	Present	Present	Absent
Caste system	Present	Present	Absent	Sometimes
Frequent passive/ active resistance	Present	Present	Absent	Sometimes
Generalized technological development	Absent	Absent	Absent	Present

Maturity: 1798-1828

The colonial mission system was similar to capitalism in only a few aspects. Our overall conclusion is, therefore, that the system was in important respects similar to but different from both slavery and feudalism.

The Spanish who established the mission system were probably trying to set up a feudal type of system and the result thus bears some similarity to feudalism. But the overlay of colonialism inherent in the invasion of the Spanish into California and the imposition of their alien political, economic, and social practices on the Native Californians also created a system which resembled slavery. The famous early California historian Herbert Bolton called it "practical slavery;" Robert Archibald, whose book on the California missions was published by the Academy of American Franciscan History, called it "slavery in fact although not in intent;" and leading California anthropologist Robert Heizer argued that "the neophyte in the mission was, in fact, a slave" (Bannon 1964:191; Archibald 1978b:181; Heizer 1991:169). This conclusion is reinforced by the fact that military expeditions prior to 1829 often seized and held Indian children as domestic slaves in the presidios and pueblos. One source states that by the late 1820s there were "large numbers of them scattered from place to place" (Hittell 1885 II:116). In October of 1829, however, Governor Echeandia issued an order abolishing slavery in California and ordered Indian child slaves restored to their parents or, ironically, delivered to the nearest mission (Hittell 1885 II:116).

The Alta California mission system was, in sum, an extreme example of the disastrous impact dependent colonial relations had on native populations. This was, of course, not the original intention of the colonial planners and those who implemented the policy. The result was intentional, however, in the sense that Indian labor was critical to maintaining the entire structure of colonialism and achieving the goals of the Spanish crown. This central role continued even after the native peoples began to die off. Colonial officials could see that the Indians were dying on a mass scale, but they made no real adjustments in their policies or practices. They apparently felt that the superiority of their culture, world view, society, and economy meant that they should continue to push their missionization and other programs regardless of the outcome. Their colonial policies resulted in elimination or near-elimination (i.e., genocide or culturecide) for entire groups of Native Americans.

"Genocide" is defined as the deliberate and systematic destruction of a racial, political, or cultural group. It is clear that the Ohlone/Costanoan and other California Native American groups were in fact destroyed during the period of 1769 to 1846. The question is, was this destruction in any sense deliberate?

On the one hand, the missions and higher civil authorities had the goal of Christianizing a heathen population (which for the Spanish included inculcating "civilized living" as they defined it). From their perspective, the death of a large percentage of the population was an unfortunate but unavoidable and unintended result. On the other hand, the Spanish authorities, from the governor down to the mission padres, knew at an early date (certainly no later than the early 1800s) that the converted Indians were not surviving at the missions. Since they were dying at a horrible rate, was not a corrective policy needed? When it was a known fact that a majority of a given group of Indians who joined a mission would be dead within a few years, was not a change required? Did the failure to change this policy not amount to the deliberate killing of a race? Why could not the Indians be converted in their villages, trained as agriculturalists, and left there? Therefore, "genocide" appears to be the correct word to use to describe the results of Spanish colonial policy. The effects on Inigo's own family and other Indian families in the area are abundantly evident. There was a successful Indian population in the Santa Clara Valley prior to 1777. But when these Indians were missionized, they died en masse. The authorities knew this and did nothing, making the effect clearly genocidal.

Eight of Inigo's own young children and his wife died due to the colonial situation and the difficult conditions at Mission Santa Clara. Inigo's wife Viviana, only 46 years old, and his two-and-a-half-year old son, José Tomás, both died on the same day, February 19, 1828. This must have been a heavy blow for the 47-year old Inigo, who was left with three young children: Maria Magdalena, aged 16; Manuel, 13; and Juana Francisca, 9. That same year of 1828 also saw the continuation of a series of dramatic events which were to seriously impact the viability of Mission Santa Clara, and it is to these events that we now turn.

Endnotes:

1. Reprinted from INDIAN LIFE AT THE OLD MISSIONS by Edith Buckland Webb by permission of the University of Nebraska Press. Copyright 1952 by the heirs of Edith Buckland Webb.

CHAPTER 4

MIDDLE AGE: WAR, MISSION SECULARIZATION, AND RETURN TO SAN BERNARDINO, 1828-1847

In 1828 Inigo turned 47 years old and became a widower. The next 18 years, corresponding roughly to his "middle age," were a time of rapid change both for him and his world. First, a large-scale Indian rebellion and resulting war in 1828-29 heavily impacted Mission Santa Clara, and the process of secularization during the 1830s finished off what was by then a dying institution. Secondly, the end of a viable Mission Santa Clara, together with Inigo's close connections and long service to the colonial power structure of Santa Clara Valley, made it possible for Inigo to claim land in the area known as San Bernardino, at or near his birthplace and the locale of his earliest memories. Third, obtaining land allowed him in turn to develop a farmstead, remarry, and hold his new family together. Fourth, the raiding by Yokuts people from the San Joaquin Valley and the arrival of numbers of Anglo-Americans resulted in continued change. This change became decisive in early 1847 when the Californio forces were defeated by the U.S. Army in a battle only a few miles from Inigo's home. The new force in the valley was to be the Anglo-Americans, and Inigo had to once again think about how to adapt to a new situation.

Background to War: Origins of the Estanislao-Cipriano Rebellion, 1826-27

The essential context within which the dramatic events of the 1827-1829 years took place—events which eventually involved Inigo and his friend Marcelo—included especially the key facts about the nature of mission life as recounted in prior chapters. As a semi-slave and semi-feudal system built on Indian labor in the present and otherworldly salvation sometime in the future, there were ample reasons for native people to be restive. This was especially true of the Yokuts, who came from far away and who often had the option of returning to their home villages and prior lifestyle. The intense love of these Native Americans for their own territory also came into play much more than for Indians like Inigo whose homeland was at or very close to the mission.

The more immediate causes of the Estanislao-Cipriano rebellion can be traced to mid-1820s developments, which had their origins in Mexico and the United States. The success of the Mexican War for Independence resulted in a new and liberal republican constitution in 1824 and a new governor in California soon thereafter. In July of 1826, this new governor, José Maria de Echeandia, issued a circular for the emancipation of some mission Indians, specifically those who might be in all ways qualified for Mexican citizenship. To obtain emancipation, such Indians had to reside in the part of California from Monterey south and had to present a petition asking for their freedom and supplying information about themselves, such as the name of the missionary they served under. This missionary then had to approve the application. In another reform, Governor Echeandia also limited to 15 the number of lashes which could be meted out at one time to an Indian. In late 1828 the idea of Indian pueblos, towns where freed neophytes could live, was also suggested (Hittell 1885:II:91-93). In practice almost nothing concrete came of these attempted reforms; only a few Indians were actually freed (others who applied had their applications vetoed by their padres), and the idea of Indian pueblos was soon dropped. It is also unknown if whippings actually decreased. In any case, it is unclear if such a "reform" is worthy of the label. Mere mention of such changes did make the Indians more disorderly and rebellious, however, and gave them ideas about the possibility of another life outside the missions (Hittell 1885:II:93; Engelhardt 1912:III:240-241).

During this same time period, the first foreign explorers/trappers began to arrive in California, making the great Central Valley and eastern part of the state an international frontier. The first to come was a small group of trappers from the United States led by Jedediah S. Smith. Smith and his men arrived in Southern California in 1826. Disobeying Mexican government orders to leave the state, they instead traveled north up the Central Valley exploring the territory and trapping for beaver pelts. Smith, representing American fur-trading interests, had mostly friendly encounters with the Valley Indians, especially once the Native Americans realized that Smith's party were not Californios (Morgan 1953:417 fn. 36; Sullivan 1936:95, 99; Weber 1990:17-19).

Smith's presence in the Central Valley and good relations with the gentile Indians soon generated problems for the missions and Californio government authorities along the coast. In mid-May of 1827, Padre Narciso Duran of Mission San Jose reported to the presidio commander in San Francisco that fully 400 Yokuts neophytes had just run away from the mission to return to their home villages in the Central Valley. The reason they left was, according to Duran, because " . . . the Anglo-Americans sent several communications to people in that part of the country, offering them protection to abandon the mission and Christian obligations and return to their villages to live and die gentiles" (quoted in Sullivan 1936:99). Ignacio Martinez, a top military leader at the San Francisco Presidio, quickly investigated the matter and blamed a Christian Indian named Narciso who he said used the presence of the Anglo-Americans as a "pretext" to encourage a mass escape from the mission (Morgan 1953:209; Sullivan 1936:102). Given the large numbers of runaway neophytes, however, Californio military leaders feared a massive Indian uprising, like the one a few years before at La Purísima in Southern California, possibly with help this time from the Anglo-Americans (Weber 1990:34-35).

Meanwhile, Smith decided that he had to return to the trappers' yearly rendezvous site in Utah, and so went over the Sierra Nevada with a few other men, leaving most of his party to spend the summer among friendly Indians at a secure camp on the Stanislaus River, reportedly near today's Oakdale (Weber 1990:20; Hurtado 1988:40). An investigatory Californio military expedition found them there during June of 1827, but since the trappers were well-armed, were causing no obvious problems, and Smith's men promised to leave very soon, they were simply given a lecture and not threatened or told to leave (Weber 1990:28-31).

Smith returned to California in mid-September 1827, and after some conflicts with the government authorities, again left California early in 1828. Within a few months of his departure, however, large numbers of Yokuts again ran away from both San Jose and Santa Clara missions. A war of rebellion as serious as any in California history was soon underway. Its leaders were two Indians named Estanislao and Cipriano.

War: The Estanislao-Cipriano Rebellion, 1828-1829

Estanislao was a Mission San Jose Indian from the "Lacquisimas" (*Lakisamne*) Yokuts tribelet. He was reportedly tall, about six feet in height, of slender build, and an excellent horseman. He had been a *vaquero*, mule trainer, and an *alcalde* at his mission (Phillips 1993:78). Less is known about the Yokuts Indian Cipriano, whose Indian name was Huhuyat. He was from the *Pitemas* tribelet, having been baptized at the age of 25 at Mission Santa Clara (SC-B 6297). In late 1828 these two Indians became a serious threat to the colonial system and its power structure. They led mass escapes from the two missions and were an example that others might follow, and they united a variety of Indians into one resisting force. The two Indian leaders were confident and defiant, sending a message from their Central Valley encampment to Padre Duran that their people were rising in revolt and they no longer feared the Californio soldiers. Duran recognized the threat, notifying Commander Martinez that "Lacquisimas" Yokuts Indians from San Jose, Santa Clara, and even from San Juan Bautista had rebelled and were joining together at one *rancheria*. Duran added darkly that:

> We cannot remain indifferent to all this. Everything depends upon capturing dead or alive the Indian Estanislao from San José and another from Santa Clara called Cipriano. Once we have them, the rest will surrender [Duran 1828; Phillips 1993:78].

Key background factors to this Indian rebellion included the issues discussed in the prior chapter, especially methods of recruitment, the nature of the mission system, and punishments. Estanislao was the main leader of this rebellion and his home village, near Knight's Ferry on the river which was later given his name, was probably where the Indians gathered. This location was only a few miles up the Stanislaus River from Oakdale where Smith's men had camped at a secure spot during the summer of 1827 (United States 413 ND).

In planning their attack the Californio leadership could depend upon old antagonisms among the Indians themselves. Inigo's own Ohlone/Costanoan tribelet had long been in conflict with the Yokuts, reportedly due to Yokuts infringement of territorial rights. Trade had also taken place between the two groups, but wars were not at all unusual (Levy 1978:488; Wallace 1978:463-465). Ohlone/Costanoan Indian auxiliaries who were enemies of the Yokuts could thus be depended upon. A second factor was superior military technology. The Californios had rifles and even cannons. The Indian rebels had the advantages of knowing the local area where the battle would take place and potentially greater numbers of men. They were also on the defensive and could hide behind fortifications. When the Californio troops first confronted Estanislao and Cipriano in early 1829, they found that their Indian enemies had indeed built a fairly extensive system of trenches and log fortifications on a large hill sited on a steep bluff overlooking the Stanislaus River. This first Californio attack was easily defeated and the party had to return to San Jose, forcing the Californios to redouble their efforts with a new expedition.

The second expedition took place in May of 1829 and was led by José Antonio Sanchez. Since up to 70 Indian auxiliaries loyal to the mission traveled with Sanchez to the Stanislaus River area to battle Estanislao, it is probable that Inigo was fighting with Sanchez against Estanislao and Cipriano. In the May 1829 battle between the Sanchez and Estanislao/Cipriano forces, Sanchez tried to use a cannon to dislodge the Indians from a stockade and trenches they had constructed. At least two Mexican-Californios were killed and eight wounded along with eleven Indian auxiliaries. Eight rebels were reportedly also killed. This attack failed, however, and when he retreated, Sanchez left a prisoner, Andrés Mesa, in the hands of the Indians. Estanislao then invited Indians from area villages to celebrate the victory and see the execution of the prisoner. Mesa was reportedly hung by one foot from the branch of a tree and his body shot with arrows until he was dead. His body was then burned (Phillips 1993:79).

The Indian victory and the loss of Californio lives must have enraged the entire Californio community. The commander of the San Francisco presidio immediately ordered Mariano G. Vallejo to organize a third and more powerful expedition, stating that

> The Indian rebels from Mission San Jose and Santa Clara have gathered together at the rivers, resolved to die rather than surrender. They are extremely insolent, committing murders and stealing horses . . . seducing other Christians to accompany them in their evil and diabolical schemes, openly insulting our troops . . . They are relying upon the manpower of the wild Indians, on the terrain and positions which they are occupying[1] [quoted in Phillips 1993:80].

The commander further ordered Vallejo to "administer a total defeat to the Christian rebels and to the wild Indians who are aiding them leaving them completely crushed" (quoted in Phillips 1993:80).

Vallejo left San Jose on May 26, 1829, with a powerful force of over a hundred soldiers and mobilized civilians, together with about fifty Indian auxiliaries from missions San Jose and Santa Clara. The Indian auxiliaries were commanded by Inigo's old friend and fellow Ohlone/Costanoan leader Marcelo and all were " . . . reputed to be long-standing enemies of the Lakisamnes" (Hurtado 1988:44). Vallejo's party had the most advanced weapons available, including at least one cannon. While we do not have lists of those present on this expedition, Inigo and other committed mission Indians, probably overwhelmingly Ohlone/Costanoans, must have made up the bulk of the auxiliary force. In a few days, Vallejo's party arrived at the site of the previous battle where another battle then took place. This battle site is today State

Historical Landmark Number 214 (Hoover et al. 1990:349). Vallejo used his cannon to destroy the Indian fortifications, killing many. The Indians were defeated and retreated. Vallejo's group then followed the Indians to their village and inflicted another defeat there. The soldiers then seized and executed on the spot a number of Indians, including three non-Christian old women (Phillips 1993:81). In addition, the Indian auxiliaries captured and murdered a runaway Christian Indian rebel from Santa Clara (whose name is unknown), whom many of the auxiliaries must have known personally. Joaquin Piña left an account of this particular incident in his diary:

> The Indian auxiliaries . . . managed to find a Christian Indian from Santa Clara. After capture he confessed that he had been the one who had burned the bodies of the two dead soldiers who had been killed on the previous expedition under Don José Sanchez. On learning this the Indian auxiliaries . . . began to beg the Commander for permission to kill the prisoner . . . . They were given this permission. So the Indian auxiliaries formed a semicircle, placed him in the middle, and four of them began to shoot arrows at him . . . . Finally seeing that he did not die, a cavalry officer shot him in the head with his carbine . . . From there they took him to an oak tree and hung him up[2] [quoted in Phillips 1993:81].

The rebel Indians had been defeated and an unknown number of them killed. Table 6 gives the names of the known killed and other available information from baptismal and death records.

Thus at least 14 of the rebel dead, which included Cipriano himself, were Indians from Mission Santa Clara, aged 14 to 74 years old. Four women were among the dead. We do not know how these women died, but possibilities include death while actively fighting, death by accident because they were at or near the battle site, and death by execution following capture. Especially notable is the fact that these 14 individuals came from 11 different Yokuts tribelets, indicating that Estanislao and Cipriano (Huhuyat) had achieved a measure of unity across tribelet boundaries perhaps unique in the Central California Indian struggle against colonial domination. Also interesting is the fact that a majority had been mission Indians at Santa Clara for eight years or more and only three had served the mission less than three years prior to joining the rebellion.

Table 6
Mission Santa Clara Indian Rebels Killed
in the Estanislao-Cipriano Rebellion, May-June 1829

Indian Name	Christian Name	Tribelet	Sex	Baptism Date	Age at Death	Baptism No.
Huhuyat	Cipriano	Pitemas	M	05/06/15	39	6297
Zulectay	Leandro	Achachaians	M	10/13/20	49	6955
Ayaputtu	Ana Maria	Chipeyquis	F	10/18/23	26	7451
Mouhicsi	Dimas	Mayemas	M	10/12/16	53	6440
Chacaquis	Hospicio	Pitemas	M	05/06/15	44	6296
Elleuti	Andres	Pitemas	M	05/06/15	64	6292
Lanitt	Andrea	Pitemas	F	03/06/15	74	6265
Chachaquis	Miqueas	Cuyens	M	03/27/13	23	6096
Volojeyot	Respecio	Tozozes	M	04/21/27	42	7996
Tilellame	Ninfa	Tuuhalmes	F	04/15/22	27	7275
Tasuamatme	Maria Trinidad	Tonul	M	01/09/22	14	7149
Chipelqui	Montano	Chugea	M	01/14/26	63	7791
Guaycatche	Peregrino	Lacquisimas	M	06/03/16	53	6391
Chocono	Petronilo	Gualansemnes	M	03/20/28	31	8131

It is clear, then, that these Indians knew Mission Santa Clara well and nevertheless escaped and took up arms against this institution and the entire colonial establishment. It was a damning indictment of the entire system that Indians who knew the mission so well became armed enemies of the authorities and killed Californio soldiers. Finally, in a foreshadowing of things to come, the Vallejo expedition returned to San Jose with 18 horses Indians had stolen from the missions or valley settlements (Phillips 1993:81).

After learning that Indian prisoners had been murdered, the governor ordered an inquiry which resulted in a mild punishment meted out to one soldier. On the other hand, Father Duran was able to convince the governor to pardon some rebels, if they returned to the missions. Estanislao himself then returned to Mission San Jose in order to save his life, since he probably would have been executed had not Father Duran intervened.

It is interesting to speculate on the relationship between Jedediah Smith's visit to the Central Valley and the Estanislao-Cipriano rebellion. It appears quite possible that the fortified hill of the Indians was at the same spot where Smith's men camped during the summer of 1827. It would have been logical and necessary for Smith and his men to find a safe location and fortify it since they were in potentially hostile territory. Having such a location as their own fortress would give the Indians confidence and encouragement in their rebellion. Also worth noting is the fact that Californio soldiers reported that Estanislao and Cipriano's men had rifles, which were strictly forbidden for Indians to possess. The Indians had only powder, however, and no bullets, so while they reportedly fired their guns, they had no real effect on the battles (Sanchez 1829). Where did the Indians get their guns? From Smith and his men?

Effects on the Mission

The Estanislao/Cipriano rebellion had a strong effect on Mission Santa Clara. Recruitment of new converts to the mission immediately collapsed and did not even partly recover until 1834. Whereas an average of over a hundred new converts had arrived at Mission Santa Clara each year during the 1826-1828 years, the average was only eight converts a year during the 1829-1833 years. Table 7 gives these and other available statistics.

The deficit created by the excess of deaths over births, and the failure of recruitment to make up the difference meant the eventual end of the mission. Another factor—running away—was also at work, as indicated by existing statistics on Mission Santa Clara's total population (see Table 7). Whereas this mission still had a population of 1,098 in 1833, one estimate indicates only 800 present in 1834. Firm figures do not exist for the key period of the mid-1830s because the two old padres, Catalá and Viader, who had operated the mission for so many decades, were both gone by 1833. Catalá had died and Viader returned to Spain. Zacatecan Indian priests from Mexico replaced them, and they did not keep accurate or complete records. It is clear, however, that large numbers of Indians were leaving the mission, especially Yokuts, who could return to home territory which was unoccupied by the Californios.

The next firm count of Mission Santa Clara population was made in September 1839, when only 291 Indians were present (Hartnell 1839). Secularization had, in the meantime, intervened. The secularization process at Mission Santa Clara began in early 1837 (discussed below). Indians could more easily leave the mission during the secularization process, and a few were formally emancipated. Others simply left and the government no longer attempted to recapture them. The result was that about 800 people had disappeared from the mission rolls in the space of only six years (1833-1839). Since only 389 died, 167 were born, and 222 were recruited, the mission population should have remained steady at about 1,100. That it declined to only 291 in late 1839 illustrates that the Indians themselves had decided to withdraw support for the institution and find other means of survival in their home villages.

As Table 7 illustrates, there was a brief revival of conversions between 1834 and 1837. This revival may have been due to the devastating effects of the 1832-1833 epidemic on the San Joaquin Valley's Indian population. Only one person was baptized in those epidemic years and the 1834-1837 revival may have been because individuals and small remnant groups who had nowhere else to go came to the mission for aid. The number of recruits reached over 60 a year in 1835 and 1836 before dropping back to a very low level again by 1838 and subsequent years. Death rates at the mission continued at a high level, which had a serious impact on the low mission population. Overall then, for the whole period, there was a tremendous decline in Mission Santa Clara population. The San Joaquin Valley Indians had, in effect, gone on strike against the mission system, a milder form of the Estanislao-Cipriano pattern of escaping from the mission and rebelling against Californio control.

A closely related feature of Indian resistance was the increasingly frequent guerrilla-type raids mounted by San Joaquin Valley Indians against the coastal missions, pueblos, and ranchos. These raids, mainly carried out by horse-riding Yokuts, had the primary aim of stealing live-

Table 7
Indian Births, Deaths and Convert Recruitment
at Mission Santa Clara, 1829-1847

Mission Date	Births	Deaths	Deficit	Converts	Population
1829	20	134	114	8	1269
1830	18	68	50	12	1226
1831	21	83	62	19	1184
1832	15	76	61	0	1125
1833	21	95	74	1	1098
1834	18	66	48	51	800
1835	27	62	35	65	?
1836	37	76	39	60	?
1837	27	58	31	27	?
1838	27	79	52	8	?
1839	31	48	17	11	291
1840	27	74	47	9	344
1841	37	72	35	21	?
1842	19	38	19	5	300
1843	35	57	22	34	?
1844	26	62	36	8	?
1845	14	38	24	4	130
1846	21	31	10	9	?
1847	37	61	24	13	?

stock, especially horses, from these Californio-controlled settlements. The horses were then used either for transportation, trade, or food. The raiding had begun years prior to the decade of the 1830s but increased greatly following the 1828-1829 rebellion. Already by late 1832, Father Narciso Duran of Mission San Jose could report that the Pueblo of San Jose and nearby settlements were:

Almost on the verge of ruin by reason of the incessant robberies of horses committed by apostate Christian Indians in league with gentiles . . . . Their unpunished insolence constrains us to foretell that, before many years, we shall see ourselves obliged to abandon our posts and reunite at one point for common defense[3] [quoted in Phillips 1993:109].

An alternative to the bunker mentality of Father Duran was the more aggressive approach of Governor José Figueroa, who in 1833 ordered that " . . . from every presidio a military expedition shall set out each month and scout those places where the robbers shelter themselves" (quoted in Beck and Haase 1974:23).

During that same year Figueroa also authorized civilians to capture stock thieves if they could catch them in the act. This soon led to abuses, however, as San Jose residents again kidnapped young Indians to use as slaves, leading to a revision of these regulations (Phillips 1993:109). Successful Indian raids still continued, and by February 1835 the *alcalde* of San Jose reported that the pueblo had lost all its horses to the raiders and the town was " . . . in a lamentable condition, having no way to round up its cattle scattered in the fields" (quoted by Phillips 1993:109). Over the decades of contact with the Spanish and Californios, the San Joaquin Valley Indians had been converted from peaceful, largely sedentary, local groups into semi-warlike, semi-nomadic bands living off raiding. As the more accessible herds of animals located in the eastern part of the Santa Clara Valley were depleted, raiding was extended to Mission Santa Clara. As a result, the mission's herds began to seriously decline. Still at a high point in 1834, by 1840 numbers of stock animals at the mission had dropped by between 66 percent and 80 percent. Some of this decline was due to the effects of secularization, but much of it was a result of raiding. Table 8 offers available figures (from Bancroft 1886 III:227-228) on this topic.

A related occurrence was the sharp decline in crops planted during the 1828-1832 period. Planting of wheat was still at a reasonably high level in 1828, for example, but dropped by more than half in the 1829-31 years (Jackson and Castillo 1995:120).

Table 8
Livestock on Hand, Mission Santa Clara, 1834-1840

Date	Cattle	Horses	Sheep
1834	14230 (includes mules)	1230	15000
1839	5620	353	6500
1840 (May)	3717	218	4867
	(-73 percent)	(-82.3 percent)	(-67.6 percent)

Life at Mission Santa Clara During Its Last Phase

Although the Estanislao-Cipriano rebellion impacted Mission Santa Clara and was a key factor in its decline during the 1830s, it still remained a functioning mission for a number of years. As such, it continued with many of the day-to-day activities—festivals, religious pageantry, celebrations of weddings, births and baptisms, and mourning of deaths—as it had for over 50 years. Colorful ceremonies had long been a factor in maintaining Indian support for the missions, and they probably became relatively more important during this period of decline.

Two interesting descriptions of festival days exist and are worth recounting here because they represent examples of the ways used to keep Indians tied to Mission Santa Clara, and because Inigo undoubtedly attended events like these. Such descriptions are also important because they show surviving Indian lifeways during the 1830s and illustrate the emerging Californio frontier culture of the period. The first description is of the feast of St. Joseph that took place at Mission Santa Clara in March of 1831 or 1832:

> It was growing late, and we started for the Mission of Santa Clara, which is about twenty leagues distant from St. Juan. A short ride brought us to the "Pueblo de San José," when we quickly passed up through the beautiful "Alameda," and stopped at the door of the Mission. Being the festival eve, many of the Indians were starting off in numbers; and ere the sun had set, hundreds were upon the road for St. Jose. Father Viader was to go in the morning, before breakfast, and, it being but a short ride, we concluded to remain and accompany him.

The morning presented the same lively scene of people going to the feast; and, at an early hour, the Padre's carriage was brought to the door. It was a singular contrivance, invented by himself, and built by the Indian mechanics under his direction—a narrow body, of sufficient width for one person only, hung on a pair of low wheels; and the whole frame was covered with brown cotton. The seat, well stuffed with lambs' wool, served to compensate for the absence of springs; and the harness, which he had made from green hide, twisted into rope, though not very ornamental, was sufficiently strong, and answered every purpose.

All being in readiness, Padre Viader got into his carriage. We mounted our horses, and off we started in grand equestrial order. The carriage was drawn by a fine black mule, astride of which sat a little Indian boy, who assisted in guiding the animal, in connection with a more experienced Indian, who, mounted on a fiery steed, led the mule with a "reata" fastened about his neck. On each side were two "vaqueros," with lassos fixed to the axletree, by which they facilitated the movement of the carriage over the road, and essentially aided the mule in ascending steep places. Three or four of the priest's pages attended him also; and in the rear followed a number of Alcaldes of the Mission. All were attired for the occasion, and from their hats were flowing red and blue ribbons, which, like pennons, fluttered in the wind.

A quick movement brought us to a view of the Mission from a neighboring rising ground, from whence we saw the gathering multitude; and as we approached nearer, the bells of the church rang a merry peal, in honor to the priest, which continued until the two missionary brothers were fast locked in an embrace; when the ringing ceased, and we retired within . . . .

Mass was soon commenced, and Padre Viader at the usual period of the ceremony ascended the pulpit, and delivered an explanatory sermon relative to the celebration of the day. The music was well executed, for it had been practised daily for more than two months under the particular supervision of Father Narciso Duran. The number of the musicians was about thirty; the instruments performed upon were violins, flutes, trumpets, and drums; and so acute was the ear of the priest that he would detect a wrong note on the part of either instantly, and chide the erring performer. I have often seen the old gentleman, bareheaded, in the large square of the Mission beating time against one of the pillars of the corridor, whilst his music was in rehearsal.

After mass was concluded we passed out of the church to the priest's apartment though a shower of rockets, which were fired off incessantly in every direction. Dinner was served early to give us time to witness the performances of the Indians, and as there were many strangers at the Mission, a very lengthy table had been prepared, so as to accommodate all. An abundance of good things appeared and disappeared, till at length the cloth was removed; cigars were smoked, and the good old friars retired to enjoy their "siesta" whilst we repaired to the front corridor to behold the fun.

At a signal from their "Capitán," or chief, several Indians presented themselves at the corner of one of the streets of the 'Rancheria" and gradually approached towards us. They were dressed with feathers, and painted with red and black paint: looking like so many demons. There were several women amongst them. Soon they formed a circle, and commenced what they called dancing, which was one of the most ludicrous specimens of grotesque performance I had ever seen. It did not appear to me that they had any change of figure whatever; but fixed to one spot, they beat time with their feet to the singing of half a dozen persons who were seated upon the ground. When these had performed their part, they retired to an encampment beyond the building and another party appeared, painted and adorned rather differently from the former, whose mode of dancing also, was quite dissimilar. They retired after a while, and arrangements were made for a bear fight. Whilst these amusements were going on, the Padres had risen, and we were called to chocolate; but the enthusiasm of the Indians hardly gave us time to finish, when we heard them crying "Aqui traen el oso!" He was soon ready, though almost dead from confinement, and the bull made but a few plunges, ere he laid him stiff upon the ground. This part of the amusement concluded, Deppe and I walked to the encampment, where the

Indians were dancing in groups, as we had seen them at the Mission. Around the large space which they occupied were little booths displaying a variety of ornaments, seeds, and fruit. All was hilarity and good feeling; for the prudence of Father Narciso had forbidden the sale of liquor. At sundown the bells were rung—rockets were let off—guns were fired; and long after supper, at a late hour of the night, we could hear from our beds the continued shouts of the multitude [Robinson 1851 (1846):95-98].

The second example of such a festival took place at Santa Clara on August 12, 1837, and is recounted as follows in the diary of Faxon Dean Atherton:

> Saturday, August 12. This being the anniversary of the foundation of this Mission, the day was ushered in by the ringing of bells, firing of guns, and all the customary noise on such occasions. The first news I heard in the morning was the death of the bear that had been caught the evening before and being a fine large one had given promise of great sport, but probably while tied to the tree ruminating on his movements being so grievously curtailed by the lazo and no doubt having a slight touch of the blues in the cold fog (and who the devil would not) which is enough to chill a dish of colache [made of squash, cheese, and corn] in two minutes, he through rage slipped his life lines and he left his carcass tied to a willow tree where it was found next morning, cold as Catholic charity and great was the lamentation thereof. However, the majority of the people were determined not to be cheated out of their sport and after Misa, they let bulls into the square singly and after sawing off the tips of their horns to prevent them from injuring their horses, they commenced what is here known by the name of "Torear," which means playing or fighting with bulls, which is done by a man on horseback or on foot running up to and shaking a red cloth or blanket in the bull's eyes, who being greatly irritated by it, rushes head foremost at the man, who then exerts his greatest skill and dexterousness to keep clear from him, and is rewarded more or less by the cheers of the spectators according as he shows himself

skillful. The Indians showed much greater courage and dexterity than the whites, they taking a blanket and going on foot would shake it (in) the bull's eye, and as he rushed towards them would throw it over his horns and jump to one side with an agility truly astonishing, notwithstanding which some three or four got thrown down and trampled upon pretty severely, Mr. Bull putting his horns under their bodies and rolling them over and over like boys rolling a large ball of snow. However, not one of them were much hurt as they had taken the precaution to deprive Mr. B[ull] of the power of doing so by sawing off the ends of his horns.

In the afternoon the Indians had a grand dance and acted a number of tricks, which were of not much account. Their dresses were very savagely fine being almost entirely covered with beads about the neck and breasts, heads full of feathers, and loins covered with a feather blanket, the rest of their bodies being painted in all manner of grotesque figures imaginable. Their songs or dances I could not make much of [Atherton 1964 (1836-39):64-65].

The prominence of Indian dancers in the festivities of the later mission period probably indicates a conscious attempt on the part of the mission power structure to provide a more welcoming environment for the native people who had recently arrived and still remained at the mission. This concession was quite logical given what had transpired in recent years, the prevention of further rebellions and escape from the mission being a prime concern.

Holy Week at Easter was another period of intense religious activity at Mission Santa Clara. Encarnación Pinedo later reported what occurred during this week:

On Holy Thursday a solemn high mass was chanted, the Indians joining in the responses, and at the end of the mass, the clergy and acolytes, robed in their richest vestments and carrying crosses and lighted candles on poles, and the people in gala attire, formed a procession which reverently issuing from the church, escorted the Holy Sacrament around the plaza and back to the sanctuary, where it was deposited with every manifestation of deepest devotion. During the ceremonies solemn hymns and psalms were chanted and prayers were offered to the divine Redeemer, while incense was constantly burned, sometimes ascending in clouds . . . . In the afternoon of Holy Thursday, the ceremony of the washing of feet took place. The oldest Indians in the rancheria were crowned with flowers and brought to the church, where they were seated on benches prepared for the occasion. The priest in his alb, and carrying a white towel and a pitcher of water scented with bay leaves, then washed their feet and wiped them, after which he ascended the pulpit and preached the sermon on true Christian humility and brotherhood, typified by the ceremony just performed . . . [quoted in Webb 1952:268-269].

The humility shown by the priests in this ceremony must have been impressive to the Indians. It showed an aspect of the mission and priestly rule which should be noted: the ability of the padres to teach values and lead by example. It is difficult to square with the violent and oppressive aspects of the colonial situation the Indians had to live under, and it is difficult to know exactly how such ceremonies would have been received.

Encarnación Pinedo told the story of the "Way of the Cross" or Christ's journey to Calvary performed on the *Alameda*, or road to San Jose. This was conducted on Good Friday by three men dressed in white linen vestments. They carried a "very heavy crucifix" along the *Alameda* halfway to the Pueblo of San Jose, stopping at the Stations along the way (Webb 1952:270).

It is quite possible that Inigo was himself among the old Christians whose feet were washed by the padres during the last years of Mission Santa Clara, and he may have at some point carried the cross along the *Alameda*. At a minimum, he must have at least observed these things and all the religious and other pageantry going on around him. At this time, Inigo was, of course, culturally more a Californio Catholic than an Indian.

Music played an important part in many of these festivals, and Inigo was active in both the mission band and choir. Inigo had received his musical training at San Jose with the famous Father Duran, who was probably the best music teacher in Northern California. Inigo also was said to have performed, presumably with the band and choir, at Mission San Jose and " . . . had a fine singing voice and played instruments well" (Hogle 1975:12-13).

Another way in which life continued during the 1830s was in the recorded cycle of marriages, births, and deaths. In 1830 Inigo became a grandfather when his daughter Maria Magdalena gave birth to a son, Casimiro. Fifteen-year old Maria Magdalena had been married to the 35-year old Casimiro in June of 1827. The couple had three more children before Casimiro died in June of 1838. She then married her second husband, Simon. They had one child in 1839, but it died in 1840.

Also in 1830, Inigo's 16-year old son Manuel was married to 13-year old Ysidra of the *Totote* (probably Yokuts) tribelet. By 1833 Manuel and Ysidra were having children together, but their first five children (born 1833-1840) all died within two years of their birth. So while Inigo was being made a grandfather many times over during this period, the death of so many of his grandchildren must have been painful in itself, but also must have brought back equally painful memories about so many of his own children dying in past years.

Finally, Inigo's 14-year old daughter Juana Francisca married the 48-year old Froylan in April 1833. They had no children and Froylan died in 1840. Testigos (witnesses) for this marriage included Inigo's old compatriot Marcelo, who with Inigo, Gorgonio, and Roberto, were all Mission Santa Clara Indians who were later able to gain land grants during the late 1830s and early 1840s.

Secularization and the Rise of the Rancheros

Desertion by Christian Indians and raiding by rebel Christians and San Joaquin tribal people were only two of the reasons why Mission Santa Clara declined during the 1830s. During this same period a new local ruling class was rising in California, a close-knit group of families best labeled the Californio ranchero oligarchy. This class had been slowly created during the decades of Spanish and Mexican rule prior to the 1830s by migration from Mexico and occasionally even from Spain and by a high birthrate once in California. By the 1830s this population of people was numerous enough to demand the mission lands, its livestock and other property, its Indian work force, and the political power needed to acquire them. Their leaders, men like Mariano G. Vallejo, José de Jesus Vallejo, José Castro, and Juan Bautista Alvarado, led the fight to expropriate mission property and its Indian labor force so that they, along with their allies and relatives, could benefit. The demographic background to this drive to seize mission property and the process of granting ranchos (often from mission lands) to private individuals is detailed in Table 9.

The gradually increasing number of Californio births registered at Mission Santa Clara over the 1810-1847 period reflects the increasing

Table 9
**Californio Births (Baptized at Mission Santa Clara),
Pueblo Population, and Santa Clara County
Private Land Grants, 1810-1847**

Births	Santa Clara	San Jose Population	No. Santa Clara Landgrants
1810	10	125	3
1811	20		
1812	11		
1813	12		
1814	13		
1815	12		
1816	14		
1817	11		
1818	17		
1819	18		2
1820	30	240	3
1821	15		3
1822	23		9
1823	19		8
1824	33		2
1825	29		1
1826	20		
1827	34		4
1828	27		4
1829	30		6
1830	34	540	2
1831	41		5
1832	43		

1833	41		21
1834	32		39
1835	38		41
1836	42		35
1837	39		31
1838	35		16
1839	42		48
1840	48	750	40
1841	54	936	56
1842	44		51
1843	45		61
1844	45		120
1845	43		67
1846	72		81
1847	74		

population of the Pueblo of San Jose and nearby Californio settlements, many of them on private land grants. Births increased from a yearly average of only 13.8 during the 1810-1819 decade, to 26 during the 1820-1829 years, and to 45.8 average annual births for the 1831-1847 period. While Californio births were rapidly rising, Indian births at the mission were stagnant during this same period and ranged from 14 to 37 a year after 1827 (see Tables 3 and 7). The population of the Pueblo of San Jose was almost doubling every decade, resulting in great pressure for new land grants. Since the San Joaquin Valley Indians had made their territory virtually off-limits to any but large armed expeditions, only the mission and other government controlled lands were left. Beginning with the speeding of the secularization process in 1833, the number of land grants in Santa Clara County increased tremendously, growing from a mere handful during the 1820s to many hundreds during the 1830s and 1840s (see Table 9). These grants included some from Mission San Jose as well as Mission Santa Clara.

    The actual process of expropriation of the 21 California missions was called secularization and it proceeded in a step-by-step fashion during the 1830s. It had originally been the intent of the missions to "civilize" the Indians and bring them into the mainstream of Spanish/Mexican life, then return their land to them to farm for themselves. Instead, the new Spanish/Mexican settlers stepped into the void left by the extermination of the Indians and the failure of the mission authorities to return land to "trained" Indians.

As pointed out above, there were false starts toward secularization as early as the mid-1820s. Political struggles between conservatives who wanted to delay or prevent the process and liberals who wanted to speed it up went on during the early 1830s both in Mexico and California. The key breakthrough came in mid-1833 during the governorship of José Figueroa, when the Mexican congress passed a sweeping law mandating the beginning of actual secularization. This involved several steps. First of all, the missions were removed from the administration of the Spanish-born Franciscan priests (religious order priests) and put in the hands of Mexican-born secular clergy (diocesan priests). The latter came from the Zacatecas College in Mexico and were brought into California from Mexico during Governor Figueroa's administration (Conmy 1938:1). Secondly, a secular administrator, basically representing the interests of the new ranchero ruling class, was appointed to emancipate those Indians considered by the mission and secular authorities to be ready to live on their own, and help distribute (together with the governor) the land, livestock, and other property to favored relatives and allies within the ranchero class. On rare occasions Indians also received land and other property grants, but this was the exception. This was true even though regulations called for them to receive land, tools, animals, and seed. In other words, there was often a big difference between the law's stated intent and its actual execution.

Figueroa implemented the 1833 Mexican law with an 1834 decree which planned to secularize ten missions in 1834, six in 1835, and the remaining five in 1836 (Bean 1973:67). Mission Santa Clara was one of the last to be completely secularized, for although the aged Father José Viader was replaced in 1833 by two Zacatecan priests (fathers Garcia Diego and Rafael Moreno), an administrator was not appointed until late December 1836 and he did not occupy his office until early 1837.

The new administrator for Mission Santa Clara beginning in early 1837 was José Ramon Estrada, a brother-in-law of the governor, Juan Bautista Alvarado. Estrada also had close ties with other key families of the ranchero oligarchy. For example, he married a member of the Castro family. One of his uncles was Luis Antonio Arguello, governor of California from 1822 to 1825, and one grandfather was Joseph Dario Arguello, who had been the commander of San Francisco, Monterey, and Santa Barbara presidios and acting governor of California in

1814-1815. Besides these connections, he also had family ties to other old and powerful California ranchero families, including the Berryessa, Peralta, Bernal, and Vallejo families (Northrop 1984, 1987). Appointed to administer Mission Santa Clara by his brother-in-law the governor, Estrada's formal job was to distribute the property fairly to all Californios, including Indians. Informally, of course, his job was to manipulate the situation in order to distribute the mission's property to favored members of the ranchero oligarchy (especially relatives) and the government itself. It was a common practice during Alvarado's administration, for example, for the governor to see mission property as a kind of bank deposit or tax fund to be drawn on as needed. A draft for a number of cattle from a specific mission would be issued by the governor to pay a debt. In this way the oligarchy enriched itself on the property of the missions, including Santa Clara (Hittell 1885:II:206; Dana 1840:210-211; Langston n.d.:138-139; Bancroft 1886:IV:50, 194; Staniford 1975:86).

When Estrada took over in early 1837 the Mission Santa Clara lands were still intact. The land base of the mission had been described in 1828 as consisting of an area about six leagues long in a north-south direction, and three leagues wide in an east-west direction. The northern boundary was the Bay of San Francisco, the southern boundary was near the headwaters of the Guadalupe River, and this river also formed the Mission's eastern boundary. The western boundary was San Francisquito Creek (Bowman n.d.:29). This area, about 18 square leagues or 80,000 acres, encompassed some of the best agricultural land in California, perhaps the world. The most loyal of the mission's Indians, including Inigo himself, were still present, but their number was dropping fast, as the Indians deserted a dying institution. In 1837 there was only a relatively small number of loyal Indian families left at Mission Santa Clara. Because of inadequate recordkeeping during this era we do not know exactly how many, but it was probably less than a hundred families. The reasonable and just approach would have been to divide much of the 80,000 acres among these Indians. Good-sized farms of 500 acres could have been distributed to all Indian families and there still would have been ample land left to distribute to the Californios both at the mission and in San Jose. This, of course, is not what occurred, as a result of the desire of the new ranchero class to take nearly all the land.

While full details are lacking, Estrada's initial actions apparently focused on "loaning" the mission's livestock, and allowing various non-Indian Californios to squat on prime pieces of the mission's lands. They included people associated with the mission (as lay teachers, for example) and leaders of the Pueblo of San Jose. They could then establish claims prior to petitioning the governor for formal grants. At the same time, conditions deteriorated for those Indians who remained at the mission. Because of secularization, raiding, and desertion, morale must have been low and declining both among the new priests now leading the mission and among the Indians themselves. In this situation agricultural production and general maintenance of the mission inevitably declined (Jackson and Castillo 1995:120). When the English Captain Belcher visited the mission in 1838, for example, he reported that it was "fast falling to decay" (Belcher 1843:I:117). In early 1839, an order was given to send 5,000 mission sheep to Sonoma as a "loan" for five years. The Indians still remaining at the mission protested and the sheep were not sent (Bancroft 1886:III:728). The Indians, observing what was happening to the lands and property they had long been assured were theirs, were in an assertive mood.

The "Yoscolo Rebellion" of 1839

By the late 1830s a Yokuts Indian leader, variously called Yoscolo, Yozcolo, or Djoscolo, was leading attacks (apparently to seize horses) against the Santa Clara Valley settlements. Existing accounts of the life and activities of this Indian and his followers are so full of discrepancies and mixed with myth that it is unusually difficult to sort out fact from fiction. For example, while Yoscolo was reportedly a baptized Mission Santa Clara Indian, his name does not appear in the official baptism lists. Perhaps he was never baptized or "Yoscolo" was his gentile name and went unrecorded. Even the exact date of his raiding activities is unclear, although the weight of existing evidence puts it in July of 1839. Apparently the frequency of Indian raids during this period resulted in the false attribution of a number of separate events to this one person and his small raiding party, magnifying his and his group's importance. During his career, Yoscolo supposedly attacked ranchos to steal livestock, and Mission Santa Clara itself to capture both livestock and Christian Indian women. He was reportedly in love with one of them, a woman named Perfecta, and wanted to free her. These attacks probably actually took place over a number of months or even years.

The events surrounding Yoscolo's demise, together with his followers, are more clear. This apparently came in late July 1839 when, after killing a Mission Santa Clara Indian guarding a cornfield, Yoscolo and his band were chased into the Santa Cruz Mountains by a group which reportedly included José Ramon Estrada (administrator), Juan Prado Mesa (commander of the soldiers at the mission), and Manuel Peña, as well as other soldiers and some Indian auxiliaries from the mission (Phillips 1993:112-13; Bancroft 1886:IV:75-76). In the fight that followed, Yoscolo and his people were all killed. Two Californios, the Cibrian brothers, also reportedly died. By this time, the struggle between the Indian raiders and the Californios had become so bitter that the decision was made to make an example of this Indian rebel. Yoscolo's head was cut off, stuck on a lance and carried first to San Jose and, after being paraded around the plaza for a time, carried down the *Alameda* to Mission Santa Clara. There the severed head was nailed to a pole next to the large cross in front of the church, where it was left for two or three months as a warning to all thieves and rebels (Phillips 1993:113).

The "Yoscolo rebellion" resulted in a further disintegration of Mission Santa Clara. When William E. P. Hartnell, the newly appointed visitor-general of missions, arrived at Santa Clara in September of 1839, he counted only 291 neophytes present (Bancroft 1886:III:727). The Indians at the mission were still considered "neophytes," even though many, like Inigo, had been part of the mission for many decades. The herds of livestock were also down substantially. With little or no work being accomplished and the land being seized by those who had enough power to do so, Inigo must have recognized that the time had clearly come to also attempt to gain the parcel of land he wanted through whatever channels were open to him.

Return to San Bernardino

Inigo had been born, sometime in 1781, in the area east of Mission Santa Clara, an area generally known as San Bernardino. This was the region he returned to by late 1839. The land to which he returned had at least two shell mounds, remnants of precontact occupation. It is likely that one of these represented the site of Inigo's childhood home. By late 1839 Inigo had "obtained his liberty" from Mission Santa Clara. Also by that time, he had squatted on and occupied "El Posida de las Animas" (the little well of the souls), a place the Indians called *Sojorpi*, in the southwestern corner of what later became the Posolmi land grant. Inigo built a traditional straw house there and reportedly also planted fruit trees at this location. Then, on November 23, 1839, he submitted a petition to José Castro, the Prefect of the First District, requesting that he be allowed to continue to occupy "El Posida de las Animas," which the "general" (presumably Castro) had given him permission to occupy. Inigo's actual words, as written by one of the mission padres or other helper, are instructive for their language and tone. This document is one of the few signed by Inigo with his "X" in the form of a cross, since he could not write:

Middle Age: 1828-1847

He prays your Honor for the sake of humanity forwards this petition to His Excellency the Governor of the Department that he may be favored with a small number of cattle and horses for his work. Your Honor can be informed of all the services he has rendered to aid the progress of said ex-missions of the Senores Don Luis Peralta, Don José Sanchez, Don Mariano G. Vallejo, Don José Tiburcia Castro, etc. etc. And he wishes to obtain from your Honor that his Son . . . be given to him, who is the Neophyte Manuel, and yet a boy, whom he brought up, naming him Manuel 2nd, who also wishes to live with him. And therefore he earnestly beseeches Your Honor intercede for this unfortunate person, in which he will receive favor and peace. And he swears that this is not done from malice, leaving to your Honor to do what is just, and he did not execute this on stamped paper as there was none.

Signed, Inigo, his mark [United States 410 ND: 78-79]

In early December of 1839, José Castro, Prefect of the First District, responded to Inigo's petition by suggesting that he apply to Governor Alvarado for the favor he sought, adding that the Prefectura believes that Inigo's "services and advanced age" entitle him to this favor (United States 410 ND:79). The governor was then petitioned, and one report states that Inigo himself traveled to Monterey and made a personal appearance before the governor to make his land grant request (United States 410 ND:20-21). If Inigo did indeed personally visit Governor Alvarado, it did not officially result in a grant to him; his petition was instead referred back to Mission Santa Clara Administrator José Ramon Estrada. The governor requested that Estrada report on whether Inigo was entitled to that which he requested and how large a land grant he should receive. Estrada responded that, since Inigo had served the Mission as a magistrate, this was "unmistakable proof" of his good conduct and he should be granted the land, together with 15 head of cattle, two yoke of oxen, and three horses (United States 410 ND:79-80). Governor Alvarado then ordered, on January 20, 1840, that Inigo should receive the following property from the government (which was seen as the owner of Mission Santa Clara assets) (United States 410 ND:47):

-- 10 tame breeding cows
-- 5 bulls
-- 15 mares with a stallion

-- 2 yoke of oxen
-- 5 milk cows
-- 4 tame horses
-- 50 sheep
-- 10 mules
-- 1 cart
-- 1 plow
-- his son Manuel and grandson Casimin

It is important to note that the granting of Indian human beings was handled in a similar manner as tools and animals, just as would be the case in a slave system. It was apparently the intention of the governing authorities to maintain the mission (albeit much reduced in size and function) and its labor force as a productive asset for as long as possible. Inigo was not officially granted any land with this order, however, and apparently did not receive the above items. This may have been due to the fact that in May of 1840 José Ramon Estrada was brought to Monterey to work closely with Governor Alvarado. Estrada was replaced as Mission Administrator by Ignacio Alviso, a man who seems to have been less well-disposed toward Inigo and his claim, and who apparently resisted turning over the property as ordered by the governor. As a result, on July 8, 1841, Inigo again petitioned the governor, stating in a respectful manner that none of the property promised had been received and requesting "his excellency" that it be granted. In addition, since his daughter Magdalena was very ill, Inigo requested that her husband Simon and two children, Maria Candelaria and José Rafael, be freed from being neophytes at Mission Santa Clara (United States 410 ND:80-81). Inigo was at least somewhat successful in his request for the promised livestock since, on July 26, 1841, Inigo officially registered his brand for cattle and other livestock (United States 410 ND:81).

During this period Inigo also began to build the houses and other structures on what he considered to be his land. Eventually Inigo built at least four structures, two of adobe and two of wood. The most elaborate of Inigo's houses was reportedly built in 1842 and was described by Padre José Maria Vasquez del Mercado of Mission Santa Clara as follows:

Table 10
Key Grants from Mission Santa Clara Lands, 1839-1845

Date	Name	Grantee	Acres
1839	San Antonio	Juan Prado Mesa	7982
1840	Rincon de Los Gatos	Sebastian Peralta & José Hernandez	6631
1840	La Purisima Concepcion	José Gorgonio & José Ramon (Indians)	4439
1841	Rincon de San Francisquito	José Pena	8418
1841	Quito	José Noriega & José Zgnon Fernandez	13310
1841	Riconada de Arroyo de San Francisquito	Maria Antonia Mesa	2230
1842	Pastoria de las Borregas	Francisco Estrada	4894
1844	Posolmi	Lope Inigo (Indian)	3042
1844	Los Coches	Roberto (Indian)	2219
1844	San Juan Bautista	José Augustin Narvaez	8880
1844	El Potrero de Santa Clara	James Alexander Forbes	1939
1845	Ulistac	Marcelo, Pio, & Cristobal (Indians)	2277

Total Acreage: 66,201

To Indians (4 grants): 11,917 acres (2,979.25 average, about one-sixth of total)

To Californios and Anglo Allies (8 grants): 54,284 acres (6,785.5 average, about five-sixth of total)

> Here in Posolmi he built last year a very good wooden house with a shingle roof, consisting of a small parlor and a small chamber, and another separate room for his son Manuel and his family, the lumber, and building of the house he paid for in grain and by other and honest means . . . [United States 410 ND].

This house was located in the southeastern corner of Inigo's land grant, just west of where the road connecting Mountain View and Alviso passed. He had moved his headquarters to this part of his land because of flooding at "La Posida de las Animas." He also built an adobe close to this frame house. Here Inigo lived and ran his ranch operations during these years. He had about a hundred head of sheep, as well as a number of cattle and horses. He also raised field crops, including beans, corn, wheat, barley, onions, potatoes, and pumpkins. Finally, he had a loom and made articles of wool on this machine (United States 410 ND).

Inigo still faced his most serious problem, however, for despite his requests, he had never been officially granted the land upon which he resided. As the process of granting Mission Santa Clara lands proceeded during the 1839-1843 period, it soon became clear to Inigo that there was an increasing chance that his claim would be absorbed and taken by one of the other nearby ranchero grants. During the 1839-1842 years, seven large parcels from mission lands, amounting to about 48,000 acres, had been officially granted to private parties, with only one of them, La Purísima Concepción, going to two Indians. Table 10 lists these grants, their size, grantee(s), and date of the grant.

The grant which posed the biggest danger to Inigo's interests was the Pastoria de las Borregas grant, which surrounded Inigo's land, and the grantee of this land steadily tried to encroach on it. Figure 2 shows the respective boundaries of these two grants. The 1842 grantee to Pastoria de las Borregas was none other than Francisco Estrada, the grandnephew by marriage of Ignacio Alviso (the current Mission Santa Clara Administrator), who was also a younger brother of former Administrator José Ramon Estrada, now a top adviser to Governor Alvarado in Monterey. Inigo must have soon realized that Francisco Estrada and Ignacio Alviso were trying to dispossess him and absorb his land into the Pastoria de las Borregas grant. Inigo knew this because Alviso had not once, but twice "lost" the official papers Inigo had prepared to formally request a grant of the land which he claimed. These papers were never seen again and are not today a part of the extant documentary record for this land. Alviso probably destroyed Inigo's two petitions for his land grant and might have succeeded in ousting Inigo and turning the land over to his grandnephew were it not for the fact that

Middle Age: 1828-1847

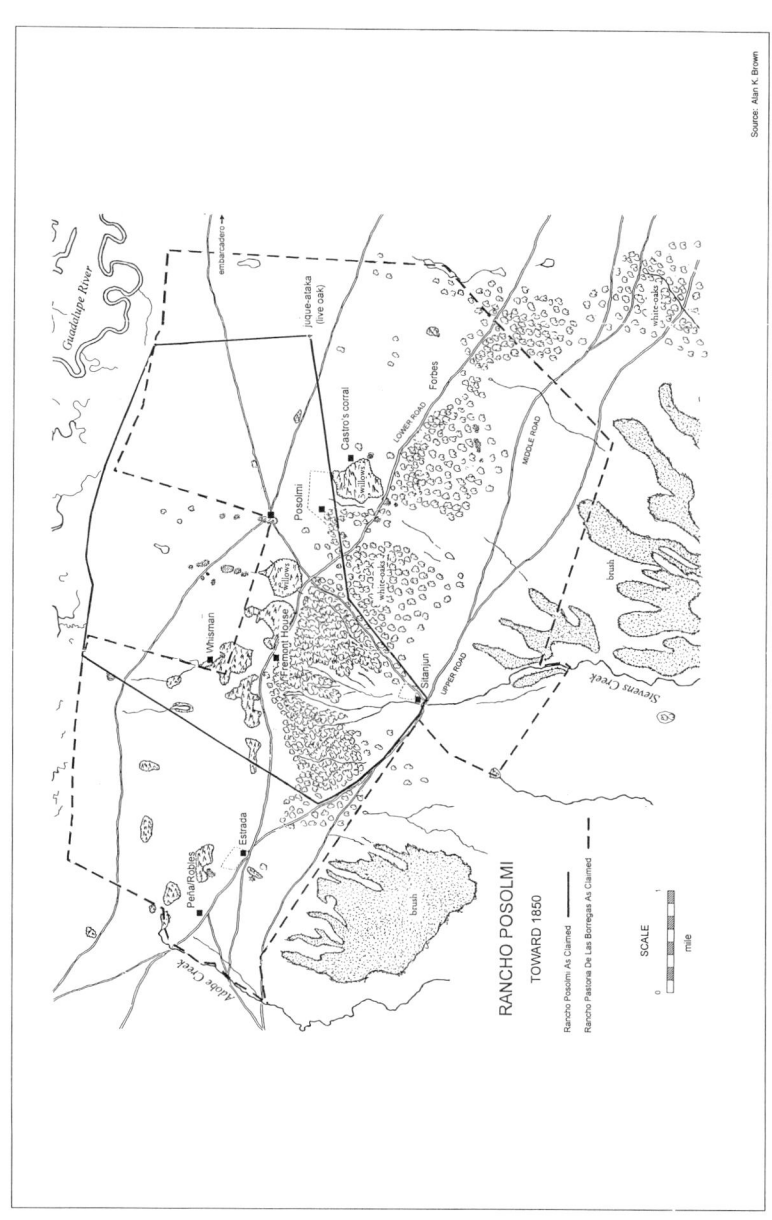

Fig. 3. Rancho Posolmi, About 1850

Governor Alvarado was replaced in late 1842 by a new governor named Manuel Micheltorena.

When Governor Micheltorena took office, he found that there was no money in the government treasury and that even the soldiers and civil functionaries had not been paid. This gave impetus to the previously floated idea of restoring some of the missions so that they could be taxed to provide an income for the government. Toward this end, in 1843 Micheltorena issued a proclamation to restore to priestly control 12 of the 21 missions, among them Santa Clara. The mission priests were then given back what land and other property still remained in the hands of the mission administrators, and the Christian Indians were rounded up and returned to the mission. The process of recapturing available Indians, most of whom were probably either idle or working for Californios on local ranches or in San Jose, must have been difficult. The plan called for one-eighth of the total annual production of each mission to be applied to the relief, sustenance, and clothing of the soldiers and civil employees of the government (Hittell 1885:II:323-324). The proclamation also specifically stated that those private land grants and other property transfers already made would not be disturbed, nor would Indians lawfully freed from mission control be returned to the missions (Hittell 1885:II:324). The governor did, however, issue several orders to try to return idle and not yet legally free Indians to Missions San Jose and Santa Clara. On April 4, 1843, for example, an order was issued from Monterey to Antonio Suñol, Sub-Prefect in San Jose that Indians not yet set free but now in San Jose be required to report to the Administrator of the Mission. Those who were "emancipated" must find useful employment, but might choose their own employment and were to be justly treated by the courts [Pueblo of San Jose 1843:328].

On January 18, 1844, the instructions were even stronger; the governor ordered the *Alcalde* of San Jose to " . . . Round up all stray neophytes and other idle Indians and put them to work at the Mission and elsewhere" (Pueblo of San Jose 1844:350). Thus the unemancipated neophytes were essentially viewed as a labor force to be used to bolster government revenue. While the 1843 proclamation to restore the missions eventually proved a failure, it did immensely strengthen the power of at least some mission priests, and conversely dissolve the power of the administrators of the missions. In the case of Santa Clara, this meant that the powers of Ignacio Alviso were severely weakened, and the powers of the resident priest Jesús Maria Vasquez del Mercado were greatly strengthened. Apparently recognizing the new situation, Inigo pressed his claim, submitting a statement to Father Mercado on June 19, 1843, which pointed out that he had occupied his land at the end of 1839 and that his papers had been taken twice by Ignacio Alviso and neither returned nor submitted to higher authorities. Inigo said, therefore, that he was occupying land which he could not prove that he owned. That same month Inigo also appealed to Sub-Prefect Antonio Suñol, telling him he had been in actual possession for over three years. While Father Mercado could not locate any documentation for Inigo's claim other than orders for cattle and similar property to be distributed to Inigo, he concluded on July 29, 1843, that the land was owned by Inigo. He added that Francisco Entrada claimed this land "inopportunely." In October of 1843, Inigo communicated to the new governor with a document probably written by Father Mercado, requesting that the land be granted to him, stating that Ignacio Alviso had hidden his papers so that he could establish his grandnephew, Francisco Estrada, on the land. He also added that Ignacio Alviso had given false information against his right. With this evidence before him, Governor Micheltorena finally granted the land known as Posolmi to the Indian Inigo in February 1844 (United States 410 ND). The original grant was 3,042 acres, although only 1,696 acres were later confirmed by the U.S. government, the remainder being taken by other claimants (see Fig. 2).

During 1844 and 1845, Micheltorena gave at least four other land grants from Mission Santa Clara lands to private parties. Two of these were granted to Indians. These were Los Coches to Roberto in 1844 and Ulistac to Marcelo, Pio, and Cristobal in 1845. Table 10 lists all the key land grants from Mission Santa Clara lands. Not only did eight of the twelve listed grants (66 percent) go to Californios or allied Anglos, the average size of the four Indian grants was less than half that of the Californio-Anglo group (2,979.25 acres vs. 6,785.5 acres). It should be added that the Indians who received land were all older Ohlone/Costanoan Indians with long and successful service to the Californios and a multitude of ties both with each other (as godparents for each others' children and witnesses for marriages) and with key members of the Californio power structure, including people like Juan Prado Mesa and members of the Arguello, Berryessa, Higuera, and Peralta families.

While this group of Indians were usually allies and served as godparents and witnesses for each other's children at baptisms and marriages, one story about a conflict between Inigo and his old friend Marcelo dates to this period and is interesting enough to repeat and offer informed speculation about. In April of 1833, Marcelo had served as a witness (*testigo*) at the marriage of Inigo's daughter Juana, indicating that the two Indian leaders then still had good relations. Both men were single in 1833. Inigo had had only one wife, but Marcelo had had three, each of whom had died childless within two years of her marriage to Marcelo (Fabiana, Rita, and Eusebia, who died respectively in 1806,

1810, and 1824). A rumor existed that Marcelo had killed them by giving them ground glass with their food. Sometime during the First World War, Mrs. Fremont Older (wife of the prominent newspaperman) wrote a series of colorful stories about Santa Clara County history. These stories included a few on the last Indians who lived in the area. They were published as newspaper articles which mixed a generous amount of legend with some accurate information, and they should be seen as a kind of recorded oral history combining myths, racist attitudes, and erroneous information with some verifiable or likely facts. One of these newspaper articles recounted a serious quarrel between Marcelo and Inigo:

> *WHEN SANTA CLARA COUNTY WAS YOUNG*
> The colorful, romantic story-history of Santa Clara valley written by Mrs. Fremont Older, prominent journalist and leading student of local history, especially for *The News* readers.
>
> * * *
>
> San Jose history does not disclose many duels. However, there was one. It had great intensity, and was fought between two Indians, Marcello and Inygo. Each was a chief. Each had been a great man at the Mission Santa Clara. Their duel was not a punctilious, code duello affair. It was fought to the death, with clubs. Like all duels of romance, it was fought for a woman. The woman was Marcello's wife, his fourth.
>
> "She was very pretty," said Marcello in Spanish to the Fentons, on whose ranch he lived. "Prettier than any of your American women, prettier than Spanish women either . . . ."
>
> . . . One day in Marcello's absence, without warning or without explanation, Mrs. Marcello fled with Inygo to his rancheria. Marcello returned to his deserted dwelling. His tribesmen explained what had happened. At first he grunted, then he yelled his anger. His squaw had left him, him the great Marcello . . . .
>
> . . . Brandishing a club, Marcello went swift as a jack rabbit to the Inygo ranch. He confronted the guilty lovers. What did they care about the fathers or the church? What did they care about the gringo's law made to protect gringo thieves? Mrs. Marcello and Inygo loved each other. They defied the fathers, the laws and Marcello. Such a whoop from Marcello! He had not

forgotten when long afterward he tranquilly told the Fentons how he attacked Inygo with his club, how Inygo defended himself. Quite tranquilly he told how he beat his rival's club out of his hands, how he made him look like quivering red jelly, how in a climax of anger he bit off his ear and left him for dead.

Inygo did not die, but always after that duel he was a broken man. His face was scarred and marred by a swelling on one side of his head. The missing ear has puzzled historians. Frequently I had wondered about it, and asked its whereabouts. I was told that Inygo lost his ear "while being civilized." Marcello regained his wife by taking her roughly by the arm and leading her back to the rancheria. Once more in possession of the beautiful woman, Marcello had no anger against Inygo. Nor did he lose faith in women. He married two more, but even after they died there shone always in his memory like a star the face of his beautiful fourth wife . . . . [Older n.d.]

While the story is embellished, it is nevertheless very interesting and undoubtedly at least partly true. For example, a photo of Inigo taken in the mid-1850s shows a prominent bump or swelling on the left side of his face, apparently the result of the blow struck by Marcelo. Other known facts also fit well with the story. Marcelo (54 years old) and his fourth wife Escolastica (18 years old) were married in late April of 1839. Inigo settled on his land in late 1839. Escolastica had two children (in 1841 and 1843) while married to Marcelo. Since none of Marcelo's other three wives had had any children with him, it is possible that he was either impotent or infertile. Inigo, having sired 11 children with Viviana, obviously did not have this problem and was a widower during this period. Was Inigo the father of these two children? We will probably never know. Unfortunately, both the two children and Escolastica herself were dead within a few years. Her children died first, then she died in February of 1844. Marcelo, who lived until 1875, apparently told this story to members of the pioneer Felton family, who in turn passed it on to Mrs. Older. Marcelo, who had been a witness at a number of key events of Inigo's family earlier, never appeared as a witness for Inigo after the early 1840s.

The timing of Inigo's second marriage is also interesting given the fact that Marcelo's wife Escolastica died in February 1844. The next month, March 1844, saw the death of Simon, husband of a 24-year old Eustaquia, both of Mission San Francisco. On May 18, 1844, less than two months after Simon's death, Inigo married a woman named Eustaquia at Mission Santa Clara. Circumstantial evidence is strong that this was the widow of Simon.

The End of Californio Dominance

The backdrop to all these events was the continuing uncertainty of life and an inability to feel confident about the future. Attempts to resurrect the mission system failed. The loss of the mission as an institution which mediated between secular society and the native people was one cause of the chaos which developed. Bad for Indians as it was in so many respects, the exploitation at the mission was at least measured and had some limits. Food, housing, clothing, work, and family life were more or less assured. The new regime was different. Remaining Indians had to survive by performing occasional work on ranches or in cities, or failing that by begging, theft, or raiding. Deprived of their land, secure regular employment, or even a minimal social safety net, they usually could not maintain normal family life and their numbers rapidly declined. Combined with this situation was the constant raiding by Yokuts, the most numerous intact Indian group. Their indiscriminate raiding did not distinguish between Californios and Ohlone/Costanoan Indians. La Purísima Concepción, the ranch of Inigo's friend and fellow Ohlone/Costanoan, Gorgonio, located a few miles to the southwest of Inigo's Posolmi Rancho, was, for example, attacked by "Tulare" (Yokuts) Indians during this period, and both Gorgonio's son and daughter-in-law were injured. Horses were stolen from Gorgonio during this incident and his house was also burned down (United States 130 ND:20-21). The Yokuts apparently saw Gorgonio as simply another Mexican Californio.

The situation seems to have worsened after the final decline of the missions during the late 1830s and early 1840s. An unusually good summary of the situation was written following an 1841-1842 visit to the Santa Clara Valley by Charles Wilkes, a U.S. Naval officer:

> During the troubles of 1836, the Indians of many of the missions were cast off or neglected, and in fact deprived of the proceeds of their labour. They had reason to believe, as had been impressed upon them by the Spanish padres, that they were interested in the proceeds and wealth that had been accumulated by their labour; and this belief had naturally tended to attach them to the soil.

The ravages of the small-pox, two years prior to our visit, completed the destruction of these establishments; for it swept off one-half of the Indians, and served to dispirit the rest. Many of them have joined the wild Indians, and are now committing acts of violence on the whites; they are becoming daily more daring, and have rendered a residence in single farm-houses or estancias not without danger. In looking at the state in which these poor Indians have been left, it cannot be denied but that they have cause to be dissatisfied with the treatment they have received . . . .

The administradors have made themselves and those by whom they were appointed, rich upon the spoils of these missions; and so great have been the drafts upon some of these missions, that they have not been able to support their neophytes. The mission of San José, for instance, during the year of our visit, was obliged to order off five hundred of its proselytes, to procure their subsistence as they best could. These acts seem to be committed without any kind of consideration, or idea that there is any injustice practised: the property acquired by the missions is looked upon as belonging to the state; the claims of the Indians are entirely overlooked, and in the event of their taking the cattle that in truth belong to them, they are severely punished. This naturally irritates them, for not only can they perceive the injustice of others appropriating the fruits of their labour, but are exasperated by seeing them living upon the common stock, while they are obliged to seek a precarious subsistence in the forest.

In consequence of this state of things, depredations are continually committed by the Indians; and, a month previous to the arrival of the squadron, they had driven off three hundred horses. Retaliatory measures on the part of the Californians were adopted; a party was collected and dispatched to punish them, which proceeded towards the interior, came to a village, and without any inquiry whether its dwellers had been the aggressors, it was set on fire, and reduced to ashes; some of the defenseless old men, who from their infirmities could not escape, were put to death, and forty or fifty women and children carried off as prisoners. This was not all: these prisoners were apportioned as slaves to various families, with whom they still remain in servitude, and receive very harsh treatment. Smarting under such wrongs, it is not surprising that the Indians should retaliate [Wilkes 1845:V:172-174].

Wilkes also visited the Embarcadero of Santa Clara at the mouth of the Guadalupe River, Ignacio Alviso's rancho near the Embarcadero (today's Alviso), and Mission Santa Clara itself. His rich descriptions of these places and their inhabitants are worth quoting from at length. Traveling up the mouth of the Guadalupe River, he pointed out that the river

> . . . runs in a tortuous direction to the Embarcadero. Its course more resembled the turn of a corkscrew than any other thing to which I can liken it. I think we counted twenty-nine bends before we reached the point at which we were to disembark, which was nearly at the head of the creek. We were compelled to haul the boat along by the grass and rushes on each side, and it was near midnight before we achieved our object. As we passed through this narrow inlet, the birds that were lodged for the night, alarmed by the noise we made, flew in thousands from the marshes. Their fluttering was so great as to resemble the rushing of a vast wave; for as they rose, thousands seemed to follow thousands, until the sound died away in the distance, and again seemed to approach in an opposite direction. In the pitchy darkness, not a bird was to be seen, although they must have passed only a few feet above our heads.
> At the Embarcadero we found no house or accommodations of any kind; but the guide soon led us to what he termed the road, which was found marked by the huge ruts made by the ox-carts. The walk was of service to us, as we had become chilled with the cold and damp air.
> After proceeding a mile over a level plain, we reached the estancia [Alviso's Ranch]. The first notice we had of it was a broken corral, and the ground covered with vast quantities of bones, hoofs, and horns. Over these we stumbled continually, until, on turning the corner of the coural, we were set upon by a pack of dogs, some fifty in number, which barked in every tone, from the snappish note of the pug to the sonorous voice

of the bull-dog. All came forward, intent upon arresting our progress towards the large adobe building, which was now in dim outline before us. The bones served us as missiles to keep them at bay, and thus to protect our approach to the premises; and when we reached the porch, we gave the discourteous curs a full discharge. We knocked lustily for some time, but no answer was returned, nor could we see any light; but on a frequent repetition, each time redoubling our efforts, we at last heard light footsteps, and the door was suddenly opened by a little Indian girl, who ushered us into a large room, which, from the tables, chairs, and closets with china, we found to be the salle a manger. Here we had a full view of the interior; and the light which was burning in the adjacent rooms, showed us the occupants fast asleep. We had scarcely time to look around us, when a huge Californian, more than six feet in height, and proportionately large, stalked towards us in his shirt. His whole figure and countenance indicated a savage, and carried me back at once in idea to the Feejee cannibals. In a gruff tone he demanded our wants, and when he had satisfactorily ascertained who we were, and received a cigar or a token of friendship, he called up the whole family, consisting of a mother, two daughters, and several other children. These, after dressing themselves, came forth, and greeted us with genuine hospitality, with such pleasant faces and cheerful talk, that it was really delightful to find ourselves in such quarters; and our surprise was the greater, in consequence of the exterior having proved so uninviting. They immediately set about providing us with supper, consisting of tea, tortillas, valdivias, ollas, with eggs and a steak; and while this was in preparation by some, others were arranging the beds and changing the furniture of the sleeping-room. All this was done whilst the mother was talking and waiting upon us; and after supper was over, she pointed to our room, and then excused herself, by saying she must provide something for the sailors who had accompanied us; whilst we retired to rest, much fatigued with our jaunt.

    The room was furnished differently from what we had been accustomed to, yet it was quite comfortable. The only piece of furniture that was not new to us was a high-post bedstead, evidently from our own country, though bedecked with old Spanish tapestry, in the way of tester, curtains, and valance. Instead of drawers, there were huge trunks, that put to shame those of modern construction. These contained the household linen and the finery of the females of the family, and were raised from the floor, that a broom might be passed underneath them. Here and there on the walls hung a new-made dress, of ample dimensions, and several Spanish sombreros, those that were of more recent date hanging highest; at least I judged them to be the best ones, from the careful manner in which they were covered up. There was no wash-stand; but a French ewer and basin, of the lozenge shape, of white and gold porcelain, were placed on a chair. A single looking-glass was hung high over it, its head inclining outwards. The dimensions of the frame were small, and the glass still smaller, owning to a figure of a patron saint occupying the larger part of the upper surface. Of chairs we had five, two with leather seats and high backs; the others were of home manufacture. A large grated window, well barred with iron, with the thick and massive walls of an adobe house, gave it the look of security for confinement within, or against attack from without. Half a dozen coloured prints of the saints, ten inches square, in black frames, graced the walls. Our beds, and every thing connected with them, were comfortable; and the manner in which we had been provided for made the entertainment doubly welcome. We found in the morning that we had occupied the sleeping-room of our hostess and her daughters, and that they had given it up expressly to accommodate us [Wilkes 1845:V:199-201].

Traveling on to the mission, Wilkes states that:

> The league between the Embarcadero and Santa Clara occupied us somewhat over an hour, for it was unbearable to attempt to ride faster than a walk. After ten o'clock, we came in sight of the mission of Santa Clara, and as we approached it the little ponds and damp places on the prairie were literally covered with wild geese, which would but barely open a way for us to pass through. They were far more tame than any barn-door

geese I ever saw, and I could not easily divest myself of the idea that they were not domesticated.

The mission of Santa Clara has, at a distance, a respectable appearance; but on our drawing near the long line of huts, formerly occupied by the Indians, which are now destroyed, excepting a few, the ruin and neglect that have taken place are evident enough. The church and mission-house adjoining have also a dilapidated look; their tile roofs and whitewashed walls require extensive repairs, as well as all the wood-work of the doors, posts, etc. The church flanks the mission-house on the north, and is about one hundred and fifty feet long by forty wide, and about fifty feet high; it is surmounted by a small steeple. The mission-house is of only one story, with a corridor extending its whole length, of one hundred and fifty feet. This dwelling is now occupied both by the administrador and the padres, and a wall divides the premises into two parts, separating the temporal from the spiritual concerns of the establishment. The padre has his own servants, cooks, etc. [Wilkes 1845:V:203].

In 1844, Inigo settled in with his new bride at the ranch he now owned. But the dramatic events which had frequently marked his life were by no means over. The United States, the rising imperial power to the east, had its eyes on California and saw this section of Mexican territory as part of its "Manifest Destiny." An aggressive and expansionist power soon confronted a much weaker one with predictable results. The Mexican-American War of 1846-1848 was mostly fought in Mexico, as United States forces pressed their attack, aiming at forcing the annexation of California and other parts of the West. But a few small battles were also fought in California, one of these only a few miles from Inigo's Rancho Posolmi. This battle, called The Battle of the Mustard Stalks, took place January 2, 1847, in fields and woods near Mission Santa Clara. The Californios were led by Francisco Sanchez and the Americans by Captains Weber, John M. Murphy, and others (Hittell 1885:604-605). The battle was preceded by several months of maneuvering and included the capture by Sanchez and his troops of a United States foraging party. Superior numbers and military equipment resulted in a United States victory after a short battle, and Sanchez soon surrendered. The Santa Clara Valley and the greater Bay Area were in American hands for good.

With the Anglo-Americans the new local and statewide power, Inigo again had to adjust to new circumstances. Thus, the first years of the American era marked another turning point in his long life.

Endnotes:

1. Reprinted from INDIANS AND INTRUDERS IN CENTRAL CALIFORNIA, 1769-1849, by George Harwood Phillips by permission of the University of Oklahoma Press. Copyright (c) 1993 by the University of Oklahoma Press, Norman, Publishing Division of the University.

2. ibid.

3. ibid.

CHAPTER 5

OLD AGE: SQUATTERS, LAND TRANSFERS, AND FINAL YEARS, 1847-1864

The defeat of the Californios in early 1847 secured the Santa Clara Valley for the United States. Almost at once numerous land-hungry pioneers began to arrive, the advance wave of what was to become an avalanche of humanity over the next few years. The structure of power, including the land tenure system, would soon undergo yet another revolution, and Inigo had to adapt to the new situation or face the possible dire consequences of failing to do so.

Squatters, a *Patrón*, and Land Transfers, 1847-1850

Change caused by the arrival of American farmers and the emergence of American institutions accelerated during 1847 and continued during 1848, even though the discovery of gold in the Sierra Nevada had yet to be felt. In 1849, however, a horde of goldseekers invaded the state. Within a short time many newcomers realized that money was to be made in the coastal valleys, raising food for the miners. "Squatting" then became a problem for landholders in the Santa Clara Valley. Most of the best land was already occupied by those Californios, foreigners, and Indians to whom it had been granted during secularization. But the Californio rancho owners were cattlemen, and not primarily farmers, so much of their land did not really look occupied to the would-be farmers from the States. Many newcomers considered such land to be open to the public, and therefore seized it without any legal right to do so.

By early 1851 squatting had become so common in Santa Clara Valley that one paper complained:

> The valley of Santa Clara has been bespattered with squatters. And some of them are so shameless in their acts that they have even squatted in the orchards of the old inhabitants of California. Orchards that have been in the possession of the same families for fifty years are all at once taken possession of by these highwaymen, who say they will contend against the proprietors, paying the expenses of the suit out of the proceeds of the orchards. If this is not high handed robbery, what can be. And worse than all, high officials and lawyers are leagued with these squatters for the purpose of robbing in this way the honest owners of the property . . . [San Francisco Alta, February 11, 1851:2].

The first of many squatters on Inigo's land seems to have been John Whisman. An account by journalist Bayard Taylor indicates that Whisman had squatted and built on Inigo's land by 1848 (Taylor 1850:67). In 1850, Taylor stopped for dinner at Whisman's house and ranch located near Posita de las Animas spring at the southwest corner of Rancho Posolmi:

> At Whisman's ranch, two miles further, we stopped to dinner. The sight of a wooden house gladdened our eyes, and still more so that of the home-made bread, fresh butter and milk which Mrs. Whisman set before us. The family had lived there nearly two years and were well contented with the country. The men go occasionally to the mines and dig, but are prudent enough not to neglect their farming operations [Taylor 1850:67].

Taylor mentioned that on the way to Whisman's house he stopped at a nearby ranch to water his mules, using an Indian basket "so closely plaited that scarcely a drop found it way through" (Taylor 1850:66). This ranch was probably Inigo's.

Inigo had to be alarmed about the squatter situation. He was an Indian with possessions coveted by the invading Anglo-Americans, and he was becoming surrounded by men who hated Indians, many of whom were quite willing to use violence against them. As we have seen from the first part of this study, Inigo grew up and matured as a member of a subordinate race in a semi-slave and semi-feudal system. This experience made him acutely aware of the necessity for *patróns*, allies against those who would abuse or deny the few rights he had. He had gained his land and possessions only through long service and the patronage of many, including the priests of Mission Santa Clara. Now, as a landowner from an oppressed race during a revolutionary transfer of power, he again had to find a protector from among the new invaders. In the summer of 1849, Inigo found his *patrón* for the new era in the person of Robert Walkinshaw.

Robert Walkinshaw had arrived in Santa Clara County in May of 1847, only a few months after the Battle of the Mustard Stalks. Walkinshaw, from Scotland, had lived on the west coast of Mexico for some years as an employee of the British commercial firm of Barron-Forbes. In 1846, Barron-Forbes acquired a two-thirds interest in the soon-to-be-famous New Almaden mercury mine, located about 20 miles southeast of Inigo's land. Walkinshaw was one of the owners of the two-thirds share. In 1846, the remaining third of the mine was owned by Father Real, the current priest at Mission Santa Clara, and Secundino and Teodoro Robles (Lanyon and Bulmore 1967:8-9; Johnson 1963:25). Walkinshaw, who reportedly had a "Spanish" wife and must have known both the Spanish language and Latin American culture, was sent to take charge of the mine's operations. At first Walkinshaw lived in a house at New Almaden near the mine, but the mine's great success during the Gold Rush years (when mercury was in great demand for separating gold from gravel and rock in sluicing and milling operations) and the dangers of mercury poisoning due to the proximity of his house probably led him to look elsewhere for a place to live (Lanyon and Bulmore 1967:11).

By June of 1849 Walkinshaw had become connected with Inigo. In that month a year later he purchased a substantial portion of land from Inigo for $2,500, a section which was called "Rancho San Bernardino" in the land case (Walkinshaw 1852).

During the early 1850s all the Mexican- and Spanish-era rancho landowners (not only Indians) of California were forced to become involved in a series of protracted court proceedings to defend their titles against squatters and make them legal in the eyes of the U.S. government. The initial focus was in the hearing rooms and the courts, but a struggle also took place over actual possession. The size of Inigo's overall grant and the amount he sold to Walkinshaw and others was thus in constant dispute during this period, both by squatters and other grantees. This threat to Mexican grantees in general was all the more reason for Inigo, who as an Indian was the least powerful of grantees, to ally with a powerful man.

Inigo did not fare well in the land court proceedings and struggles with squatters. His original claim was for 3,042 acres. But when the boundaries of Inigo's Posolmi grant were finally officially settled in extended court cases and surveyed and drawn during the late

1850s, Rancho Posolmi amounted to only about 1,700 acres. Walkinshaw (who had purchased his acreage from Inigo) had 847.98 acres, Inigo 448.2 acres, and Thomas Campbell (who had also purchased some of Inigo's land) 400 acres (Healey 1859). The claimants of adjacent Rancho Pastoria de las Borregas and others had successfully annexed part of Inigo's original claim.

While Inigo lost land during the squatter and court battles of the late 1840s and 1850s, he was, nevertheless, one of only a very few California Indians who retained any land whatsoever during this era. At a time when Indians were being barred from the state and local courts, kicked off their lands and onto reservations, and even sometimes hunted down and killed like animals, Inigo remained with his small family in possession of his houses and a substantial piece of land.

Two reports from the early twentieth century, accounts which appear to be basically accurate, stress how Walkinshaw protected Inigo and treated him well:

> When Inygo was an old man the fathers obtained for him a grant called "Posolomi," adjoining the Murphy ranch near Sunnyvale. It consisted of several hundred acres and had long been the home of Indians in the valley. For years Inygo lived in a little house on his ranch. He was protected in his property by Robert Walkinshaw of Tepic, Mexico. Walkinshaw was a Scotchman, who had married a Spanish woman. He was one of the first owners of the Almaden mine. The Walkinshaws often drove with Inygo in their great carriage. They had a large rambling one-story house on the Inygo ranch where they entertained the fashionable people of San Francisco and the important families of the Santa Clara Valley [Older n.d.].

The second account stated:

> The old Indian Chief Inygo [sic], used to live in the usual Indian style on his Posolmi ranch, three miles distant from Mountain View. After a while the Walkinshaws, who were very cultivated Scotch people at one time part owners of the New Almaden mine, decided that it was no good for an Indian to have land and took possession of the Posolomi. However, the Walkinshaws were very good to Inygo . . . . They gave him wine to

drink and . . . killed him with kindness [*San Jose News*, February 11, 1918].

It is interesting to speculate about how Walkinshaw and Inigo became connected. It could have been through activities at the old Mission Santa Clara church and Father Real's ties to the New Almaden Mine. This possibility suggests that Inigo had an ongoing relationship with the old mission and that he remained a "good Indian" from the point of view of those in power. Another possible connection between Inigo and Walkinshaw could have developed from ties Inigo may have had to the place which became the New Almaden Mine. Local Indians were initially the principal workers at the mine in 1846-47. They dug the ore out of the hill for others to process (Egenhoff 1953:99-104). Native Americans had also long used this cinnabar mine. As one of the last of the older Native Americans of this vicinity, Inigo may have continued a connection to this place that had been visited by native people coming from great distances away. In late 1851 the *San Joaquin Republican* newspaper ran the following story about the "discovery" of the New Almaden Mine, which, while clearly embellished, also appears to reflect a core of truth:

> Many years ago the Padre of the Mission of Santa Clara was informed by some neighboring Indians, who had grown wealthy by extensive dealings in vermilion with other tribes, that they would show him a stream of living water, as they expressed it. The Padre . . . agreed to accompany them to the mountain side . . . . After traveling into the neighborhood of New Almaden . . . [the Indians showed] the Padre an excavation in the hill-side, some 100 feet in extent, and on proceeding to the furtherest extremity of the tunnel found numerous skeletons of human beings, who had been killed by the falling in of the earth. Out of this excavation ran a small stream of quicksilver . . . (*San Joaquin Republican*, November 12, 1851:20).

Life During the 1850s

During the 1850s, Inigo lived in one or more of the three houses which made up a small complex at the southeastern corner of Rancho Posolmi. The September 1859 U.S. Surveyor's Plat of the Rancho Posolmi clearly shows this area and the adjacent road between Mountain

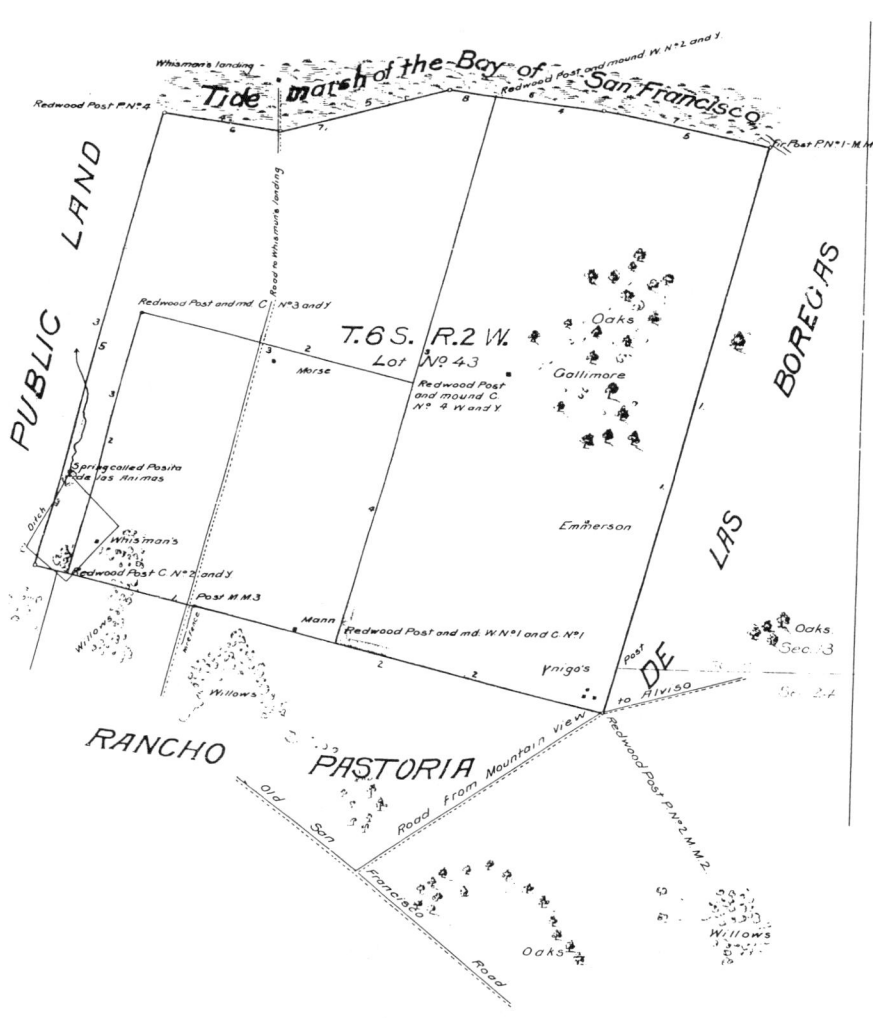

Fig. 4. Plat of the Rancho Posolmi, September 1859

View and Alviso (Fig. 3). This plat shows that Walkinshaw owned the eastern half of Rancho Posolmi. Campbell owned the large square plot in the southern part of the western half. Whisman held, as a squatter, a small, roughly square area in the southwest corner, and Inigo held the remainder, mostly in the northwest corner. The map indicates that at least by 1859, Walkinshaw had the area in the southeast corner of Posolomi where Inigo had built his houses. The other names on the map—Emmerson, Gallimore, Morse, and Mann—are the names of other squatters who had put up buildings on Walkinshaw's and Campbell's land, but had not fenced a specific section as Whisman apparently had.

In 1852, Inigo, a farmer, was living on his ranch with his wife Eustaquia and four other younger Indians. The group is listed as follows on the 1852 census list (California 1852:158):

Name	Age	Sex and Race
Ynigo	60	MI
Stoja (i.e., Eustaquia)	50	FI
Maria	20	FI
Fernanda	25	FI
Antonio, José	18	MI
Rafael, José	20	MI

One of these, José Rafael, is clearly Inigo's grandson (born in 1834), the son of Maria Magdalena and her first husband Casimiro. The "Maria" listed in the census could have been either Maria Candelaria (born 1832), the daughter of Maria Magdalena and Casimiro, or Maria Petronila (born 1840), the daughter of Eustaquia and Simon, her first husband. While the age listed (20) for the Maria in the census is correct for Maria Candelaria, it is clearly wrong for Maria Petronila, who was only 12 years old in 1852. But it also seems strange that the young Maria Petronila would not be living with her mother Eustaquia. The connection to Inigo and Eustaquia of the other two young Indians listed in the census is unclear. Inigo, whose actual age was 71 in 1852, and Eustaquia, whose actual age was 32 in 1852, had had one child, also named Maria Magdalena, in 1847, but she had died in 1849. The family increased in March 1854 when Inigo and Eustaquia had a daughter, Maria Angela (see Fig. 1).

During the early 1850s, Inigo reportedly lived in "a very good adobe house," had several other small wood houses, and was cultivating 300-400 acres of land. Crops included wheat, corn, beans, potatoes, pumpkins, and onions. Wheat was apparently the largest crop; it was grown in strips up to two hundred yards wide (Mendenhall 1861; Alviso 1853, 1862; Bennett n.d.). Inigo also had several corrals and about 200 head of cattle, 300 sheep, and 25 horses (Alviso 1853). These crops and animals were no doubt the main means of life for Inigo and his family. Inigo, while an old man, was apparently still able to work hard, however, since he reportedly was "up in the redwoods getting lumber" when a group of people came to look for him during this era (United States 410 ND:35-36).

In 1855 or early 1856 Inigo was apparently used as an informant by the Reverend Father Gregory Mengarini of Santa Clara University who was compiling a vocabulary of "the Indian Language at Santa Clara." The work, later published in *Contributions to American Ethnology* (Vol. III:536-539, 1877-93), was based on interviews with "an old Chief." University of Santa Clara archivist Arthur Dunning Spearman later concluded that the informant was Inigo because of Inigo's advanced age at the time that Mengarini was working and the fact that Inigo was an Indian leader and had had a long close connection with the mission and its priests (Spearman 1963:131-133).

Inigo traveled to San Francisco during this period and had his photo taken by photographer William Shew. The earliest known use of this photograph, which is reproduced here (see Fig. 5), was by the *San Francisco Chronicle* on August 23, 1903. There had been some confusion as to whether this photograph was of Inigo or Marcelo, but the *Chronicle* identified it as a photo of Inigo and said that Edward A. T. Gallagher, a personal friend of Inigo, had supplied it:

> One cannot think of the California missions without seeing the neophytes wandering in and out among the arcades, tilling the grounds about the rambling adobes or coming at the call of the bells to worship the God of their new-found faith. But, for all that, they seem to belong to the very far away, and it is not easy to believe that there is any one living to-day who had personal acquaintance with one of these Indians who lived under the influence of the padres. But there is. Edward A. T. Gallagher, one of the best-known pioneers of this State, is the man, and to him the "Chronicle" is indebted for the accompanying illustration of Ynego, called the curator of the Mission of Santa Clara in the days when he was "the last leaf on the tree," and before the fine old adobe was turned over to the care of the Jesuits of Santa Clara.
>
> Mr. Gallagher knew Ynego when he was living in that part of the State, in the days when he owned great tracts there, when he settled Alviso. He says his

good old Indian friend was a rarely fine old fellow, and that he was as solicitous of the Mission as a mother could be of her first born. The accompanying picture is reproduced from a copy of an old ambro-type taken in 1856 upon one of the occasional visits he made to San Francisco. He died in the early sixties.

The photo also clearly shows a large area of swelling on the left side of Inigo's face, probably the result of the fight with Marcelo so many years before.

Also during this same period, a marriage occurred which must have been a joyful event for Inigo and Eustaquia. On September 17, 1855, Inigo's grandson, José Rafael (age 20), married Maria Petronila, Eustaquia's daughter (age 15) from her first marriage. The witnesses for this wedding included Inigo himself, José de la Cruz, José de Jesus, and one Fulgencio. The presence of these other Santa Clara Indian men at the wedding indicates that the old networks, formed during the mission era, were still in place in the mid-1850s despite the rapid changes which had occurred.

The happiness of a late summer wedding soon gave way to tragedy, however. Inigo and Eustaquia's two-year old daughter Maria Angela died suddenly on May 1, 1856. A few months later, in October 1856, and only 13 months after his wedding day, Inigo's grandson José Rafael died. But the worst was yet to come. Inigo and Eustaquia had a third child, Francisco, born in March 1857. Eustaquia's pregnancy may have been difficult. When a local settler, Alfred Doten, traveled on horseback over to Inigo's ranch to ask her to do some washing in January 1857, she turned down the work. As Doten later wrote in his diary:

> Jan 5 . . . Morning I rode up to Senati's place on Becky and took the washing along, but not being able to find anyone to do it, I had to leave it at old Indigo's, for his squaw to wash - Sunset, I was up to Indigo's and his squaw told me she could not do it because she has "a picaniny in her belly," so I had to take the bundle back home - Jane will do the washing . . . [Doten 1973 (1857):328].

Eustaquia may have had a difficult birth or later complications, for she died in mid-April 1857. She was 37 years old. Without a mother, the infant Francisco survived only a few more weeks, dying in May 1857. Inigo was left almost alone. He had seen both of his wives, at least twelve of his own children, and at least eight of his grandchildren die. Due to poor recordkeeping during the 1850s, we do not know the fate of two other children and six grandchildren. One or more of them, or Eustaquia's daughter Maria Petronila, may have been present to try to ease Inigo's pain, but we do not know.

We do have information from Alfred Doten's journals that in April and May of 1858, at least, Inigo was active and still in good health. In mid-April 1858, for example, Doten rode with Inigo and recorded a part of Inigo's conversation:

> When I went up this morning, old Ynego rode up with me, as far as M.V. [Mountain View] - The old fellow says when he was a little boy, his tribe was numerous about here - but all have died, and he is the only one left - says the bears were there - very numerous all through the woods, and they killed lots of the Indians - says he thinks God sent the bears to kill all bad Christians - lucky there are no bears here nowadays - [Doten 1973 (1858):410].

On May 1, 1858, Doten saw Inigo at a May Day picnic, reporting as follows on what happened after the crowning of the May Queen and "attendant speeches":

> . . . all dispersed to dinner, which was placed on cloths spread on the ground under a big oak - candy, nuts, raisins, white-bread, oranges, cheese, figs, peppermints and apple pie was laid out in plenty, and it soon disappeared - the ladies all had the first chance at it and squatted down all around it and the men all came in outside - Old Norato was there, and Old Indigo was there also and got a whole sack full of the remnants of the feast to carry home - He struck a good lead, and no doubt wished such parties were a little more frequent . . . [Doten 1973 (1858):413].

With few, if any, surviving family members, Inigo probably faced increasing isolation and poverty during these years, and needed to gather "remnants of the feast" whenever he could. He still was respected and had friends, as evidenced by his attendance at public events such as May Day. But life must have been both lonely and at times very hard for him during his final years.

In 1858 Inigo's patron Robert Walkinshaw died during a trip to his native Scotland, leaving a wife and several children behind (Arbuckle 1968:25). Walkinshaw's large estate, listed as being worth $75,000 in the 1870 census, was by then managed for the family by one Samuel Price (U.S. Census Bureau 1870a). Neither the Walkinshaw family nor Inigo appear in the 1860 census for Santa Clara County; perhaps they were missed by the census taker.

Inigo's Final Years, 1860-1864

While Inigo must have felt alone with his numerous memories during his last years, at the same time life must have been intensely interesting. He was a man who had lived through amazing changes, but these changes were now coming more and more rapidly. And they were coming close to his home, to nearby Mountain View, to the Santa Clara Valley, and all over Northern California. Perhaps most striking was the immense wealth that was already flowing out of Inigo's Posolmi land grant. In the Gold Rush economic boom times of the 1850s, the squatters who had seized Inigo's land were doing very well. The 1860 United States agricultural census gives statistics on the farms of a number of these squatters. The returns for three squatters who were known to be living on parts of Inigo's grant in 1860 will be reviewed. Table 11 summarizes this information.

It will be recalled that the entire Posolmi grant, as confirmed by the U.S. courts, amounted to about 1,700 acres. These three farms together were only 687 acres, or less than half. Yet these 687 acres were valued at $17,500 in 1860, had grazing animals which were worth another $13,870, and had produced 3,275 bushels of wheat and barley and 1,916 pounds of butter and cheese the previous year. These were large figures for the time and they well illustrate that the Posolmi property was indeed a very valuable one. There were thus strong incentives to be a squatter and to try to dispossess Inigo of his land.

We know from the Doten journal that Inigo visited the nearby town of Mountain View in 1858 and probably in later years as well. The place that Inigo observed was a type of small-scale frontier farm-supply and transportation boom town. In the early 1860s Mountain View had a population of about a hundred, and had a hotel, a grocery store, general merchandise store, post office, and blacksmith shop. Two daily stages connected the town with San Francisco and San Jose. Inigo also probably visited the town of Santa Clara, a bit further away from Mountain View, especially since this is where the mission was located. In the early 1860s,

Table 11
Agricultural Returns and Values for Three Farms on Rancho Posolmi, 1860*

	W. Gallimore	S. B. Emmerson	J. Whisman
Acres	227	300	160
Farm Value	10000	5000	2500
Value of Farm Implements	700	500	100
Animals Owned	58	241	42
Value of Animals	3220	10000	650
Yearly Harvest Wheat/Barley (bushels)	2000	1000	275
Yearly Production Butter/Cheese (pounds)	216	1500	200

* Source: U.S. Census Bureau 1860:25-27

Santa Clara was a much larger boom town (2,559 people in 1860), with a number of new brick buildings, a hotel, general merchandise store, dry goods, grocery, and hardware stores, a book store, drug store, bank, and lawyers' and physicians' offices. Stages connected the town with San Francisco, Alviso, San Jose, and other points (Knight 1860-1862; U.S. Census Office 1864:31).

Inigo's last days of life saw the arrival of one of the key symbols of the new industrial age which was being born in California. The San Francisco and San Jose Railroad arrived in Mountain View, Santa Clara, and San Jose in January 1864. This railroad could travel 40 miles an hour and represented the power available to those who could develop science and technology. This marked a final important change for Inigo, who had been born among his own people in a nearby village 83 years earlier, and who had lived through some incredible changes during his long and eventful life.

On the 28th of February, 1864, about a month and a half after the arrival of the railroad, Inigo reported that he felt ill and had to go to his adobe home. Mary J. Gates recounted the local tradition of his death as follows: "Telling his friends that he wished to be buried by a cross he had planted, and receiving shortly afterward the blessing of the priest, this kindly representative of an ancient race passed away . . . " (Gates 1895:13).

The *San Jose Patriot* (March 2, 1864) reported on Inigo's death as follows, exaggerating his age as was common during this era:

> Death of an Old Indian
>
> An honest old Indian named Inigo, who it is supposed had arrived at the age of 104 years, died on Sunday the 28th of February on the Inigo Ranch near Mountain View in this county. This neighborhood has been his residence for a century.

We do not know who buried Inigo, or if any of his relatives, such as his son Manuel or Eustaquia's daughter Maria Petronila, were still alive to help bury him. The location of Inigo's grave was on what L.L. Loud called in 1912 the "smaller Ynigo Mound" (Loud 1912). This was about a half mile north of the southwestern corner of the Posolmi grant, which was near the Mountain View-Alviso Road. His grave site was close to where the Walkinshaw family had their ranch complex. The place had been a village site, perhaps the same village where Inigo was born in 1781. He was thus put to rest with many of his own people.

Fig. 5. Lope Inigo in 1856 (University of Santa Clara Archives)

CHAPTER 6

AFTER INIGO: RANCHO POSOLMI FROM WALKINSHAW TO MOFFETT FIELD, 1860s-PRESENT

Since Inigo's death in 1864, there has been a succession of owners of Rancho Posolmi. Until 1930 farming was the focus of economic activity. Since 1930 military and aerospace uses have been developed, gradually supplanting farming. Over this 130-year period, almost all traces of the past—buildings, shell mounds, and Inigo's very grave—were systematically removed.

The Walkinshaws, 1864-1882

The Walkinshaw family owned a 688-acre parcel of the Posolmi grant, including the land where Inigo was buried. One of the Walkinshaw daughters had a cross erected over Inigo's grave and a fence built around it (Older n.d.). In the early 1860s three single Walkinshaw sisters lived in the Santa Clara area, perhaps at times on the Posolmi grant itself. In the summer of 1861, however, William H. Brewer found them living at the New Almaden Mine with their married sister, who was the wife of mine superintendent John Young (Brewer 1966 [1861]:157, 160). Brewer recounted in his journal a horseback ride he took with the Walkinshaw sisters:

> Mrs. Young's Scotch father, Robert Walkinshaw, having died, the children now live here. There are several girls left, all beautiful. Professor Whitney thinks one is the most lovely lady he has seen in the state. I hardly go to that length. They ride every afternoon and invited us to ride with them. Three of them, with Miss Day, a Miss Clark of Folsom, a young

Englishman, Averill, and I made up the party. It was the pleasantest time I have had in the state. We started at five o'clock and rode five or six miles east to the top of a hill that commands a lovely view of the Santa Clara Valley and the opposite mountain chain.

I wish you could see those Mexican ladies ride; you would say you never saw riding before. Our American girls could not shine at all. There seems to be a peculiar talent in the Spanish race for horsemanship; all ride gracefully, but I never saw ladies in the East who could approach the poorest of the Spanish ladies whom I have yet seen ride. I cannot well convey an adequate conception of the way they went galloping over the fields—squirrel holes, ditches, and logs are no cause of stopping—jumping a fence or a gulch if one was in the way. The roads are too dusty to ride in, so we rode over the hills and through fields, sometimes on a trail, sometimes not. We took tea at Mrs. Day's, then were invited to Mr. Young's, where we spent a pleasant evening. My lame knee was better, but still bad enough as an excuse for not dancing [Brewer 1966 (1861):160-161].

The 1870 United States agricultural census lists the "Walkinshaw Estate," along with four other farms which also occupied parts of Inigo's land grant. This census report illustrates how productive and valuable the land had become by that time. Table 12 presents these data. The figures in Table 12 of butter produced in only one year are striking, and illustrate the rapid accumulation of wealth possible on many Santa Clara Valley farms.

The 1870 population census shows two distinct groups living on the Walkinshaw Estate. The first group, which occupied one dwelling, consisted of Charles Slade, the farm manager, and 15 workers—11 farm laborers, a carpenter, a cook, a house servant, and a gardener. All were listed as white males, except for the cook and house servant who were Chinese. All were between the ages of 21 and 46.

In a second dwelling resided Samuel and Francisca Price, Robert and Guadalupe Walkinshaw, and seven other people. Samuel Price is listed as "agent for estate." The two Walkinshaw children were both minors, 18 and 16 respectively. The others included house servants, a housekeeper, and a Chinese washman. Following this listing are found the families of Gallimore, Frink, Jenkins, and Bailey (U.S. Census Bureau 1870a).

Table 12
Agricultural Returns and Values for Five Farms on Rancho Posolmi, 1870*

Farm**	W	G	F	J	B	Totals
Acres	600	305	75	165	300	1445
Value	75000	20000	8000	13000	20000	136000
Value of Farm Implements	1800	1500	200	300	1000	4800
Animals Owned	43	51	20	16	17	147
Value of Animals	1260	2830	2000	1200	1200	8490
Yearly Harvest Wheat/Barley (bushels)	9273	2300	650	1200	2400	15823
Yearly Production Butter/Cheese (pounds)	1200	50	200	200	500	2150

* Source: U.S. Census Bureau 1870b

**W: Walkinshaw Estate; G: W. Gallimore; F: D. Frink; J: E. Jenkins; B: J. Bailey.

An 1876 map lists all five of these landowners and shows how the "Ynigo Reservation" was divided at that time (see Fig. 4). In 1876 the Walkinshaw family still controlled both the largest section (about 680 acres) and the corner near the Mountain View-Alviso Road, which had contained Inigo's adobe house. This map also shows the location of Walkinshaw's house, which was reportedly close to the location of Inigo's grave (Loud 1912).

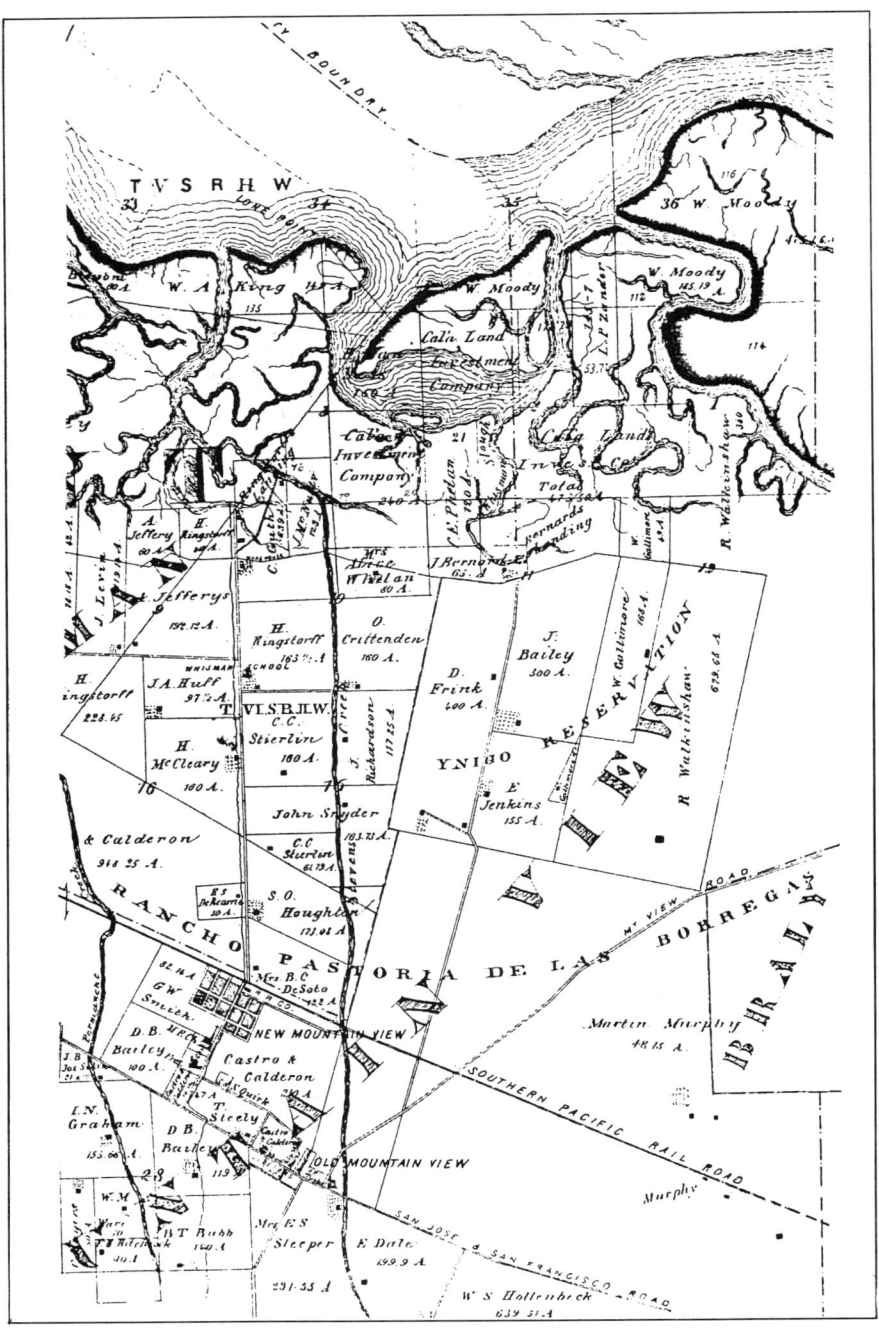

Fig. 6. The "Ynigo Reservation" in 1876

Curtner, Cunningham, and Holthouse, 1882-1929

In October of 1882 Robert Walkinshaw, Jr., sold his farm of approximately 680 acres containing the Inigo grave site to Henry Curtner for $75,000 (Joyce 1972:1; Bailey and Phillips 1887). Curtner was a Santa Clara Valley cattle rancher and a land speculator who purchased large farms or ranches and subdivided them for settlers (Sawyer 1922:423-424). Curtner held the land for about a decade, perhaps using it for grazing cattle, then sold it in turn to James F. Cunningham in 1891 (Joyce 1972). The 1900 census lists the 55-year old Cunningham and his 50-year old wife Sarah as owners of the farm, which was mortgaged. Cunningham was born in Canada and was a naturalized United States citizen. His wife was born in Massachusetts, and the couple, married for 26 years, had no children. Living with them were a mother-in-law, a sister-in-law, and two farm hands who worked with Cunningham on the farm (U.S. Census Bureau 1900).

In 1903 the Cunninghams put the "Ynigo Rancho," as it was then called, up for sale. An advertisement for the property, listed as 688 acres in size, stated:

> There is a 9-room house with bath, large barn with room for 24 horses, a warehouse 50 x 100 feet that will hold 500 tons of hay, a blacksmith shop, good buildings for hired help, 5 artesian wells ranging from 96 to 180 feet deep . . . 25 acres in sugar prunes, balance in high state of cultivation . . . . This property will be sold as a whole or in subdivisions for $150 per acre, one-half cash, the balance on easy terms [*Mountain View Register*, March 27, 1903].

There were apparently no purchasers for the subdivided acreage and Cunningham leased the land, eventually selling the 688 acres to the Hirsch Land Company. The land was first leased, then sold to members of the Holthouse family, who also owned and operated another farm in the vicinity for many years (Foote 1888:480; Sawyer 1922:835-836; Older n.d.).

In 1912, during the period when the Holthouse family was leasing the ranch, archaeologist L. L. Loud visited the area, recording the prehistoric Indian mounds of the Mountain View vicinity. He surveyed the Holthouse Ranch and wrote that Inigo was buried on the smaller of two "Ynigo Mounds," which was located 2 3/4 miles E.N.E. of Mountain View on the road to Alviso, where the farm buildings of the J. F. Cunningham estate stood in 1912. Loud noted that

... the fence about his grave was standing less than 20 years ago. This mound, 25 ft. above sea level, is a deposit several hundred ft. in diameter . . . probably 5 ft. or more deep . . . A second mound was . . . 1/3 mile to north of above mound near a set of farm buildings" [Loud 1912].

Pinpointing the exact location of the "Smaller Ynigo Mound" and Inigo's grave site is thus, according to L. L. Loud at least, equivalent to finding the location of the Cunningham/Holthouse ranch buildings. Two detailed maps from the mid-1890s are of help (figs. 5 and 6). These two maps, a U.S. Geological Survey map (surveyed in 1895 and published in 1899) and a U.S. Coast and Geodetic Survey map (surveyed in 1897 and published in 1900) both show that the center of activity on the 688-acre Walkinshaw/Curtner/Cunningham/Holthouse Ranch during the mid-1890s was an area about one-half mile due north of the southeast corner boundary of the Rancho Posolmi landgrant. A tree-lined road paralleled the eastern boundary of the Posolmi grant from its southeast corner northward about a half mile, then turned northwest and ran about one-eighth mile to a cluster of buildings (see figs. 5 and 6). About a half-mile to the north stood two more buildings (Fig. 5). If L. L. Loud is correct, then Inigo's grave and the Smaller Ynigo Mound were located near the largest set of buildings shown on the maps, about one-half mile north of the southeast corner of the Posolmi grant. No buildings or other cultural features are shown at the southeastern corner of Posolmi, where Inigo's dwellings were shown on the 1859 Surveyor General's map (Fig. 3). This indicates that by the mid-1890s the area where Inigo's main adobe house had stood had already been destroyed and the land there used to grow crops. Perhaps one of his other houses still stood in the area where the main Walkinshaw/Cunningham/Holthouse farm buildings existed during this era.

The two younger Holthouse brothers, Mark H. (born in 1872) and Joseph F. (born in 1878), intensively farmed the 688-acre property where Inigo's houses stood and where his grave apparently lay. Both of the brothers had large families who helped them work the land. They also employed hired men who were housed in the old buildings on the property (Sawyer 1922:835-836; U.S. Census Bureau 1910, 1920; Older n.d.). Sometime a few years after Loud's 1912 survey, the Holthouse family reportedly destroyed at least one of the Ynigo Mounds (probably the smaller one as it was nearer the road and the Walkinshaw house) to plant alfalfa. This may have also destroyed the Inigo grave site. In the process, they unearthed and collected many "Indian skulls and bones"

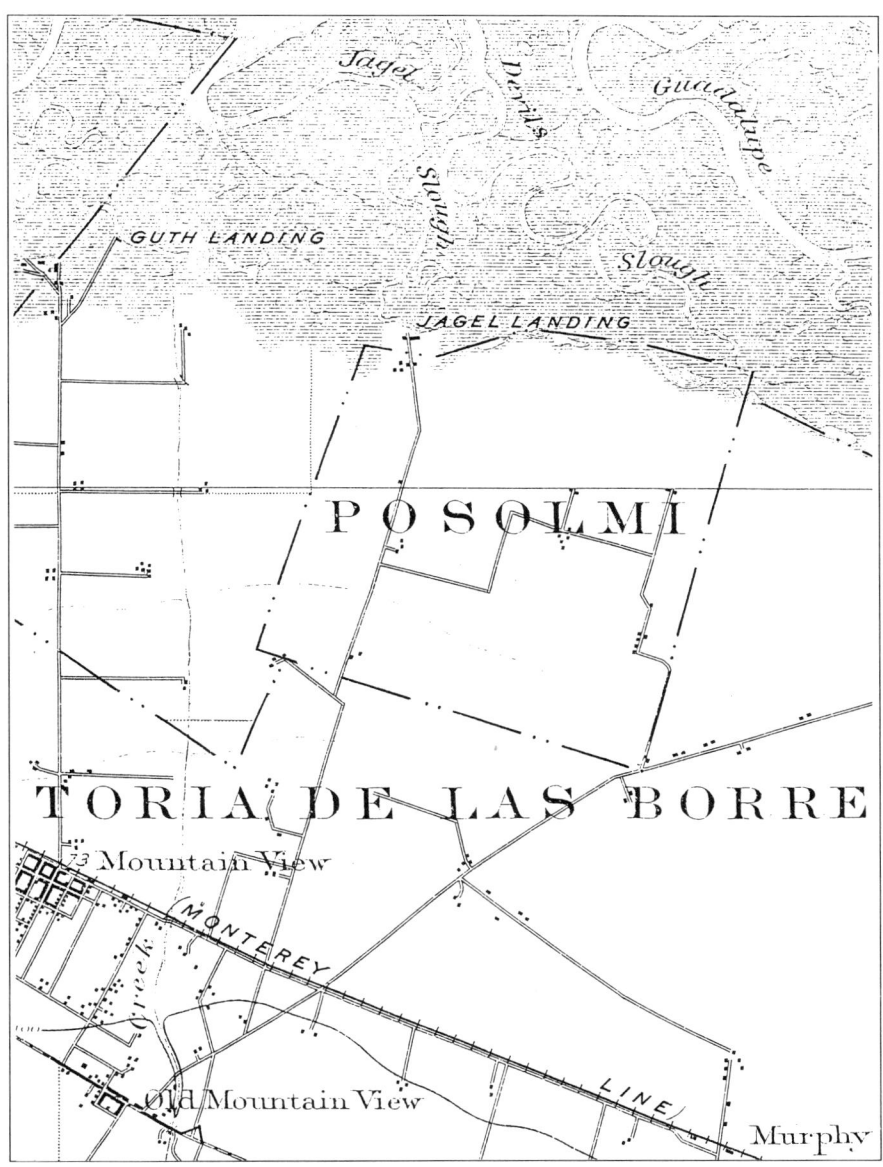

Fig. 7. Posolmi, 1895-1899

(Older n.d.). Sometime between 1912 and 1917 Mrs. Fremont Older visited the "Inygo ranch" and later wrote about the visit in a newspaper column:

> Some time ago I visited Inygo ranch. I drove across two rows of bare, brown poplar trees to the old, low, grey, double-winged Walkinshaw house. The windows were missing. The walls had been defaced, the marble mantels broken and the rooms deserted. In the rear of the house I heard a noise. In that direction I made my way.
>
> In a large, bleak room I found a strong, handsome American woman, the wife of the tenant of the property, cleaning the bedrooms of the workmen. I asked her to show me where in the adobe field on the right had been the Indian mound.
>
> She pointed toward a great field, level as a billiard table, lying between the ranch house and the main highway. "There is the mound," she said. "My son scraped it off a week ago for alfalfa. The ground must be level. Last week my son, Mark Holthouse, dug up some of the Indian skulls and bones."
>
> ### SKULLS DUG UP
> She led me to the veranda on the north side of the house. There, lying under the porch floor, were some skulls. She shrank from touching them. When I took them up I found that two were very small and had evidently been women. The large one had plainly been a man. The teeth were in excellent condition.
>
> "May I have one of these skulls?" I ventured.
>
> With the touch of amusement she granted my request. "There are a lot more bones in the field," she said. "My son dug a hole in the ground and buried them. He didn't want to be bothered at his work by scraping up bones."
>
> "Who owns Inygo's ranch now?" I asked.
>
> "Since the Walkinshaws went away it has often changed hands. Now it belongs to a stock company. One of the principal owners is Mr. Hirsch."
>
> Holding the grey skull in my hand, I drove back past the alfalfa field which has become a new grave, the grave of California history [Older n.d.].

Older added cryptically that Inigo's grave marker and fence had been destroyed and that she had information that Inigo's bones had been removed from his grave by a vandal. She wrote, "Only the memory of man marks where Inygo rested. There is reason to believe that one zealous collector of rarities in California many years ago dug up Inygo's skeleton and carried it away" (Older n.d.).

Mark Holthouse also reportedly tore down a "small one story" adobe house in 1914. This location was about fifty feet east of where the Holthouse ranch house stood in 1940. A garage was then built on the site (Hendry and Bowman 1940:888).

In 1919 the Holthouse brothers purchased the 688-acre ranch which they had been leasing. Electric-powered wells were installed on the land, pumping water for irrigation of crops. Over time, such pumping significantly impacted the level of flowing water in the Santa Clara Valley, and creeks and marshes were reduced in size or dried up entirely. The pumping allowed additional crops, including alfalfa, tomatoes, sugar beets, and peas to be added to the hay, grain, and dairy farming which had been the farm's prior focus (Sawyer 1922:835-836; Jacobsen 1984:51). The Holthouse family then used Inigo's fame to help sell their fresh peas. These peas were sold under the brand name of "Ynigo, . . . with a picture of an Indian chief who was portrayed—uncharacteristically—wearing a bonnet of the Plains Indians" (Jacobsen 1984:51).

Moffett Field and Adjacent Development, 1929-Present

In 1929-1930 agriculture was by far the mainstay of Rancho Posolmi and the Santa Clara Valley generally. Some light industry existed in the valley, but varied agricultural produce was the key factor in the economy. During these years the United States Navy was looking for a West Coast base to house dirigibles, the lighter-than-air craft which were then seen as having important military uses. A large number of communities were interested in hosting the facility. To attract the Navy, the San Jose Chamber of Commerce successfully raised almost $500,000 to purchase 1,000 acres, which were then given free to the Navy in 1931. The 1,000 acres included most of the Posolmi landgrant (U.S. Naval Air Station 1958:4-5). Construction began in 1931 and continued off and on for several years. By the early 1950s a large hangar (the floor alone covered eight acres) and immense landing field covered almost the entire 1000 acres. The 1953 U.S. Geological Survey map shows developments by that time (see Fig. 7).

150   *Inigo of Rancho Posolmi*

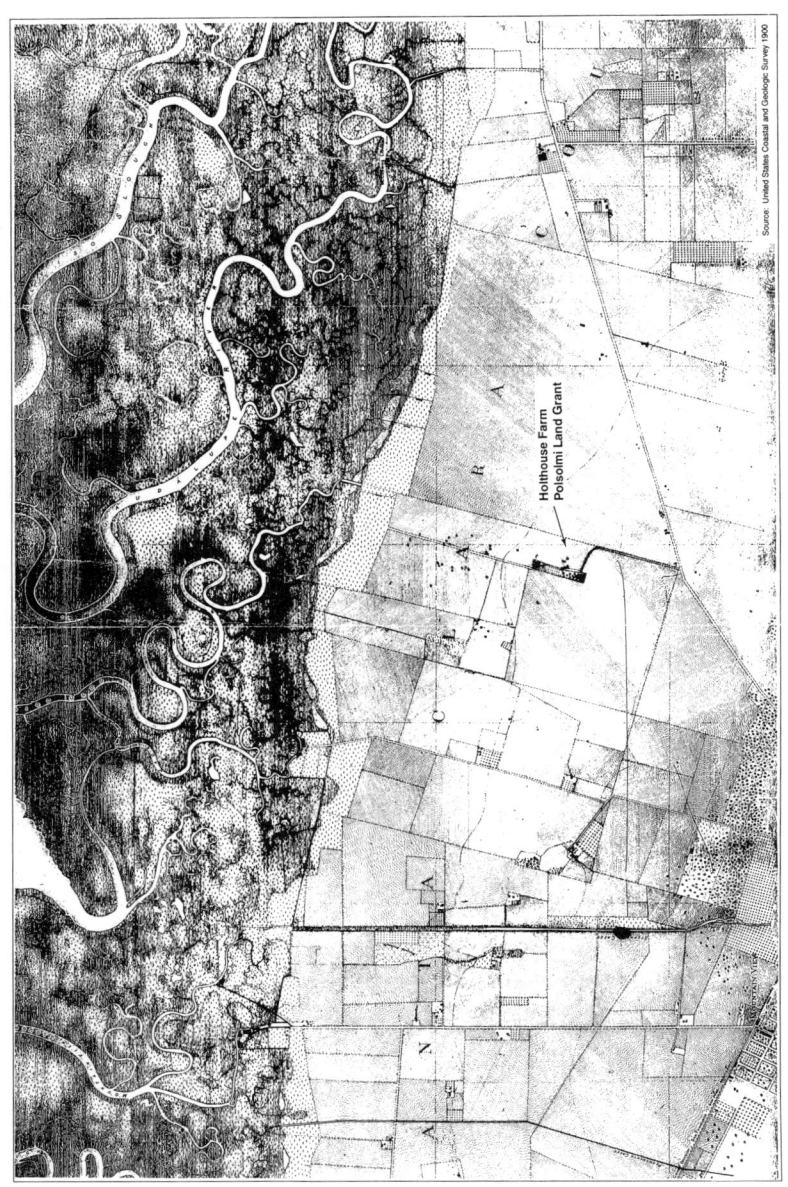

Fig. 8. Posolmi, 1897-1900

After Inigo: 1860s-Present

The Holthouse family continued to own and operate its farm on reduced acreage on the eastern edge of the Posolmi grant until the early 1960s. During this time, the Holthouse family maintained the two complexes of farm-related buildings shown on the maps of the mid-1890s (see figs. 5, 6, and 7). The Holthouse family sold out to the Lockheed Corporation in the early 1960s. Lockheed then constructed the military-related aerospace facility that currently stands on the site. All of the buildings related to the Holthouse family's occupation appear to have been torn down by 1981, although some small-scale farming continued until about 1990 in the southeastern corner of the Posolmi grant (U.S. Geological Survey 1981; Fig. 8). Today there are no above-ground structural remains of the nineteenth century on the Posolmi landgrant. The main Holthouse ranch buildings were located where the Lockheed Credit Union building stood in the 1980s (*Lockheed Star* September 10, 1982). As is the case for most of the Santa Clara Valley, urbanization and industrial development have eclipsed the rural past and those, like Lope Inigo, who inhabited a very different world.

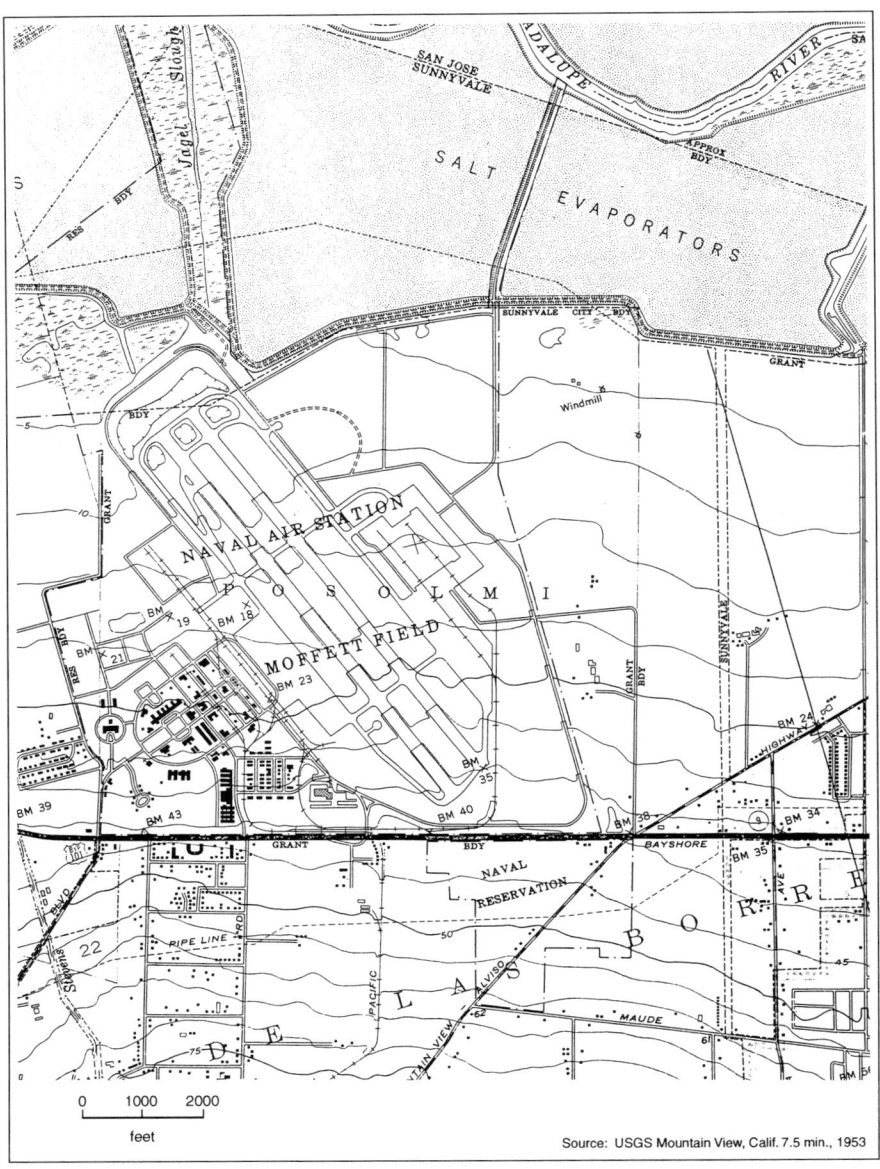

Fig. 9. Posolmi and Moffett Field, 1953

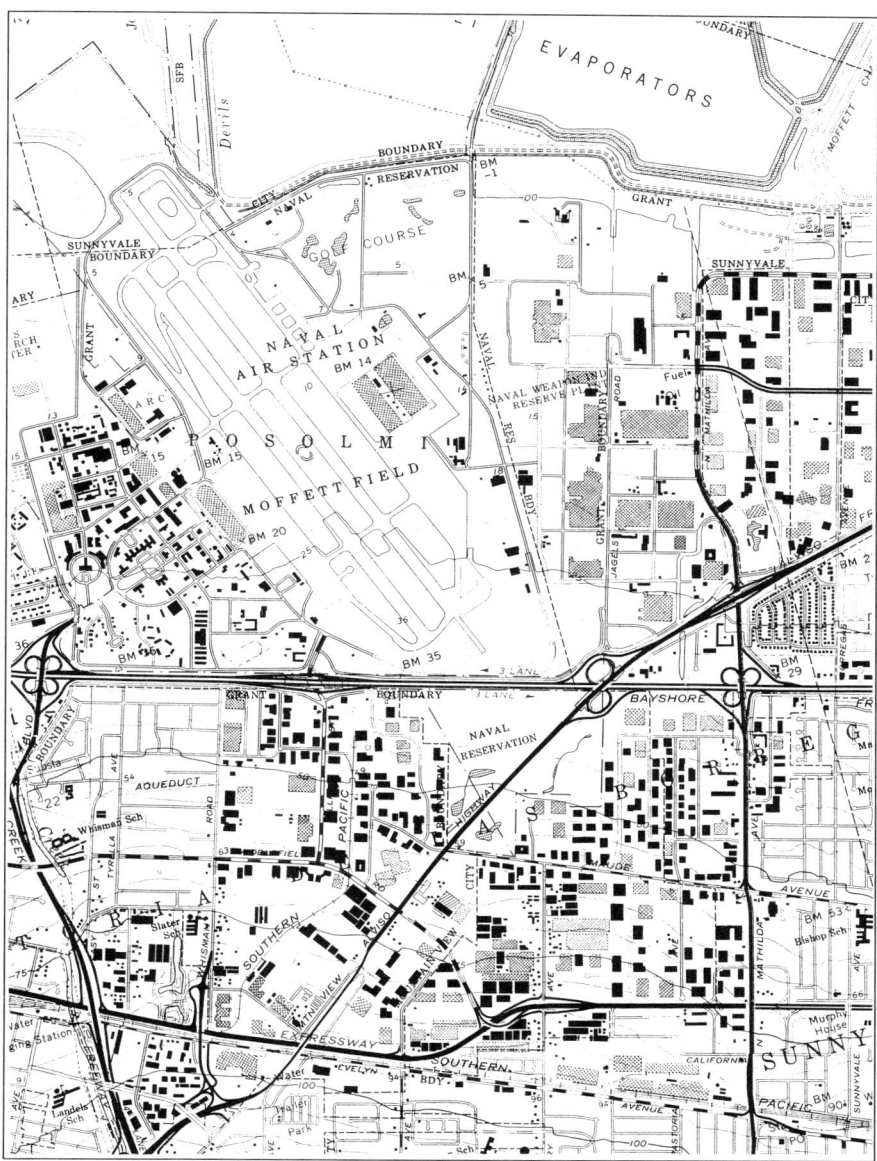

Fig. 10. Posolmi and Moffett Field, 1981

EPILOGUE

THE LEGACY OF THE PAST

With their shell mounds and annual burning practices, Inigo's people made only minor marks on the land. Even the Spanish and the Californios who followed lacked the science and technology to heavily impact the natural features of the Santa Clara Valley. Both cultures, the Native American and Latin American, therefore, left relatively little behind in the way of physical remains. This is not so in the case of the period since Inigo's death in 1864.

The power of modern industrial society over the land is nearly absolute. As a result, almost all of the Santa Clara Valley's original natural and cultural landscape is now hidden from memory, lost in the past. Only small fragments of the great bayside marshlands and meadowlands remain, the rest have been drained or paved over. The formerly tree- and brush-covered valley floor is now closely packed with the monuments of the aerospace and silicon chip industries. They, in turn, are bordered everywhere by commercial enterprises and residential development. Surrounding and connecting these uncounted tens of thousands of buildings is a circulatory network of great and small highways, between which are found the old railroad lines and towns of the more recent past. The shell mounds and rough adobes of the Indians and their Spanish/Californio successors are mostly gone. Even remains of the more recent agricultural and ranching heritage have mostly disappeared. Thus little remains of the natural or cultural heritage of the Rancho Posolmi area.

During the second half of the 1990s, a section of the old Rancho Posolmi became part of a transportation corridor for the Tasman Light Rail system. Passengers traveling on this train move between a chain of modern urban and suburban locations—places like San Jose, Sunnyvale, and Mountain View—where both the original landscape and remains of the region's early historical development have been either removed entirely or, at minimum, hidden from view. Yet, as we have seen from this study, the Rancho Posolmi area has had an unusually rich and interesting history. This history is one of change, and the light rail system itself is another phase of that long tradition.

A monument to Inigo and his people is planned for the Bayshore/NASA stop on the Tasman Light Rail line, a marker reminding us of the rich history and heritage left by these fellow human beings who once lived on this part of the earth. This monument will include a picture of Inigo and read in part as follows:

Inigo
1781 - 1864

Standing here near his village of long ago, Inigo reminds us of his people—the Tamien Ohlone—who first made this valley their home. When the mission church came, their world changed. Years passed . . . and the boy who was baptized Inigo grew, married, and had children of his own. Then his world changed again, from Spanish to Mexican rule, and he and others were released from the mission compound. For faithful service, Inigo was granted land, which was rare for an Indian. This land grant—Rancho Posolmi—held his village, his childhood home . . . . Then change came yet again. Americans arrived in ever-increasing numbers, and with statehood Indian people lost their citizenship rights. Much of Inigo's ranch was lost, yet he lived out his years on the land of his birth. Here he stands again, a reminder of the past and of a people who endured great changes, adapting so their descendants might find a future.

REFERENCES

Alvarado, Juan Bautista
    n.d.   Historia de California 1769-1824. Ms. on file, Bancroft Library, University of California, Berkeley.

Alviso, José Antonio
    1853, 1862   Deposition. Land Case 410 ND. Ms. on file, Bancroft Library, University of California, Berkeley.

Anza, Juan Bautista de
    1930 [1776]   *Anza's Diary of the Second Anza Expedition, 1775-1776. Anza's California Expeditions,* Vol. III. Herbert Bolton, editor. University of California Press, Berkeley.

Arbuckle, Clyde
    1968   *Santa Clara County Ranchos.* Harlan-Young Press, San Jose.

Archibald, Robert
    1978a   *The Economic Aspects of the California Missions.* Academy of American Franciscan History, Washington, D.C.

    1978b   "Indian Labor at the California Missions: Slavery or Salvation." *Journal of San Diego History* 24(2):172-182.

Arguello, José
    1788   Arguello al Gobernador Pedro Fages sobre pelea de Indios. San Francisco Presidio, April 30, 1788. [Paraphrase of destroyed original.] Archives of California (C-A 1-63) 4:261-262. Bancroft Library, University of California, Berkeley.

    1804a   Arguello al Gobernador Arrillaga. San Francisco Presidio, June 30, 1804. Ramo Californias, Tomo 9:439- 441. Archivo General de Nacion. Palacio Nacional, Mexico City. (Microfilm at Bancroft Library).

    1804b   Arguello al Gobernador Arrillaga. San Francisco Presidio, October 26, 1804. [Paraphrase of destroyed original.] Archives of California (C-A 1-63) 11:358-359. Bancroft Library, University of California, Berkeley.

    1805   Arguello al Gobernador Arrillaga. San Francisco Presidio, February 28, 1805. [Paraphrase of destroyed original.] Archives of California (C-A 1-63) 12:39-40. Bancroft Library, University of California, Berkeley.

Arguello, Luis
    1805   Informe a Teniente Jose Arguello sobre un plan de Indios para quemar la Mision de Santa Clara y matar a los Padres. Mission San Jose. May 10, 1805. [Paraphrase of destroyed original.] Archives of California (C-A1-63) 12:30. Bancroft Library, University of California, Berkeley.

Arrillaga, José Joaquin de
    1804   Arrillaga al Virrey José de Iturrigaray. Monterey. May 11, 1804. Ramo Californias, Tomo 9:433. Archivo General de Nacion. Palacio Nacional, Mexico City. (Microfilm available, Bancroft Library).

1806   Arrillaga al Alferez Luis Arguello. Monterey. May 20, 1806. [Paraphrase of destroyed original.] Archives of California (C-A 1-63) 26: 262-265. Bancroft Library, University of California, Berkeley.

1807a   Arrillaga al Macario Castro, comisionado del pueblo de San Jose. September 4, 1807. Archives of the City of San Jose, 1807, Doc. 24. San Jose Historical Society, San Jose, CA.

Arroyo de la Cuesta, Felipe
   1976 [1814]   Reply to the Interrogatory of 1812 from Mission San Juan Bautista. May 1, 1814. [Reprinted in *As the Padres Saw Them*, Maynard Geiger and Clement Meighan, editors.] Santa Barbara Archives, Santa Barbara.

Atherton, Faxon Dean
   1964 [1836-9]   *Diary*. California Historical Society, San Francisco.

Bailey and Phillips
   1887   *Map of Santa Clara County, California*. The Bancroft Company, San Francisco.

Bancroft, Hubert Howe
   1886   *History of California*, Vol. II, III, and IV. The History Company, San Francisco.

Bannon, John F. (ed.)
   1964   *Bolton and the Spanish Borderlands*. University of Oklahoma Press, Norman.

Bean, Lowell John (ed.)
   1994   *The Ohlone: Past and Present - Native Americans of the San Franciso Bay Region*. Ballena Press Anthropological Papers No. 42. Ballena Press, Menlo Park.

Bean, Walton
    1973   *California: An Interpretive History*. McGraw-Hill Book Company, New York.

Beck, Warren A., and Ynez D. Haase
    1974   *Historical Atlas of California*. University of Oklahoma Press, Norman.

Beechey, Frederick W.
    1968 [1831]   *Narrative of a Voyage to the Pacific and Beering's Strait, to co-operate with the polar expeditions: performed in His Majesty's ship Blossom, under the command of Captain F. W. Beechey . . . in the years 1825, 26, 27, 28 . . .*, Vol. II. Henry Colburn and Richard Bentley, London.

Belcher, Captain Edward
    1843   *Narrative of a Voyage Round the World, performed by Her Majesty's ship Sulphur, during the years 1836-1842, including deails of the naval operations in China from Dec. 1840, to Nov. 1841*. Vol. I. Henry Colburn, London.

Bennett, Winston
    n.d.   Deposition. Land Case 410 ND. Ms. on file, Bancroft Library, University of California, Berkeley.

Bowman, Jacob N.
    n.d.   The Area of Mission Lands. Ms. on file, Bancroft Library, University of California, Berkeley.

Brewer, William H.
    1966 [1860-4]   *Up and Down California in 1860-1864*. Francis P. Farquhar, ed. University of California Press, Berkeley.

Brown, Alan K.
    1973   Indians of San Mateo County. *La Peninsula: Journal of the San Mateo County Historical Association* 17(4), San Mateo.

Buelna, Feliz
    1862   Deposition. Land Case 410 ND. Ms. on file, Bancroft Library, University of California, Berkeley.

Butler, Rev. Alban
    1961 [1745]   *The Lives of the Fathers, Martyrs and other Principal Saints*, Vol. I. William Clowes, London.

California, State of
    1852   Census of Santa Clara County, 1852. Ms. on file, California State Archives, Sacramento.

Campbell, Thomas
    1853   Deposition. Land Case 410 ND. Ms. on file, Bancroft Library, University of California, Berkeley.

Castillo, Edward
    1991   The Native Response to the Colonization of Alta California. In *Native American Perspectives on the Hispanic Colonization of Alta California*, Edward Castillo, editor. Garland Publishing Company, New York.

Catalá, Magín, and José Viader
    1820   Catalá e Viader al Gobernador Sola. Mission Santa Clara, May 3, 1820. Letters of the Catholic Missionaries of California 1772-1849. Ms. on file, Library of the Academy of Franciscan History, Pacific School of Religion, Berkeley.

    1976 [1814]   Reply to the Interrogatory of 1812 from Mission Santa Clara, November 4, 1814. [Reprinted in *As the Padres saw Them*, Maynard Geiger and Clement Meighan, eds.] Santa Barbara Archives, Santa Barbara.

Companys, F. Boneu
    1983   *Gaspar de Portolá: Explorer and Founder of California*, Alan K. Brown, translator. Instituto de Estudios Ilendenses, Lleida, Spain.

Conmy, Peter T.
   1938   Secularization of the California Missions 1831-1845. Ms. on file, Bancroft Library, University of California, Berkeley.

Contra Costa Gazette
   1867   (December 21).

Cook, Sherburne F.
   1957   The Aboriginal Population of Alameda and Contra Costa Counties, California. *University of California Anthropological Record* 16(4):131-156, Berkeley.

   1976   *The Conflict Between the California Indian and White Civilization.* University of California Press, Berkeley.

Cook, Warren L.
   1973   *Flood Tide of Empire: Spain and the Pacific Northwest.* Yale University Press, New Haven.

Cowan, Robert G.
   1956   *Ranchos of California.* Academic Library Guild, Fresno.

Crespí, Juan
   1969 [1769]   Excerpts from the Journal of Juan Crespí. In *Who Discovered the Golden Gate?* Frank M. Stanger and Alan K. Brown, eds. San Mateo County Historical Association, San Mateo.

Dana, Richard H.
   1840   *Two Years Before the Mast.* Harper and Brothers, New York.

Dillon, Richard H.
   1984   *Iron Men: California's Industrial Pioneers.* Candela Press, Point Richmond, California.

Doten, Alfred
   1973 [1857-58] *The Journal of Alfred Doten, 1849-1903.* Walter Van Tilburg Clark, ed. University of

Nevada Press, Reno.

Duran, Narciso
1828   Duran al Ignacio Martinez, San José Mission November 8, 1828. Letters of the Catholic Missionaries of California 1772-1849. Ms. on file, The Library of the Academy of American Franciscan History, Pacific School of Religion, Berkeley.

Duran, Narciso, and Buenaventura Fortuny
1976 [1814]   Reply to the Interrogatory of 1812 from Mission San Jose, November 7, 1814. [In *As the Padres Saw Them*, Maynard Geiger and Clemen Meighan, eds.] Santa Barbara Archives, Santa Barbara.

Engelhardt, Zephyrin
1912   *The Missions and Missionaries of California*, Vol. II and III. James H. Barry Company, San Francisco.

Engenhoff, Elisabeth (comp.)
1953   De Argento Vivo: Historic Documents on Quicksilver and its Recovery in California Prior to 1860. *California Journal of Mines and Geology*, San Francisco.

Fages, Pedro
1937 [1775]   *A Historical, Political, and Natural Description of California*, Herbert I. Priestley, ed. University of California Press, Berkeley.

1969 [1772]   Excerpts from the Journal of Pedro Fages during the Fages-Crespí Explorations of 1772. In *Who Discovered the Golden Gate?* Frank M. Stanger and Alan K. Brown, eds. San Mateo County Historical Association, San Mateo.

1972 [1772]   Diary . . . in Search of the Port of San Francisco . . . Fages as Explorer, 1769-1772. Theodore S. Treutlein, ed. *California Historical Society Quarterly* 51:338-356.

Font, Pedro
    1930 [1776]   *Font's Complete Diary of the Second Anza Expedition. Anza's California Expeditions*, Vol. IV. Herbert E. Bolton, ed. University of California Press, Berkeley.

Foote, H. S.
    1888   *Pen Pictures from the Garden of the World*. The Lewis Publishing Company, Chicago.

Forbes, Alexander
    1937   *California: A History of Upper and Lower California*. John Henry Nash, San Francisco.

Galindo, Nasario
    1959 [1883]   Early Days at Mission Santa Clara. *California Historical Society Quarterly* 38(2):101-111.

Gates, Mary
    1895   *Contributions to Local History: Rancho Pastoria de las Borregas, Mountain View California*. Cottle and Murgotten, San Jose.

Gayton, Anna H.
    1935   Areal Affiliations of California Folktales. *American Anthropologist* 37(4):582-599.

Geiger, Maynard, and Clement Meighan
    1976   *As the Padres Saw Them: California Indian Life and Customs as Reported by the Franciscan Missionaries, 1813-1815*. Santa Barbara Mission Archives, Santa Barbara.

Gifford, Edward W.
    1927   Southern Maidu Religious Ceremonies. *American Anthropologist* 29(3):214-257.

Hall, Fredrick
    1871   *The History of San Jose*. A. L. Bancroft and Co., San Francisco.

Harrington, John P.
    1921-1938   Mutsun Fieldnotes. Ms. on file, National Anthropological Archives, Smithsonian Institution, Washington, D.C. (Microfilm available at San Jose State University).

Hartnell, William Edward
    1839   Diario. Ms. on file, Mss. C-E 77, Bancroft Library, University of California, Berkeley.

Healey, Charles T.
    1859   Plat of the Rancho Posolmi. On file, Bureau of Land Management, Sacramento.

Hendry, G. W., and J. N. Bowman
    1940   The Spanish and Mexican Adobe and other Buildings in the Nine Bay Area Counties 1776-about 1850. Part 7. Santa Clara. Ms. on File, Bancroft Library, University of California, Berkeley.

Hittell, Theodore H.
    1885   *History of California*, Vol. II. Pacific Press Publishing House, San Francisco.

Hogle, De Witt E.
    1975   *Pastoral Days of Mountain View*. Santa Clara County Historical and Geneaological Society, Santa Clara County, California.

Hoover, Mildred B., Hero E. Rensch, Ethel G. Rensch, and William N. Abeloe, revised by Douglas E. Kyle
    1990   *Historic Spots in California*. Stanford University Press, Stanford.

Hurtado, Albert L.
    1988   *Indian Survival on the California Frontier*. Yale University Press, New Haven.

Jackson, Robert H.
    1984   Gentile Recruitment and Population Movements in the San Francisco Bay Area Missions. *Journal*

of California and Great Basin Anthropology 6(2):225-239.

1994 *Indian Population Decline: The Missions of Northwestern New Spain, 1687-1840.* University of New Mexico Press, Albuquerque.

Jackson, Robert H., and Edward Castillo
1995 *Indians, Franciscans, and Spanish Colonization: The Impact of the Mission System on California Indians.* University of New Mexico Press, Albuquerque.

Jacobson, Yvonne
1984 *Passing Farms, Enduring Values: California's Santa Clara Valley.* William Kaufmann, Los Altos, California.

Joyce, Pat
1972 Ynigo Rancho. Ms. on file, Mountain View Pioneer Room, Mountain View.

Kenneally, Finbar (ed.)
1965 *The Writings of Fermin Francisco de Lasuen*, Vol. II. Academy of American Franciscan History, Berkeley.

King, Chester
1978 Historic Indian Settlements in the Vicinity of the Holiday Inn Site. In *Archaeological Investigations at CA-SCL-128, the Holiday Inn Site.* Joseph Winter, ed. San Jose.

King, Thomas F.
1974 The Evolution of Status Ascription around San Francisco Bay. In *Antap: California Indian Political and Economic Organization.* Ballena Press Anthropological Papers 2. Lowell J. Bean and Thomas F. King, eds. Ballena Press, Ramona, California.

Knight, William Henry
    1860-2   Knight's Scrapbooks. Ms. on file, Mss. C-E 200, Vol. 12. Bancroft Library, University of California, Berkeley.

Kotzebue, Otto von
    1830   *A New Voyage Round the World in the Years 1823, 24, 25 and 26*, Vol.II. Henry Colburn and Richard Bentley, London.

Kroeber, Alfred L.
    1932   The Patwin and Their Neighbors. *University of California Publications in American Archaeology and Ethnology* 29(4):253-423.

Langsdorff, George H. von
    1814 [1806]   *Voyages and Travels in Various Parts of the World during the Years 1803, 1804, 1805, 1806 and 1807. Part 2.* Henry Colburn, London.

Langston, Kathryn Lee
    n.d.   The Secularization of the California Missions 1813-1846. M.A. Thesis (History), University of California, Berkeley.

Lanyon, Milton, and Laurence Bulmore
    1967   *Cinnabar Hills: The Quicksilver Days of New Almaden.* Village Printers, Los Gatos, California.

Lasuen, Fermin F. de
    1965 [1785-1803] *The Writings of Fermin Francisco de Lasuen.* Finbar Kenneally, ed. Academy of American Franciscan History, Berkeley.

Levy, Richard
    1978   Costanoan. In *Handbook of North American Indians*, Vol. 8:California. Robert F. Heizer, ed. Smithsonian Institution, Washington, D.C.

Lockheed Star
    1982   (September 10)

Loud, L. L.
    1912   Notes on Castro mound #356, site CA-SCL-1. Manuscript 361. Ms. on file, Phoebe Hearst Museum of Anthropology, University of California, Berkeley.

McCarthy, F. C.
    1958   *The History of Mission San Jose, California 1797-1835.* Academy Library Guild, Fresno.

Mendenhall, William
    1861   Deposition. Land Case 410 ND. Ms. on file, Bancroft Library, University of California, Berkeley.

Milliken, Randall
    1983   The Spatial Organization of Human Population on Central California's San Francisco Peninsula at the Spanish Arrival. M.A. Thesis (Cultural Resources Management). Sonoma State University, Rohnert Park, California.

    1991   An Ethnohistory of the Indian People of the San Francisco Bay Area from 1770 to 1810. Ph.D. Dissertation (Anthropology). University of California, Berkeley.

    1995   *A Time of Little Choice: The Disintegration of Tribal Culture in the San Francisco Bay Area 1769-1810.* Ballena Press, Menlo Park.

Moncada, Fernando Rivera y
    1969 [1774]   Excerpts from the Journal of Captain Fernando Rivera y Moncada during the Exploration of 1774. In *Who Discovered the Golden Gate?* Frank M. Stanger and Alan K. Brown, eds. San Mateo County Historical Association, San Mateo.

Moraga, Gabriel
    1794   Informe al Teniente José Arguello. San Jose, October 30, 1794. [Paraphrase of destroyed original]. Archives of California (C-A 1-63)

8:201. Bancroft Library, University of California, Berkeley.

Morgan, Dale L.
1953 *Jedediah Smith and the Opening of the West.* Bobbs-Merrill Company, Inc., New York.

Mountain View Register
1903 (March 27)

Murguia, Antonio, and Tomas de la Pena
1777 Informe al R. P. Presidente Frey Junipero Serra. Mission Santa Clara, December 30, 1777. Archives of the Mission of Santa Barbara 9:505-509.

Noboa, Diego de, and Tomás Peña
1784-1793 Informes of Mission Santa Clara. Veronica Lo CoCo, trans. Ms. on file, Orradre Library, University of Santa Clara, Santa Clara.

Northrop, Marie E.
1984-1987 *Spanish-Mexican Families of Early California: 1769-1850*, Vol. I and II. Southern California Genealogical Society, Burbank.

Older, Mrs. Fremont
n.d. When Santa Clara County was Young. Newspaper Clippings on File, Bancroft Library, University of California, Berkeley.

Otterbein, Keith F.
1977 The Anthropology of War. In *Handbook of Social and Cultural Anthropology*, J. Honigmann, ed. Columbia University Press, New York.

Palou, Francisco
1913 [1786] *The Life and Apostolic Labors to the Venerable Father Junipero Serra.* George Wharton James, trans. and ed. Private Press of George Wharton James, Pasadena, California.

1926 [1773-83] *Historical Memoirs of New California.* 4 vol. University of California Press, Berkeley.

Peralta, Luis
1805 Diario del Expedición a la Sierra. Mission San Jose. January 30, 1805. [Paraphrase of destroyed original]. Archives of California (C-A 1-63) 12:33-34. Bancroft Library, University of California, Berkeley.

Phillips, George Harwood
1974 Indians and the Breakdown of the Spanish Mission System. *Ethnohistory* 21(4):291-302.

1981 *The Enduring Struggle: Indians in California History.* Boyd and Fraser, San Francisco.

1993 *Indians and Intruders in Central California 1769-1849.* University of Oklahoma Press, Norman.

Pueblo of San Jose
1796-1844 Pueblo Collection, Calendar and Catalogue of Spanish Mexican Archives. Ms. on file. San Jose Historical Museum, San Jose.

Riddell, Francis
1978 Maidu and Konkow. In *Handbook of North American Indians, Vol. 8: California.* Smithsonian Institution, Washington, D.C.

Robinson, Alfred
1851 *Life in California.* H. G. Colliins, London.

Sanchez, Francisco Miguel, and José Viader
1796 Informe of Mission Santa Clara, Translated by Veronica Lo CoCo. Ms. on file, Orradre Library, University of Santa Clara, Santa Clara.

Sanchez, José Antonio
1805 Sanchez al Teniente José Arguello. Mission San Jose. January 16, 1805. [Paraphrase of destroyed original.] Archives of California (C-A

1-63) 12:34-35. Bancroft Library, University of California, Berkeley.

Sanchez, José
    1829   Report on Battle with Estanislao, May 10, 1829. Ms. on file, Mss. C-A 53, Bancroft Library, University of California, Berkeley.

San Francisco Alta
    1851   (February 11)

San Francisco Chronicle
    1851   (November 12)

    1903   (August 23)

    1994   (April 5)

San Jose News
    1918   (February 11)

San Jose Patriot
    1864   (March 2)

Sawyer, Eugene T.
    1922   *History of Santa Clara County*. Historic Record Company, Los Angeles.

Spearman, Arthur Dunning
    n.d.   Mission Padre of Santa Clara: The Life and Work of Padre Magín Catalá, Holy Franciscan of Early California. Ms. on file, Papers of Arthur Dunning Spearman, S.J., Santa Clara University Archives, Santa Clara, California.

    1963   *The Five Franciscan Churches of Mission Santa Clara: 1777-1825/a documentation by Arthur Dunning Spearman*. National Press, Palo Alto.

Staniford, Edward
    1975   *The Pattern of California History*. Canfield Press, San Francisco.

Stanger, Frank M., and Alan K. Brown
    1969   *Who Discovered the Golden Gate?* San Mateo County Historical Association, San Mateo.

Stodder, Ann L.
    1986   *Mechanisms and Trends in the Decline of the Costanoan Indian Population of Central California.* Coyote Press, Salinas.

Sullivan, Maurice S.
    1936   *Jedediah Smith: Trader and Trail Breaker.* Press of the Pioneers, New York.

Suñol, Antonio
    1857   Deposition at Trial United States vs. Andreas Castillero. Argento Vivo, Historic Documents on Quicksilver and Its Recovery in California Prior to 1860. *California Journal of Mines and Geology* (October 1953).

Taylor, Bayard
    1850   *El Dorado; or Adventures in the Path of Empire; comprising a voyage to California, via Panama: life in San Francisco.* G. P. Putnam and Son, New York.

Thompson and West
    1876   *Historical Atlas Map of Santa Clara County.* Thompson and West, San Francisco.

United States
    Var.   Land Case 130 ND, La Purisima Concepción; Land Case 410 ND, Posolmi; Land Case 413 ND, Rancheria de Rio Estanislao. Mss. on File, Bancroft Library, University of California, Berkeley.

United States Census Bureau
    1860-1870b   Agricultural Census of Santa Clara County, California. Ms. on file, Bancroft Library, University of California, Berkeley.

	1864	*Population of the United States 1860.* Government Printing Office, Washington, D.C.
	1870a-1920	Manuscript Population Census of Santa Clara County, California. Ms. on file, Bancroft Library, University of California, Berkeley.

United States Coast and Geodetic Survey
    1900   Resurvey of San Francisco Bay California: Mountain View to Alviso. Ms. on file, Map Room, University of California, Berkeley.

United States Geological Survey
    1899   Palo Alto Quadrangle. Ms. on file, Map Library, University of California, Berkeley.

    1953, 1981   Mountain View Quadrangle. Ms. on file, Map Library, University of California, Berkeley.

United States Naval Air Station
    1958   Moffett Field California: Silver Anniversary 1933-1958. Ms. on file, Mountain View Pioneer Room, Mountain View.

Vallejo, Guadalupe
    1891   Ranch and Mission Days in Alta California. *Century Magazine* 41:181-192.

Vancouver, George
    1801   *A voyage of discovery to the North Pacific Ocean, and Round the World;, in which the coast of north-west America has been carefully examined and accurately surveyed. Undertaken by His Majesty's command, principally with a view to ascertain the existence of any navigable communication between the North Pacific and North Atlantic Oceans; and performed in the years 1790, 1791, 1792, 1793, 1794 and 1795, in the Discovery sloop of war, and armed tender Chatham, under the command of Captain George Vancouver.* Vol. III. John Stockwell, London.

Viader, José, and Magín Catalá
    1811   Informe of Mission Santa Clara. Veronica Lo CoCo, trans. Ms. on file, Orradre Library, University of Santa Clara, Santa Clara.

Walkinshaw, Robert
    1852   Statement of Petitioner Robert Walkinshaw, March 23, 1852. Land Case 410 ND. Ms. on file, Bancroft Library, University of California, Berkeley.

Webb, Edith B.
    1951   The Mission Indian Villages or Rancherias. Ms. on file, Bancroft Library, University of California, Berkeley.

    1952   *Indian Life at the Old Missions*. University of Nebraska Press, Lincoln.

Weber, David J.
    1990   *The Californios Versus Jedediah Smith, 1826-1827*. The Arthur H. Clark Company, Spokane, Washington.

Weber, Francis J., ed.
    n.d.   *The Laurelwood Mission: A Documentary History of Santa Clara de Asis*. Libra Press, Hong Kong.

    1991   *Prominent Visitors to the California Missions*. Kimberly, Los Angeles.

Wilkes, Charles
    1845   *Narrative of the United States Exploring Expedition 1838-1842*, Vol. V. Lea and Blanchard, Philadelphia.

Winter, Joseph C.
    1978   Tamien: 6000 Years in an American City. Ms. on file, Bancroft Library, University of California, Berkeley.

INDEX

Abortion 67, 72
Achachaians 93
Agriculture 18, 25, 52, 147
Alameda 45-47, 98, 103, 110
Alcalde 60, 69, 70, 89, 97, 99, 116
Alta California 17, 49, 55, 62, 65, 72, 83, 85
Alta California missions 62, 65, 72
Alvarado, Governor Juan Bautista 104, 107
Alviso 6, 9, 23, 122, 133, 134, 138, 139, 143, 145
Alviso, Ignacio 112, 114, 116, 117, 122
Alviso, José Antonio 133, 134
Ambilocal residence 11
Ana Maria 93
Andrea 93
Andres 91, 93
Anglo-Americans 87, 89, 126, 128
Animals 2, 3, 4, 28-30, 36-38, 40, 43, 51, 52, 97, 102, 112, 130, 134, 137, 138, 143
Anza, Juan Bautista de 5, 6, 20, 21, 22
Archibald, Robert 38, 67, 69, 71, 85
Arguello family 117
Arguello, Joseph Dario 107
Arguello, Lieutenant José 41, 42, 76
Arguello, Luis Antonio 78, 79, 107
Arrillaga, José Joaquin de 58, 74, 75, 81
Arroyo de la Cuesta, Felipe 10, 12, 13
Assimilation 69, 70
Atherton, Faxon Dean 101
Atole 41
Ausaima 8
Ayaputtu 93
Bailey 142-144
Baja California 17, 71

Bancroft, Hubert Howe 97, 108-110
Bannon 85
Baptism 3, 27-29, 31, 32, 42, 48, 93, 109
Barron-Forbes 129
Battle of the Mustard Stalks 125, 129
Bay of San Francisco 108
Beads 19-21, 55, 73, 102
Bean, Walton 62, 107
Beck, Warren A. 97
Beechey, Frederick W. 16
Belcher, Captain 109
Bennett, Winston 133
Bernal family 108
Berryessa family 108, 117
Bibiana 47
Big Sur 9
Bolbons 79
Bolton, Herbert 85
Borica, Diego de 51
Bowman, Jacob N. 51, 52, 108, 147
Brewer, William H. 2, 141
British 17, 34, 129
Brown, Alan K. 7, 17
Butler, Rev. Alban 32
Calabazas Creek 6
Californio 87, 89-91, 94-96, 98, 103-106, 117, 120, 127, 149
Campbell 9, 23, 51, 133
Campbell, Thomas 130
Canada 144
Capitalism 84, 85
Capitanes 10
Carlos III, King 17
Carmel River 19
Carquinez Strait 19
Casimiro 104, 133
Castillo, Edward 37, 51, 67, 97, 109
Castro 75

Castro family 107
Castro, Don José Tiburcia 104, 110, 111
Catalá, Father Magín 13, 38, 45, 46, 49, 50, 59, 66, 69-71, 75, 95
Celedonia 31
Celedonio 31
Cemetery 14, 39
Central Valley 50, 88-90, 94
Ceremonial dances 12
Ceremonial house 5
Chacaquis 93
Chert 4
Chiefs 11, 12
Chinese 46, 142
Chipeyquis 93
Chocono 93
Christians 44, 50, 59, 67, 73, 75-79, 81, 91, 103, 104, 136
Chugea 93
Cinnabar 56, 131
Cipriano 87-95, 98
Classic Mission Period 49, 59
Clear Lake 8
Coast Range 9, 51, 75
Colonialism 17, 18, 25, 26, 29, 44
Conmy, Peter T. 107
Contra Costa County 68
Cook, Sherburne F. 7, 72, 75, 81
Cook, Warren L. 17
Costanoan 9, 10, 17, 80-82, 85, 90, 91, 117, 120
Coyote 21
Coyote River 6, 9
Creation 12, 13, 83
Crespi, Father Juan 2, 5, 18, 26
Cristobal 113, 117
Crops 4, 29, 32, 33, 39, 43, 52, 53, 61, 97, 114, 133, 134, 145, 147
Cruz, José de la 135
Cueva, Father Pedro de la 76-78
Culture shock 66
Cunningham, James F. 144, 145
Cunningham, Sarah 144
Cunningham/Holthouse Ranch 145
Cupertino 6, 9, 22, 23, 51
Curtner, Henry 144, 145

Cuyens 93
Dana, Richard H. 108
Dance regalia 4, 13
Death 2, 13, 15, 42, 45, 62, 64, 65, 70-73, 80, 86, 92, 93, 95, 101, 104, 118-121, 138, 139, 141, 149
Descent groups 11
Desertion 104, 109
Diablo Valley 19
Diego, Father Garcia 107
Diet 4, 66, 70, 72
Dimas 93
Diphtheria 71
Division of labor 3, 4, 61
Djoscolo 109
Doten, Alfred 135-137
Dress 5, 29, 30, 66, 71, 124
Drought 43
Duran, Father Narciso 11, 88-90, 94, 96, 97, 99, 103
Dysentery 70, 71
East Bay 8, 19, 76
Echeandia 85, 88
Egenhoff 131
Elleuti 93
El Mocho 44
El Posida de las Animas 110
El Potrero de Santa Clara 113
Embarcadero 54, 55, 122, 124
Emerenciana 31, 32
Emmerson, S. B. 133, 138
Engelhardt, Zephyrin 50, 59, 88
Entrada, Francisco 113, 114, 117
Epidemic 22, 26, 70, 71, 95
Escolastica 119
Estanislao 87-95, 98
Estanislao-Cipriano Rebellion 89, 93
Estrada, Francisco 113
Estrada, José Ramon 107, 109, 111, 112, 114
Eusebia 117
Eustaquia 119, 120, 133, 135
Fabiana 117
Fages, Pedro 3, 5, 12, 15, 16, 19
Fages, Governor 41
Feast of St. Joseph 98

Index

Felton 119
Fernanda 133
Fernandez, Father Manuel 43-45
Fernandez, José Zgnon 113
Feudalism 82-85
Figueroa 97, 107
Figueroa, Governor José 97
First World War 118
Font, Pedro 14, 20, 21
Food shortages 30
Foote, H. S. 144
Forbes, James Alexander 113
Fortuny, Buenaventura 15
Franciscan missionaries 17
Franciscans 15, 17, 58, 71
Fremont Plain 12
Frink 142, 143
Froylan 104
Fulgencio 135
Fur-trading 88
Galindo, Leandro 53
Galindo, Nasario 53, 69
Gallagher, Edward A. T. 134
Gallimore, W. 133, 138, 142, 143
Galvez, José de 17
Gates, Mary J. 138, 139
Gayton, Anna H. 13
Geiger, Maynard 52, 66, 69, 70
Gender roles 61
Genocide 85, 86
Gentiles 30, 33, 39, 50, 89, 97
Gifford, Edward W. 12
Gifts 21, 22, 29, 44, 73
Giguam 31
Golden Gate 9, 18
Gold Rush 129, 137
Good Friday 103
Gorgonio 61, 104, 120
Gorgonio, José 113
Government 11, 17, 50, 51, 58, 59, 68, 75, 79, 88, 89, 95, 106, 108, 111, 116, 117
Governor of California 49, 59, 107
Grave site 139, 144, 145
Guadalupe River 5, 6, 9, 21, 23, 26, 45, 51, 55, 108, 122
Gualansemnes 93
Guaycatche 93

Guriguri 7
Haase, Ynez D. 97
Hall, Frederick 27, 38, 50-52, 56
Harrington, J. P. 10-12
Hartnell, William Edward 95, 110
Healey, Charles T. 130
Heizer, Robert 85
Hendry, G. W. 147
Hernandez, José 113
Higuera 77, 117
Hirsch Land Company 144
Hittell, Theodore H. 85, 88, 108, 116, 125
Hogle, De Witt E. 103
Holthouse 144-148
Holthouse, Joseph F. 145
Holthouse, Mark H. 145, 147
Holy Week 102
Hospicio 93
Houses 5, 19, 29, 34-36, 47, 53, 55-57, 60, 70, 112, 121, 130, 131, 133, 145
Huchiuns 8
Huhuyat 93
Hurtado, Albert L. 89, 91
Infanticide 67
Infant mortality 62
Inigo, Lope 1, 2, 3, 21, 25-27, 31-33, 36, 40, 42, 45, 47, 49, 50, 59-62, 64, 65, 69, 73-75, 77, 80-82, 86, 87, 88, 91, 98, 103, 104, 108, 110-114, 116-120, 125, 126, 127-131, 133-139, 141, 144, 145, 148, 150
Intergroup hostility 16
Intertribelet marriages 16
Inygo 118, 119, 130, 146, 147
Isabel 48
Jacinta 48
Jackson, Robert H. 28, 33, 36, 37, 51, 55, 56, 65, 71, 72, 97, 109
Jacobsen, Yvonne 147
Jenkins 142, 143
Jesus 104
Jesus, José de 135
Jorge 75, 76, 79
Joscori, Captain 75
José 6, 9, 11, 15, 17, 22, 23

25, 27, 28, 30, 34, 41, 44-48, 49-51, 58, 59, 61, 64, 71, 73, 74, 76, 78, 79, 81, 86, 88-92, 94, 96-98, 103-114, 116, 118, 121, 131, 133, 135, 137-138, 147, 149
José Antonio 90
José Gorgonio 113
José Rafael 112, 133, 135
José Thomas 61
Joyce, Pat 144
Juana Francisca 62, 86, 104
Justa 31
Kenneally, Finbar 56, 58, 66-68
King 7, 8, 17
King, Chester 8
King, Thomas F. 7
Knight, William Henry 138
Knight's Ferry 90
Konkow Maidu 15
Kotzebue, Otto von 51, 52, 56, 57
Kroeber, Alfred L. 8
Lacquisimas 90
Lakisamne 89
La matanza 54
Lamchin 20
Land grant 26, 74, 110, 111, 114, 137, 142, 150
Langsdorff, George H. von 16, 72
Langston, Kathryn Lle 108
Lanitt 93
La Purisima 89
La Purisima Concepcion 113, 114, 120
Lasuen, Father Fermin de 55, 56, 58, 65-68
Leandro 53, 93
Levy, Richard 9-11, 90
Life expectancy 65
Livermore Valley 76
Livestock 22, 28, 98, 104, 107-110, 112
Lockheed Corporation 148
Lockheed Credit Union 148
Lockheed Star 148
Los Altos 51
Los Altos Hills 51
Los Coches 113, 117

Los Gatos 9, 51, 113
Loud, L. L. 4, 67, 70, 139, 143-145
Luecha 77-80
Magdalena 62, 86, 104, 112, 133
Male line 11
Manifest Destiny 125
Mann 133
Manuel 43, 62, 86, 104, 109, 111, 112, 114, 116, 139
Marcello 118, 119
Marcelo 60, 87, 91, 104, 113, 117-119, 134, 135
Maria 38, 47, 61, 62, 86, 88, 93, 104, 112, 113, 116, 133, 135, 136, 139
Maria Angela 133, 135
Maria Candelaria 133
Maria Magdalena 62, 86, 104, 133
Maria Petronila 133, 135, 136, 139
Maria Trinidad 93
Maria Viviana 47
Maria Ysabel 61
Marriage 16, 57, 104, 114, 117, 119, 135
Marsh, John 68
Martinez, Ignacio 89, 90
Mass conversions 42, 74
Massachusetts 144
Matalans 19, 21
May Day 136
Mayemas 93
Mayordomo 34, 47, 53
Measles 71
Mendenhall, William 133
Mengarini, Reverend Father Gregory 134
Mercado, Father Jesus Maria Vasquez del 116, 117
Mercado, Padre José Maria Vasquez 112
Mercury poisoning 129
Mesa, Andres 91
Mesa, Juan Prado 109, 113, 117
Mesa, Maria Antonia 113
Mexican-American War of 1846-1848 125
Mexico 17, 22, 62, 88, 95, 104, 107,

Index

125, 129, 130
Micheltorena, Governor Manuel 116, 117
Milliken, Randall 7, 11, 16, 28, 29, 33, 39, 41-44, 58, 66, 71, 74-79, 81
Mills 53
Miqueas 93
Mission bells 40
Mission Peak 1
Mission San Carlos Borromeo 19
Mission San Francisco 7-9, 22, 76, 119
Mission San Jose 11, 15, 71, 76, 78, 79, 88, 89, 91, 94, 96, 103, 106
Mission San Juan Bautista 8, 10, 13, 59
Mission Santa Clara 3, 6-9, 13, 15, 22-24, 25, 26, 29, 30, 32, 33, 38-41, 43, 45, 49-56, 58-67, 70, 72-76, 78-80, 82, 86, 87, 89, 92-98, 102-114, 117, 118, 120, 122, 125, 129, 131
Miwok 81, 82
Moffett Field 26, 141, 147
Moncada, Captain Fernando Riviera y 19
Monjeria 29
Montano 93
Monterey 11, 12, 18-20, 58, 88, 107, 111, 112, 114, 116
Moraga, Commissioner Gabriel 43, 44
Moraga, José 28
Moreno, Father Rafael 107
Morgan, Dale L. 88, 89
Morse 133
Mortality 62, 64
Mortuary practices 15
Motsun 8
Mouhicsi 93
Mountain View 6, 23, 51, 114, 130, 137-139, 143-145, 149
Mountain View-Alviso Road 139, 143
Mount Diablo 79
Murguia, Father Antonio 8, 26
Murphy, Captain John M. 125, 130
Napa Valley 4
Narciso 11, 88, 89, 96, 99, 101
Narvaez, José Augustin 113

Native fire management 43
Neophytes 27, 29, 30, 39, 45, 50, 59-61, 65-67, 88, 89, 110, 112, 116, 121, 134
New Almaden Mine 56, 130, 131, 141
New England 54
New world 17
Ninfa 93
Noboa, Diego de 29, 30, 32, 33, 36, 38
Noriega, José 113
Northern California 103, 137
Northrop, Marie E. 108
Oakdale 89, 90
Obsidian 4
Ohlone 9, 10, 17, 80-82, 85, 90, 91, 117, 120, 150
Ohlone/Costanoans 81, 82, 91
Older, Mrs. Fremont 118, 119, 130, 141, 144-147
Origin stories 13
Otterbein, Keith F. 16
Our Mother Santa Clara 6, 9
Our Patron San Francisco 6, 9
Ownership 25
Pedro Pablo 61
Pacheco Pass 79
Pacific Coast 9, 14
Palo Alto 5, 23, 51
Palou, Father Francisco 4, 5, 7, 14, 22, 27, 28
Pastorela 39
Pastoria de las Borregas 113, 114, 130
Paternalism 66
Patron 6, 9, 124, 127, 129, 137
Patwin 8
Peña, Father Tomas de la 8, 26, 27, 29, 30, 32, 33, 34, 36, 38
Peña, José 113
Peña, Manuel 109
Peninsula 2, 7, 8, 11, 16, 19, 21
Penitencia Creek 6
People of reason 50
Peralta family 108, 117
Peralta, Don Luis 74-79, 111
Peralta, Sebastian 113
Peregrino 93
Perfecta 109

Pescadero, Village of 78
Pescadero Creek 14
Petronilo 93
Phillips, George Harwood 50, 89-92, 94, 97, 109, 110, 144
Piña, Joaquin 92
Pinedo 46, 102, 103
Pinedo, Senorita Encarnacion 46
Pio 113, 117
Pitemas 89, 93
Point Año Nuevo 5
Pomo 8
Population density 5-7
Portola expedition 18
Posita de las Animas 128
Posolmi 2, 26, 110, 113, 114, 117, 120, 125, 128-131, 133, 137-139, 141, 143, 145, 147, 149, 150
Pozole 41
President of the Missions 49, 58
Price, Francesca 142
Price, Samuel 137, 142
Pronunciation 10
Property rights 83, 84
Prostitution 71
Psychocultural disintegration 66
Pueblo 27, 28, 41, 44-46, 50, 51, 58, 59, 64, 96-98, 103, 105, 106, 108, 116
Pueblo of San Jose 27, 44-46, 50, 58, 59, 64, 96, 103, 106, 108, 116
Puichon 9
Purisima 89, 113, 114, 120
Quito 113
Raids 76, 95, 97, 109
Ramon 107, 109, 111-114
Rancheria 8-10, 79, 90, 103, 118, 119
Rancho Pastoria de las Borregas 130
Rancho Posolmi 125, 128, 130, 131, 133, 138, 141, 143, 145, 147, 149, 150
Rancho San Bernardino 129
Rape 71
Real, Father 129
Rebellion 44, 45, 50, 59, 68, 69, 78, 79, 87-90, 92-94, 96, 98, 109, 110
Recruitment 12, 62, 63 65, 73-76, 80, 81, 90, 94, 96
Regidores 50
Respecio 93
Riddell, Francis 15
Rincon de Los Gatos 113
Rincon de San Francisquito 113
Rita 117
Ritual, Christian 12, 13, 30
Roberto 104, 113, 117
Robinson, Alfred 101
Robles, Teodoro Robles 129
Ronsom 20
Runaways 39, 75-78, 80, 81
Russian expansion 17
Sacramento River 8
Saint Ignatius 31, 32
Sal, Lieutenant Hermenegildo 44
Samis 3, 21, 31
San Andreas Valley 7
San Antonio 8, 9, 23, 47, 113
San Bernardino 6, 8, 9, 22, 23, 25-28, 31, 87, 110, 129
San Bruno 7
San Carlos 8, 9, 19
Sanchez, Father José 34, 74, 75, 81
Sanchez, Francisco Miguel 45, 47
Sanchez, José Antonio 90
San Diego 18, 79
San Francisco 4-9, 11, 16, 18-23, 28, 34-38, 44, 51, 56, 69, 65, 75, 76, 89, 91, 107, 108, 119, 130, 134, 135, 137, 138
San Francisco Alta 128
San Francisco and San Jose Railroad 138
San Francisco Bay 4, 5, 7, 18, 20, 22, 51
San Francisco Chronicle 65, 134
San Francisco Peninsula 7, 8, 11, 16, 19, 21
San Francisco Presidio 28, 44, 76, 89, 91
San Francisco Solano 6, 9, 23
San Francisquito Creek 9, 18, 20, 51, 108

Index

San Joaquin Republican 131
San Joaquin Valley 58, 73, 75, 80-82, 87, 95, 97, 106
San Jose 6, 9, 11, 15, 22, 23, 25, 2?, 28, 30, 44-47, 50, 51, 58, 59, 64, 71, 73, 76, 78, 79, 88-91, 94, 96-98, 103, 105, 106, 108, 110, 116, 118, 121, 137-139, 147, 149
San Jose Chamber of Commerce 147
San Jose Cupertino 6, 9, 22, 23
San Jose Guadalupe 22, 25
San Jose News 118, 131
San Jose Patriot 139
San Juan Bautista 6, 8-10, 13, 23, 59, 90, 113
San Martin 14
San Mateo County 15
San Mateo River 7
Santa Agueda 8
Santa Barbara 79, 107
Santa Clara 1, 2, 3-9, 11-15, 17-24, 25-30, 32-34, 38-43, 45, 49-67, 69, 70, 72-76, 78-82, 86, 87, 89-98, 101-114, 116-118, 120, 122, 124, 125, 127-131, 134, 135, 137, 138, 141, 142, 144, 147, 148, 149
Santa Clara Baptism Records 28
Santa Clara Death Register 15
Santa Clara Valley 1, 2, 3-6, 8, 9, 11, 12, 14, 17-21, 23, 25, 32, 33, 42, 51, 58, 75, 80, 86, 87, 97, 109, 118, 120, 125, 127, 130, 137, 142, 144, 147, 148, 149
Santa Clara University 134
Santa Cruz 53, 56, 70, 109
Santa Ysabel 6, 9, 23
Saratoga 51
Sawyer 144, 145, 147
Scarlet fever 71
Scotland 129, 137
Scott Creek 19
Secularization 87, 95, 97, 104, 106, 107, 109, 127
Secundino 129
Serra, Father Junipero 26, 27
Seven Years War 17

Seunens 79
Shew, William 134
Sierra Miwok 51
Sierra Nevada 18, 51, 89, 127
Simon 104, 112, 119, 120, 133
Slade, Charles 142
Slavery 83-85
Smaller Ynigo Mound 139, 144, 145
Smith, Jebediah S. 88-90, 94
Sojorpi 110
Sola, Governor 59
Soldiers 2, 17, 18, 20, 28, 30, 37, 41, 44, 47, 50, 55, 56, 60, 62, 67, 68, 71, 74, 77-79, 90-92, 94, 109, 116
Sonoran Mexico 17
Spain 17, 53, 62, 95, 104
Spanish colonial system 17, 33, 51, 69
Spanish Empire 17
Spanish explorers 6, 7, 12, 14
Spearman, Arthur Dunning 46, 47, 56, 134
Squatters 127-129, 133, 137
Ssalson 20
Stanger and Brown 2, 18
Staniford, Edward 108
Stanislaus River 89-91
State Historical Landmark Number 214
Status system 12
Stevens Creek 5, 6, 9, 21
Stodder, Ann L. 55, 61, 71, 72
Stoja 133
Suñol, Sub-Prefect Antonio 116, 117
Sullivan, Maurice S. 88, 89
Sunnyvale 51, 130, 149
Supernatural powers 11, 13, 30
Sycca 7
Tamien 9, 150
Tamyen 9
Tasman 149, 150
Tasuamatme 93
Taylor, Bayard 128
Tayssen 75, 76, 79, 80
Technological development 83, 84
Temnem 3, 21, 31
Territorial boundaries 9
Thamien 8
Tilellame 93

Tonul 93
Totote 104
Tozozes 93
Tribelet 8, 9, 11, 26, 47, 66, 75, 77, 78, 89, 90, 92, 93, 104
Tuberculosis 71
Tulare 120
Tuuhalmes 93
Ulistac 113, 117
Unilineal inheritance 11
United States 26, 60, 68, 75, 88, 90, 111, 112, 114, 117, 120, 125, 127, 134, 137, 142, 144, 147
University of Santa Clara 134
U.S. Census Bureau 137, 138, 142-145
U.S. Coast and Geodetic Survey 145
U.S. Geological Survey 145, 147, 148
U.S. Navy 147
Vallejo, Don Mariano G. 74, 75, 91, 92, 94, 104, 111
Vallejo, Guadalupe 69
Vallejo family 108
Vallejo, José de Jesus 104
Vancouver, Captain George 5, 34-38, 66
Viader, José 13, 47, 49, 50, 59, 60, 66, 69-71, 75, 76, 95, 98, 99, 107
Viceroy 17, 51
Villages 2, 5-9, 14-16, 18, 19, 21-24, 27, 28, 31, 42-44, 50, 67, 77, 80, 81, 86, 88, 89, 9, 95
Violence 41, 43, 44, 65, 73, 121, 128
Viviana 47, 49, 50, 60-62, 64, 71, 86, 119
Volojeyot 93
Walkinshaw Estate 142, 143
Walkinshaw family 137, 139, 141-143
Walkinshaw, Guadalupe 142
Walkinshaw house 145, 146
Walkinshaw, Robert 129-131, 133, 137, 142, 144
Walkinshaw, Robert, Jr. 144
Walkinshaw/Cunningham/Holthouse farm 145
Walkinshaw/Curtner/Cunningham/Holthouse Ranch 145

Wallace 90
War for Mexican Independence 51
Way of the Cross 103
Warfare 11, 16
Weaving 13, 57, 60, 61
Webb, Edith 27, 38, 40, 41, 45, 47, 53-55, 61, 103
Weber, Captain 125
Weber, David J. 66, 88, 89
Whisman, John 128, 133, 138
Whitney, Professor 141
Wilkes, Charles 120, 122, 124
Willow Glen 6
Winter, Joseph C. 28, 29
Woman leader 12
Women, Leadership roles for 11
World order 13
Worship 13, 40, 66, 134
Yginio 48
Ynego 134, 136
Ynigo 26, 133, 139
Ynigo Mounds 26, 145
Ynigo Rancho 144
Yokuts 81, 89, 90, 92, 104, 109
Yoscolo 109, 110
Yoscolo Rebellion 109, 110
Young, John 141
Yozcolo 109
Ysidra 104
Zacatecan Indian priests 95
Zacatecas 107
Zulectay 93